The Double Eagle Guide to

WESTERN
PUBLIC
CAMPGROUNDS

VOLUME I
PACIFIC NORTHWEST

IDAHO · OREGON · WASHINGTON

A DOUBLE EAGLE GUIDE ™

Discovery Publishing Company
Billings, Montana 59105-0545

The Double Eagle Guide to Western Public Campgrounds
Volume I

PUBLISHED BY
Discovery Publishing
Post Office Box 50545
Billings, Montana 59105-0545 USA

Discovery Publishing is an independent, private enterprise.
The information contained herein should not be construed
as reflecting the publisher's approval of the policies or
practices of the public agencies listed.

Information in this book is subject to change without
notice.

10 9 8 7 6 5 4 3 2 1

Produced, printed and bound in the United States of America.

ISBN   0-929760-01-8
$8.95

TABLE OF CONTENTS

INTRODUCTION

Whether you're a veteran of many western camps or are planning your first visit, this series is for you.

In this, the Premier Edition of the *Double Eagle*™ series, we've included most public campgrounds along or near the major highways and byways of the 11 contiguous western United States.

Our goal is to provide you with accurate, detailed, and yet concise, *first-hand* information about the campgrounds you're most likely to want to know about.

The volumes which comprise the *Double Eagle*™ series constitute a significant departure from the sketchy, plain vanilla approach to campground information provided by other campground guidebooks. Here, for the first time, is the most *useful* information about the West's most *useable* public campgrounds.

The name for the series was suggested by the celebrated United States twenty-dollar gold piece--most often called the "Double Eagle"--the largest and finest denomination of coinage ever issued by the U.S. Mint. The Double Eagle has long been associated with the early history of the West, as a symbol of traditional value, prosperity and excellence.

So, too, the *Double Eagle*™ series seeks to provide you with information about what are perhaps the finest of all the West's treasures--its public recreational lands.

We hope you enjoy reading these pages, and come to use the information in these volumes to enhance your own recognition of the outstanding camping opportunities available in the West.

Live long and prosper.

Thomas and *Elizabeth Preston*
Publishers

CONVENTIONS USED IN THIS SERIES

State Identifier: The state name and number combination in the upper left or right corner of each page, provides an easy means of cross-referencing the written information to the numbered locations on the maps which accompany each volume.

Campground Name: The officially designated name for the campground is listed in boldface, followed by the specific forest, park or other public land in which it is located. In many instances, particularly those involving state parks, the campground has no distinctive, individual name, and thus is listed as having the same name as its parent park.

Location: This section allows you to obtain a quick approximation of a campground's location in relation to nearby major communities.

Access: Our *Easy Access*™ system makes extensive use of highway mileposts in order to pinpoint the location of access roads, intersections, and other major terminal points. (Mileposts are about 98 percent reliable--but occasionally they are mowed by a snowplow or an errant motorist, and may be missing.) Access points utilizing mileposts are given in a positive notation, e.g., milepost 62 +.6 (six-tenths of a mile beyond milepost 62). (We won't insult your intelligence by suggesting how to figure out what to do if you're approaching from milepost 63.)

Since everyone won't be approaching a campground from the same direction, we've provided access information from two, sometimes three, points. In all cases, we've chosen the access points for their likelihood of use. Distances from communities are given from the approximate midtown point, unless otherwise specified. Mileages from access points has been rounded to the nearest mile, unless the exact mileage is critical. All instructions are given using the current official highway map available from each state.

9

Facilities: The items in this section have been listed in the approximate order in which a visitor might observe them during a typical swing through a campground. Following the total number of individual camp units, items pertinent to the campsites themselves are listed, followed by information related to 'community' facilities.

It has been assumed that each campsite has a picnic table. Therefore, this item is usually not specifically mentioned.

Site types: (1) Standard--no hookup; (2) Partial hookup--water, electricity; (3) Full hookup--water, electricity, sewer.

Fire facilities have been categorized into three basic forms: (1) Fireplaces--angular, steel or concrete, ground-level, normally with a steel grillwork across the top; (2) Fire rings--circular, steel, concrete or natural stone, ground-level or below ground-level, often with a steel grillwork across the top; (3) Barbecue grills--angular steel box, supported by a steel post about 36 inches high, with a steel grillwork across the top.

Toilet facilities have been listed thusly: (1) Restrooms--"modern", i.e., flush toilets and usually a wash basin; (2) Vault facilities--"simple", i.e., outhouses, pit toilets, call them what you like, (a rose by any other name.....).

Supply points have been described at six levels: (1) Camper Supplies--buns, beans and beverages; (2) Gas and Groceries--a quick stop, like a 7-11; (3) Minimal--basic hardware items, a mechanic's shop, or other very basic goods and services, in addition to gas & groceries; (4) Limited--at least one store which approximates a small supermarket, more than one fuel station, a general merchandise store, hardware store, and several basic services; (5) Adequate--more than one supermarket, (including something that resembles an IGA or a Safeway), a good choice of fuel brands, and a number of general and specialty stores and services; (6) Complete--they have a K-Mart.

Note that we have extensively employed the use of *general* and *relative* terms in describing the size, separation and state of levelness of the campsites ("basically level", "somewhat slopey", "medium-to-large", etc). The information is presented as an educated estimate by experienced

10

observers. Please allow for variations in perception between yourself and the reporters.

Season and Fees: Fees listed are the latest available at press time, but they should be considered **minimum** fees, since agencies often do not establish their fee schedule until the start of the camping season (or, in many cases, *after* the start of the season). (As you travel, you might notice that fees charged in public campgrounds operated by concessionaires/lesees are often higher than fees charged in similar "straight" campgrounds.) Seasons listed are approximate, since weather conditions, particularly in mountainous regions, may allow or require adjustments in the opening/closing dates.

Natural Feaures: Here we've drawn a word picture of the natural environment in and around each campground. Please remember that seasonal, even daily, conditions will affect the appearance of the area. A normally "sparkling stream" can be a muddy torrent for a couple of weeks in late spring; a "deep, blue lake" might be a nearly empty hole in a drought year; "lush vegetation" may have lost all its greenery by the time you arrive in October.

Attractions: As is mentioned a number of times throughout this series, the local scenery may be the principal attraction of the campground (and, indeed, may be the *only* one you'll need). Other attractions/activities have been listed if they are low-cost or free, and are available to the general public. An important item: **Swimming and boating areas usually do not have lifeguards.**

Notes: Consider this section to be somewhat more subjective in nature than the others. In order to provide our readers with a well-rounded report, we have listed personal comments related to our field observations.

(Our staff's enthusiasm for the West's recreational offerings is, at times, unabashedly proclaimed. And if the prose sometimes sounds like a tourist promotion booklet, please bear with us--there's a lot to be enthusiastic about!)

Editorial remarks (Ed.) occasionally have been included.

A Word About Style...

In this, the inaugural edition of the *Double Eagle* series, we've utilized a free-form writing concept which we call "Notation Format". Complete sentences, phrases, and single words have been incorporated into the campground descriptions as appropriate under the circumstances. We've adopted this style in order to provide our readers with detailed information about each item, while maintaining conciseness, clarity, and conversationality. We'd appreciate knowing if this system works for *you*. Thanks.

A Word About Text...

Another departure from the norm is our use of larger-than-normal type sizes throughout the series. It's one thing to read a guidebook in the convenience of your living room. It's another matter to peruse the pages while you're bounding and bouncing along in your camper as the sun is setting; or by a flickering flashlight inside a breeze-buffeted dome tent. We hope *this* works for you, too.

And a Final Word...

...about creepy-crawlers, critters and costs...
...bugs, boors, bears, and bureaucrats...

We've tried very, very hard to provide you with accurate information about the West's great camping opportunities. But occasionally, things aren't as they're supposed to be.....

If a campground's fees or facilities were changed after this edition had already gone to press, please let us know.

If the campers in the next site keep their generator poppety-popping until midnight so they can cook a turkey in the microwave, blame the bozos, not the book.

If the beasties are a bit bothersome in that campground by the bog, note the day's delights and not the difficulties.

Thanks for buying our book. Have a terrific trip!

Idaho

Idaho is a surprise.

Mention Idaho, and most people conjure up images of The Prolific Potato Patch in the West.

It's true that thousands of acres of reclaimed land in the barrens of the Snake River Plain of southern Idaho are dedicated to agriculture. (And if you just whiz through on the Interstate, you'll probably be convinced that that *is* all there is to Idaho.)

But much of the state is mountain, and lake, and forest, and stream. Actually, some of the United States' greatest mountain wilderness lies partly or exclusively in Idaho.

Looking at a map of Idaho, you'll note that, geographically, it has two distinct regions: the Snake River Plain, in the extreme south/southeast; and the mountainous northern three-fourths of the state, topped by the verdant Idaho Panhandle. (OK, there is a region of beautifully green valleys and towering mountains in the southeast corner, but a lot of people say that country really belongs to Wyoming, anyway.)

Much of the immense, roughly triangular, region bordered by Couer d'Alene in the north, Boise in the southwest and Idaho Falls in the southeast remains undiscovered, so to speak, by the masses and throngs. This isosceles triangle of true wilderness and fairly easily accessible near-wilderness, provides camping opportunities at whatever level of adventure you may be looking for.

And for its size and population, Idaho has an unusually large number of excellent public camping areas. It's true that, except for the state parks, the majority of these camps are sans hot showers and hookups and visitor centers. A small exchange, indeed, for what you receive in return.

Idaho is a pleasant surprise.

INDIAN CREEK
State Recreation Area

LOCATION: Northern Idaho Panhandle north of Priest River.

ACCESS: From the intersection of U.S. 2 and Idaho State Highway 57 in Priest River, drive north on Highway 57 for 22 miles to the 'Coolin Corners' fork; turn east (right) at the fork and proceed 6.1 miles to Coolin; travel north on East Shore Road (paved) for 4 miles to Cavanaugh Bay (road turns to good gravel here); continue 7 miles (and past a marina); turn west (left) into the campground.

FACILITIES: 92 level sites; many sites are quite close together with minimal to average separation; parking pads are gravel; some excellent tent-pitching areas; fireplaces; b-y-o firewood is recommended; water at several faucets; restrooms with showers; holding tank disposal station near the entrance; gravel driveways; camper supplies at a store at the park entrance; limited to adequate supplies and services are available in Priest River.

SEASON & FEES: $7.00 for a standard site, $9.00 for a partial-hookup site, $10.00 for a full-hookup site, $4.00 for an extra vehicle; open all year, with limited facilities in winter; 10 day limit; reservations accepted.

NATURAL FEATURES: Located on a large, moderately forested flat on the east shore of Priest Lake; the lake stretches 26 miles north and south between 2 forested ridges; vegetation in the campground consists of sparse grass and various types of tall conifers and hardwoods.

ATTRACTIONS: Boating; fishing (world record kokanee salmon); swimming (large sandy beach); day use area with picnic shelters; ranger-directed campfire programs; nearby historical site "Vinther Nelson Cabin" is accessible only by boat; annual logging celebration.

NOTES: Though access to Indian Creek is 'over hill and dale', the facilities are excellent and the lake is beautiful.

16

LUBY BAY
Idaho Panhandle National Forests

LOCATION: Northern Idaho Panhandle north of Priest River.

ACCESS: From the intersection of U.S. 2 and Idaho State Highway 57 in Priest River, drive north on Highway 57 for 28 miles; at "Frizzy O'Leary's" turn east (right) onto a paved road; drive 1.4 miles to a "T" intersection; turn north (left); drive 0.5 mile on a gravel road to the campground.

FACILITIES: 52 sites, including 24 smaller sites close to the lake in the east (lower) loop, and 28 larger sites on a hillside on the west (upper) side of the access road; parking pads are gravel, mostly straight-ins; some may need additional leveling; sites in the upper loop may be better for larger rv's; some tent sites are rather sloped; fire rings; firewood is available for gathering in the area; water at several faucet-fountains; restrooms; holding tank disposal station in the upper loop; paved driveways; minimal supplies at a store 2 miles south on Highway 57; limited to adequate supplies are available in Priest River.

SEASON & FEES: $6.00 in the west loop, $5.00 in the east loop, 2 vehicles and 8 persons permitted per site; May to mid-September; 10 day limit.

NATURAL FEATURES: Located in a wide valley between 2 crests of the Rocky Mountains, on the west shore of 25,000-acre Priest Lake; campground vegetation consists of tall pine, limited underbrush and a thick carpet of pine needles.

ATTRACTIONS: Boating; fishing (especially deep-water trolling); hiking trails to Upper Priest Lake and Roosevelt Grove of Ancient Cedars; Hanna Flats Nature Trailhead is 1 mile west of Highway 57 and the ranger station; ranger-naturalist programs may be scheduled for weekends.

NOTES: It's worth the long trip off the main highways to see the scenes at Priest Lake. But get here early on mid-summer weekends.

PRIEST RIVER
Corps of Engineers Recreation Area

Beautiful park

LOCATION: Far northern Idaho east of Priest River.

ACCESS: From U.S. 2 at milepost 7 +.1 (just east of the Priest River Bridge, east of the community of Priest River), turn south into the park entrance, then turn right into the campground.

FACILITIES: 18 sites; sites are average to large, with typically good separation; parking pads are gravel and level, many are pull-throughs large enough to accommodate good-sized rv's; some good tent-pitching areas are sheltered beneath tall trees; fireplaces; b-y-o firewood; water at several faucets; restrooms with showers; gravel driveways; campground host; limited to adequate supplies and services are available in Priest River, 1 mile west.

SEASON & FEES: $7.00; May to September.

NATURAL FEATURES: Located in a fairly dense stand of timber, consisting of tall conifers and considerable underbrush, at the confluence of the Priest River and the Pend Oreille River; adjacent to the campground is an expansive recreational park on the grassy northeast bank of the river; the Cabinet Mountains lie to the south and the Selkirks to the north.

ATTRACTIONS: Fishing; boating; adjacent Priest River City Park has extensive day use facilities including lawns, ball diamond, children's play area, sandy beach with floating docks; annual Huckleberry Festival held in Priest River in August; public tours of Albeni Falls Dam, which spans the Pend Orielle River west of town.

NOTES: This very nice campground is just far enough from the highway to be quiet, and close enough to the town of Priest River to be convenient. The setting is beautiful--at the meeting of two rivers, and framed by distant, densely forested mountains. The adjacent city park is a bonus if you have kids or like to lawn-stroll.

RILEY CREEK
Corps of Engineers Recreation Area

LOCATION: Idaho Panhandle west of Sandpoint.

ACCESS: From U.S. Highway 2 at milepost 14 +.5 (midtown LaClede, 7 miles east of Priest River), turn south; proceed south, and then west for 1.1 miles to the park entrance.

FACILITIES: 69 sites in 2 loops; sites are level, average or better in size (some are quite 'deep'), with fairly good separation; parking pads are gravel, medium to long straight-ins; some very nice tenting opportunities in among the tall cedars; fire rings; b-y-o firewood is recommended; water at faucets throughout; restrooms with showers; holding tank disposal station; paved driveways; campground host; gas and groceries in LaClede; limited to adequate supplies and services are available in Priest River.

SEASON & FEES: $7.00; May to September.

NATURAL FEATURES: Located on a forested flat along the north bank of the Pend Orielle River, between the Albeni Falls Dam and Lake Pend Orielle; tall cedars and very little underbrush provide separation and shelter in the campground; a large, open, grassy area separates the campground from the river; forested slopes flank the river as it winds its way through the Idaho Panhandle.

ATTRACTIONS: Boating; paved boat launch and floating docks; fishing; hiking (foot trails through the park); a large day use area includes extensive lawns, playground, and sandy swimming beach; Albeni Falls Dam, located west of Priest River, is open for tours during the summer.

NOTES: Though most sites are a short distance from the river's edge, there are some sites with views through the trees of the river and the forested hills beyond. This is a *very nice* facility that's very well-maintained. *very tree*

This is the nicest of the 2 parks. Beautiful forested campsites. Big enough for bicycling.

19

SPRINGY POINT
Corps of Engineers Camp

LOCATION: Idaho Panhandle south of Sandpoint.

ACCESS: From U.S. Highway 95 at milepost 471 +.7 (3 miles south of Sandpoint, 40 miles north of Coeur d' Alene), turn west onto Lake Drive (just south of the bridge over Lake Pend Orielle); proceed 3.1 miles on a narrow, rough and twisty paved drive; turn north (right) into the campground.

FACILITIES: 36 sites in 2 loops; sites are small to average in size and have average to good separation; parking pads are small to medium, gravel, pull-throughs or straight-ins; many pads will require some additional leveling; limited tent-pitching opportunities, mostly for smaller tents; fire facilities; b-y-o firewood is recommended; water at several faucets; restrooms with showers; holding tank disposal station; resident manager; east loop has a paved drive; west loop has a gravel drive; adequate to complete supplies and services are available in Sandpoint.

SEASON & FEES: $7.00, one vehicle per site; May to October.

NATURAL FEATURES: Located on a forested slope on the south shore of beautiful Lake Pend Orielle; tall cedars and hardwoods for shelter, plus an abundance of ferns for ground cover; glimpses of the lake through the trees from some sites; great views, from the lakeshore, of tall, timbered mountains across the lake to the north.

ATTRACTIONS: Boating; paved boat ramp and floating dock; fishing; swimming; sandy beach; day use area with picnicking.

NOTES: Sites at Springy Point are rather close together with limited room for maneuvering large vehicles along the narrow driveway. All sites are within a short walk of the lake. It appears to be a very popular campground, perhaps because the city of Sandpoint is so near.

SAMOWEN
Idaho Panhandle National Forests

LOCATION: Idaho Panhandle east of Sandpoint.

ACCESS: From Idaho State Highway 200 at milepost 48 +.1 (18 miles east of Sandpoint, 7 miles west of Clark Fork), turn south onto Samowen Road; proceed south 0.9 mile; turn west (right), and continue 0.1 mile to the campground.

FACILITIES: 56 sites in 3 loops; sites are small to average, with average to good separation; sites closer to the lake are more level, but typically smaller; parking pads are gravel straight-ins or pull-throughs; some sites farther from the lake have larger parking pads which may require additional leveling; a few designated tent sites along the lakeshore; fireplaces or fire rings at each site; some firewood is available for gathering, b-y-o to be sure; restrooms; cold showers at the bathhouse; holding tank disposal station; paved driveways; campground host; minimal supplies in East Hope, 2 miles west; complete supplies and services are available in Sandpoint, 18 miles west.

SEASON & FEES: $6.00; May to October; 14 day limit.

NATURAL FEATURES: Located on the northeast shore of 43-mile-long Lake Pend Orielle; fairly dense campground vegetation consists of tall conifers, a thick forest carpet, but very little underbrush.

ATTRACTIONS: Fishing (including world record kamloops, dolly varden trout and kokanee salmon); boating; gravel boat ramp; swimming (rocky beach); day use area with picnic shelters and barbecue grills; an historically significant fur trade center, Kullyspell House, is nearby.

NOTES: Samowen Campground and beautiful, azure Lake Pend Orielle are surrounded by emerald hills and distant mountains that produce a lovely picture. Some sites have a lake view through the trees. This campground is justifiably popular, so arrival should be early on summer weekends.

ROUND LAKE
State Park

LOCATION: Northern Idaho southwest of Sandpoint.

ACCESS: From U. S. 95 at a point 8 miles southwest of Sandpoint and 36 miles north of Couer d'Alene, turn west onto Dufort Road; proceed 1.5 miles west; turn south into the park; continue on a paved access road, past the visitor center, to the campground.

FACILITIES: 53 sites in 2 loops; sites are fairly spacious and have average to good separation; parking pads are paved, most are level, and some are long enough to accomodate very large rv's; many good tent-pitching areas nestled beneath tall trees; fireplaces; some firewood is available for gathering in the surrounding area; water at faucets throughout; restrooms with showers, plus supplemental vault facilities; holding tank disposal station near the entrance; paved driveways; limited supplies in Westmond, 4 miles south; complete supplies and services are available in Sandpoint.

SEASON & FEES: $7.00; open all year, with limited facilities in winter; 15 day limit.

NATURAL FEATURES: Located on 142 forested acres surrounding Round Lake, a 58-acre glacially formed lake only 37 feet deep; Cocolalla Creek flows into and out of the lake; the lake and campground are completely surrounded by stands of tall timber and a moderate amount of underbrush.

ATTRACTIONS: Visitor center; campfire programs scheduled during the summer season; summer activities include hiking, swimming, fishing, skin diving, and boating (hand-propelled); winter sports include ice fishing, ice skating, sledding, cross-country skiing and snowshoeing.

NOTES: Round Lake State Park is a very popular park offering many, varied, nature-related activities. The campsites are nicely sheltered by towering cedars, pines and fir trees.

GARFIELD BAY
Idaho Panhandle National Forests

LOCATION: Northern Idaho on the west shore of Lake Pend Orielle.

ACCESS: From U.S. 95 at a point 6 miles south of Sandpoint and 38 miles north of Couer d' Alene, turn east onto Sagle Road; proceed east for 9 miles on this paved, but winding, county road (after 7.5 miles there is a fork in the road--take the right fork) to Garfield Bay; continue 0.4 mile beyond the boat ramp and day use area, on a narrow, steep, twisty, but paved, access road to the campground.

FACILITIES: 27 sites in 2 loops; sites are well spaced with good privacy; parking pads are medium to large enough to accommodate large rv's; some may require additional leveling; many sites have very good tent-pitching areas; fireplaces; some firewood is available for gathering in the area; water at several faucets; vault facilities (restrooms in the nearby day use area); paved driveways; campground host; camper supplies at a marina; adequate to complete supplies and services are available in Sandpoint.

SEASON & FEES: $4.00; May to September; 14 day limit.

NATURAL FEATURES: Located on a hill 200 feet above Garfield Bay on Lake Pend Orielle, the largest lake in Idaho; campground and lake are completely surrounded by densely forested slopes typical of northern Idaho; campground vegetation consists of lush ferns, underbrush and tall trees.

ATTRACTIONS: Boating; sailing; windsurfing; fishing (including ice fishing in winter); day use area below the campground has picnicking facilities and a boat ramp; a number of small lakes in the area are accessible by county roads.

NOTES: Since the campground is slightly removed from Garfield Bay's center of activity, it usually maintains a quiet atmosphere. Access to very beautiful Lake Pend Orielle is only a short walk or drive from the campsites.

WHITETAIL
Farragut State Park

LOCATION: Northern Idaho north of Couer d'Alene.

ACCESS: From U.S. Highway 95 at a point 20 miles north of Couer d'Alene and 24 miles south of Sandpoint, turn east onto Idaho State Highway 54; proceed east on Highway 54 for 4 miles to the park entrance; just beyond the visitor center, turn right, onto South Road, and continue for 1.8 miles; turn right into the campground.

FACILITIES: 93 sites in 3 loops; sites are mostly small, with limited to adequate separation; parking pads are small to medium, most are fairly well leveled; good tent-pitching possibilities; 5 walk-in sites along the bike trail; fireplaces; firewood is usually for sale, or b-y-o; water at centrally located faucets; restroom with showers; holding tank disposal station on South Road; paved driveways; campground host; limited supplies and services are available in Bayview, a few miles northeast; complete supplies and services are available in Couer d'Alene.

SEASON & FEES: $7.00 for a site, $4.00 for an extra vehicle; open all year, with limited facilities and reduced fees in winter; 10 day limit; reservations accepted.

NATURAL FEATURES: Located within walking distance of Idlewild Bay of Lake Pend Orielle (the largest lake in Idaho, with more than 100 miles of shoreline); the Bitterroot Mountains are visible across the lake to the east; campsites are situated in a light conifer forest with moderate underbrush.

ATTRACTIONS: Boating; sailing; fishing (world record kokanee salmon); boat launch and docks; swimming (sandy beach); ranger-directed programs; nature trails, bicycle routes and equestrian trails; model airplane flying field; visitor center has an historical museum.

NOTES: Farragut State Park was originally a Naval Training Station which was established during WWII, in 1942. As you can see above, there's a lot to do here.

SNOWBERRY
Farragut State Park

LOCATION: Northern Idaho north of Couer d'Alene.

ACCESS: From U.S. Highway 95 at a point 20 miles north of Couer d'Alene and 24 miles south of Sandpoint, turn east onto Idaho State Highway 54; proceed east on Highway 54 for 4 miles to the park entrance; just beyond the visitor center turn right, onto South Road, and continue for 1.9 miles; turn left into the campground.

FACILITIES: 45 sites, all with partial hookups, in 2 loops; sites are average-sized, with adequate separation; parking pads are medium to long, many are pull-throughs; most are well leveled; restrooms with showers; holding tank disposal station nearby; fireplaces; firewood is usually available for sale, or b-y-o; paved driveway; limited supplies in Bayview, a few miles northeast; complete supplies and services are available in Couer d'Alene.

SEASON & FEES: $9.00 for a partial-hookup site, $4.00 for an extra vehicle; open all year, with limited facilities and reduced fees in winter; 10 day limit; reservations accepted.

NATURAL FEATURES: Located on a gentle, forested slope near Idlewild Bay at the south end of Lake Pend Orielle; this largest lake in Idaho has a depth greater than 1000 feet; peaks of the Bitterroot range are visible to the east across the lake.

ATTRACTIONS: Boating; sailing; fishing (world record kokanee salmon); boat launch and docks; swimming (sandy beach); ranger-directed programs; nature trails, bicycle routes and equestrian trails; model airplane flying field; visitor center has an historical museum.

NOTES: Lake Pend Orielle is one of the most beautiful of the larger lakes in the Northern Rockies. Farragut State Park was first developed as Farragut Naval Training Station during World War II. Over a quarter-million sailors were trained here.

25

BEAUTY CREEK
Idaho Panhandle National Forests

LOCATION: Northern Idaho east of Coeur d'Alene.

ACCESS: From Interstate 90 at Exit 22 (9 miles east of Coeur d'Alene, 29 miles west of Kellogg), proceed south on Idaho State Highway 97 for 2.3 miles; turn east (left) onto a paved access road; continue east for 0.3 mile to the campground.

FACILITIES: 12 level sites; most sites are small to medium in size with minimal separation; parking pads are paved, fairly level, small to average in size; level, grassy tent spots; fireplaces; barbecue grills are available in the adjacent picnic area; b-y-o firewood is recommended; water at a hand pump; vault facilities (H); driveway is a narrow single lane road; complete supplies and services are available in Coeur d'Alene.

SEASON & FEES: $5.00; May to September; 14 day limit.

NATURAL FEATURES: Located in a long, narrow canyon at the eastern end of Beauty Bay on Lake Coeur d'Alene; sites are stretched out in a grassy meadow along Beauty Creek; peaks of the Coeur d'Alene Mountains rise to over 6000' just to the east; sites are separated mostly by tall grass and some brush.

ATTRACTIONS: Boating (boat ramp and dock at Mineral Ridge on the shore of Lake Coeur d'Alene); fishing; Caribou Ridge interpretive trail; a nearby BLM Mineral Ridge hiking trail leads almost 5 miles up to a Mt. Coeur d'Alene viewpoint; the city of Coeur d'Alene has museums and galleries.

NOTES: Beauty Creek Campground is located in a pleasant open canyon very near one of the most beautiful lakes in Northern Idaho. Beauty Creek meanders past the sites on its way to Lake Coeur d'Alene. A couple of sites are quite a distance to the east past the main camp area-- so don't give up looking for them.

BUMBLEBEE
Idaho Panhandle National Forests

LOCATION: Northern Idaho east of Coeur d'Alene.

ACCESS: From Interstate 90 Exit 43 at Kingston (30 miles east of Coeur d' Alene, 8 miles west of Kellogg), proceed through Kingston east/north on the Coeur d'Alene River-Prichard Road for 4.7 miles; turn northwest (left) onto Forest Road 209 (paved); drive 3 miles and turn east (right) onto Forest Road 796 (paved) for 0.2 mile into the campground.

FACILITIES: 25 level sites in 2 loops; sites are well spaced, with average to excellent separation; parking pads are gravel, and some are pull-throughs spacious enough to accommodate very large rv's; good tent-pitching opportunities beneath tall conifers; fire rings plus a few barbecue grills; firewood is available for gathering in the area; water at a centrally located hand pump in each loop; vault facilities (H); gravel driveways; campground host; limited supplies in Kingston; complete supplies and services are available in Coeur d'Alene.

SEASON & FEES: $5.00; May to mid-September; 14 day limit.

NATURAL FEATURES: Located in a fairly open forest surrounded by large, grassy Bumblebee Meadow; situated near the confluence of Bumblebee Creek and the North Fork of the Coeur d'Alene River; Bumblebee Peak rises to 4746' of altitude just a few miles to the north; campground vegetation consists of tall conifers and light underbrush.

ATTRACTIONS: Fishing; hiking; the drive along the Coeur d'Alene River passes through a very pleasant pastoral landscape.

NOTES: This quiet, secluded spot is reached by driving along the gently curving Coeur d'Alene River Road. The drive itself is worth the trip, but, in addition, Bumblebee Campground offers spacious sites in a peaceful setting.

BIG HANK
Idaho Panhandle National Forests

LOCATION: Northern Idaho east of Coeur d'Alene.

ACCESS: From Interstate 90 Exit 43 at Kingston (30 miles east of Coeur d' Alene, 8 miles west of Kellogg), proceed through Kingston east/north on the Coeur d'Alene River-Prichard Road for 21 miles to the Prichard Fork; take the left fork onto Forest Road 208; proceed north to milepost 18 +.8; turn west (left) into the campground. **ALTERNATE ACCESS:** From I-90 at Wallace, access is available over the snakey, steep (but paved) Dobson Pass Road to Forest Road 208 at Prichard.

FACILITIES: 30 level sites; sites are nicely spaced with good separation which affords considerable privacy; parking pads are paved, level, and large enough, even double-wide in some instances, to accommodate very large rv's; some very roomy tent spaces are located in grassy areas beneath tall trees; fire rings and barbecue grills; firewood is available for gathering in the area; water at several hand pumps; vault facilities (H); holding tank disposal station at the Shoshone Work Center near milepost 6; paved driveways; campground host; minimal supplies in Prichard; complete supplies and services are available in Coeur d'Alene.

SEASON & FEES: $5.00; May to September; 14 day limit.

NATURAL FEATURES: Located on the bank of the crystal clear Coeur d'Alene River in a fairly dense forest setting; campground vegetation consists of tall conifers and considerable underbrush; though the river flows within a few yards of many sites, there are no real riverside sites with open river views; often showery in summer.

ATTRACTIONS: Fishing; river floating (early in the season); hiking trails in the campground area.

NOTES: Though Big Hank Campground is located quite a distance from the main highway (I-90), we've included it in this listing because it's a really nice place.

DEVIL'S ELBOW
Idaho Panhandle National Forests

LOCATION: Northern Idaho east of Coeur d'Alene.

ACCESS: From Interstate 90 Exit 43 at Kingston (30 miles east of Coeur d' Alene, 8 miles west of Kellogg), proceed through Kingston east/north on the Coeur d'Alene River-Prichard Road for 21 miles to the Prichard Fork; take the left fork onto Forest Road 208; proceed north to milepost 13; turn east (right) into the campground. **ALTERNATE ACCESS:** From I-90 at Wallace, access is available over the snakey, steep, sometimes narrow, Dobson Pass Road to Forest Road 208 near Prichard.

FACILITIES: 19 sites; sites are generally level and well spaced, with average or better visual separation; most parking pads are paved, and some are pull-throughs or double-wides spacious enough for very large rv's; large, level tent spaces; fire rings; firewood is available for gathering in the area; water at a centrally located hand pump; vault facilities (H); holding tank disposal station at the Shoshone Work Center near milepopst 6; paved driveways; campground host; minimal supplies in Prichard; complete supplies and services are available in Coeur d'Alene.

SEASON & FEES: $5.00; June to September; 14 day limit.

NATURAL FEATURES: Located in an open forest on the west bank of the Coeur d'Alene River; most sites are situated around a small grassy meadow; tall pine, moderate underbrush and flowering beargrass provide separation and privacy for most sites; peaks of the Shoshone Range rise to over 6000' just to the east; some units have views of the river, which flows by within a few yards of some of the sites.

ATTRACTIONS: Fishing; river floating; hiking trails.

NOTES: This typically quiet, somewhat secluded spot has some very sheltered sites and some open ones. This entire stretch along the Coeur d'Alene River almost seems like part of a different world.

KIT PRICE
Idaho Panhandle National Forests

LOCATION: Northern Idaho east of Coeur d'Alene.

ACCESS: From Interstate 90 Exit 43 at Kingston (30 miles east of Coeur d' Alene, 8 miles west of Kellogg), proceed through Kingston east/north on the Coeur d'Alene River-Prichard Road for 21 miles to the Prichard Fork; take the left fork onto Forest Road 208; proceed north to milepost 10; turn east (right) into the campground. **ALTERNATE ACCESS:** From I-90 at Wallace, access is available over the serpentine Dobson Pass Road to Forest Road 208 near Prichard.

FACILITIES: 52 sites in 3 loops; most sites are level and well-spaced; parking pads are paved, many are pull-throughs or double-wides spacious enough to accommodate even the largest rv's; most tent spots are large and level; water at faucet-fountains throughout; vault facilities (H); holding tank disposal station at the Shoshone Work Center near milepost 6; fire rings and/or barbecue grills at each site; firewood is available for gathering in the area; paved driveways; campground host; minimal supplies in Prichard; complete supplies and services are available in Coeur d'Alene.

SEASON & FEES: $5.00; May to September; 14 day limit.

NATURAL FEATURES: Located along the bank of the Coeur d'Alene River, which meanders through a narrow, forested valley in this area; most campsites are surrounded by tall timber and moderate underbrush; some sites are right along the river's edge; campground elevation is 2550'; peaks of the Shoshone Range rise to over 6000' to the east.

ATTRACTIONS: Fishing; river floating.

NOTES: Kit Price Campground has recently been expanded and improved. It is typically inhabited by fishermen who stay a few days or more. The drive along the Coeur d'Alene River is eminently pleasant; the drive through Dobson Pass to or from Wallace is an adventure!

HAWLEY'S LANDING
Heyburn State Park

LOCATION: Northern Idaho south of Coeur d'Alene.

ACCESS: From Idaho State Highway 5 at a point 6 miles east of Plummer and 12 miles west of Saint Maries, turn north at a sign for "Hawley's Landing"; continue 0.3 mile on a winding, paved road to the campground.

FACILITIES: 54 sites, including several with hookups, in 2 loops; sites are average-sized with typically good separation; parking pads are gravel, medium to large, some may need additional leveling; many good tent sites; fireplaces; firewood is usually available for sale, or b-y-o; restrooms in one loop and vault facilities in the other; water at several faucets; campground host; minimal supplies in Plummer; complete supplies and services are available in Coeur d'Alene.

SEASON & FEES: $7.00 for a standard site; $9.00 for a partial-hookup site, $10.00 for a full-hookup site, $2.00 for an extra vehicle; 15 day limit.

NATURAL FEATURES: Located on a bluff above two lakes; Chatcolet Lake is separated from Round Lake by 2 long, slender, low islands--an unusual feature of the landscape; sites are forested, with 23 hilly sites and 31 on a more level hilltop; the hilltop sites have a view of the lakes through the trees; the St. Joe Mountains rise to above 5000' and are visible across the lakes to the east.

ATTRACTIONS: Boating (nearby marina has a boat launch); fishing; hiking (5 hiking trails, varying in length from 0.5 mile to 3.0 miles, lead off from the campground); trail down to a day use area, boat docks and lake access; visitor center at park headquarters; ranger-directed campfire programs.

NOTES: Heyburn State Park, the United States' first state park, was established in 1909. The campground facilities were completely revitalized quite recently.

31

BENEWAH
Heyburn State Park

LOCATION: Northern Idaho south of Coeur d'Alene.

ACCESS: From Idaho State Highway 5 at a point 11 miles east of Plummer and 7 miles west of St. Maries, turn north at the sign for "Benewah Campground" (just east of the Benewah Creek Bridge), drive north 1 mile on a paved access road, past a private resort, to the public camping area.

FACILITIES: 39 sites including 15 with hookups,in 3 loops; sites are small to medium with minimal to fair separation; parking pads are gravel; some sites are level with large parking pads, while other sites are perched on a rocky hillside with small parking spaces; a few good tent sites; fireplaces; limited firewood is available for gathering in the vicinity, b-y-o is suggested; water at several faucets; central restroom with showers; paved driveways; camper supplies at the resort store; limited supplies in St. Maries; complete supplies and services are available in Coeur d'Alene.

SEASON & FEES: $7.00 for a standard site, $9.00 for a partial-hookup site, $10.00 for a full-hookup site, $2.00 for an extra vehicle; April to September; 14 day limit.

NATURAL FEATURES: Located on a hill east of Benewah Lake in light to medium forest; most sites have some trees and brush for shelter and separation; some sites have commanding views of Benewah Lake, which is separated from Round Lake by an unusual feature--a "river between the lakes"; quantities of wild rice grow nearby in a marsh environment at the south end of Benewah Lake, home to a sizeable assortment of bird species.

ATTRACTIONS: Boating; boat ramp and public docks; fishing; visitor center at Heyburn State Park Headquarters; hiking trails, including the historic Mullan Trail, at the west end of the park.

NOTES: There are some terrific views of the lake and surrounding area from the sites on the bluff.

EMERALD CREEK
Idaho Panhandle National Forests

LOCATION: Northern Idaho between Coeur d'Alene and Lewiston.

ACCESS: From Idaho State Highway 3 at a point 4 miles south of Fernwood and 6 miles north of Clarkia (just south of the Benewah/Shoshone County Line) turn west at the "Emerald Creek Recreation Area" sign onto Forest Road 447; proceed west/south for 3.3 miles on a gravel access road; at the fork in the road take the left fork and continue 1.4 miles farther on a narrow dirt road to the campground.

FACILITIES: 18 sites; sites are roomy and spaced quite far apart, with good visual separation; parking pads are level, gravel straight-ins; many units would accommodate medium to large rv's; a number of sites are suitable for larger tents; barbecue grills; firewood is available for gathering in the area; water at hand pumps; vault facilities; gravel driveways; limited supplies in Clarkia; nearest source of complete supplies and services is Lewiston, 60 miles southwest.

SEASON & FEES: $4.00; May to October; 14 day limit.

NATURAL FEATURES: Located in a grove of trees surrounded by a grassy meadow; Emerald Creek flows past the campground and into the St. Maries River to the east; the campground is within 3 miles of the Emerald Creek Garnet Area.

ATTRACTIONS: Garnet digging--this is the primary activity in the area; (an administration building is located at the "dig" to provided information to diggers and visitors); fee for using the facility, which is usually open 8:00 to 5:00 Thursday to Monday during the summer; additional info is available from the ranger station in Clarkia; fishing.

NOTES: This secluded campground offers an inviting place to enjoy nature, whether or not you include a side trip to one of the two places in the world where star garnets can be found.

HELLS GATE
State Park

LOCATION: Western Idaho south of Lewiston.

ACCESS: From U.S. Highway 12 at the west edge of Lewiston (just east of the Snake River Bridge), proceed south on Snake Avenue for 3.5 miles (along the east bank of the Snake River); turn west (right) into the park; campground is 1.0 miles south of the park entrance.

FACILITIES: 96 sites, including 64 with partial hookups, in 3 loops; sites are mostly average-sized with minimal separation; parking pads are level and paved; some pads are long enough to accommodate the largest rv's; excellent tent-pitching opportunities; barbecue grills; b-y-o firewood; water at faucets throughout; restrooms with showers; holding tank disposal station; paved driveways; camper supplies at a nearby marina; complete supplies and services are available in Lewiston.

SEASON & FEES: $7.00 for a standard site, $9.00 for a partial-hookup site, $2.00 for an extra vehicle; March to November; 15 day limit.

NATURAL FEATURES: Located on the mostly open east bank of the Snake River; vegetation consists of mown lawns and a few planted trees; grassy bluffs to the east, behind the campground, and to the west, across the river; typically breezy; winters here are milder than at just about any other state park in Idaho.

ATTRACTIONS: Boating; fishing; swimming; children's playground; jogging and biking trails; visitor center; guided tours of the nearby sternwheeler, the steamboat Jean; float trips through the Snake River Canyon.

NOTES: As the name implies, this is the gateway to North America's deepest canyon--5500' deep Hells Canyon--and Hells Canyon National Recreation Area. The groomed lawns and mild climate make the park a very popular, three-season spot.

LAPWAII/NEZ PERCE
Winchester Lake State Park

LOCATION: Western Idaho south of Lewiston.

ACCESS: From U.S. 95 at a point 40 miles south of Lewiston and 33 miles north of Grangeville, travel west/north on Business Route 95A into Winchester; turn west (left) onto Joseph Avenue; proceed west/south 0.3 mile to the park entrance; turn east (left) into the park, and continue 0.2 mile to the camping areas.

FACILITIES: 60 sites, including 28 forested sites in the Lapwaii Campground and 32 more open sites in the Nez Perce Campground; parking pads are oiled gravel, medium to large, with the more spacious sites in the Lapwaii area; some very nice open areas for tent-pitching; leveling may be required at many sites; fireplaces; very little firewood is available for gathering in the area, b-y-o is recommended; water at faucets throughout; vault facilities; paved driveways; minimal supplies in Winchester; complete supplies and services are available in Lewiston.

SEASON & FEES: $7.00; open all year, with limited facilities in winter; 15 day limit.

NATURAL FEATURES: Located on the west shore of Winchester Lake, a 103-acre impoundment on a forested high plateau at the foot of the Craig Mountains; campground vegetation consists of tall conifers, grass and some underbrush; some sites in the Nez Perce unit have lake views; elevation 3900'.

ATTRACTIONS: Fishing (including ice fishing); motorless boating; nature trails; ice skating, sledding, and cross-country skiing; campfire programs; nearby town of Lapwaii, on the Nez Perce Indian Reservation, invites the public to pow wows peroidically during the year.

NOTES: Winchester Lake lies in one of the country's more intense climatic zones. Summers are usually short, with very warm days and cool nights. Winters tend to be long, cold and snowy.

APGAR
Clearwater National Forest

LOCATION: Idaho Panhandle east of Kooskia.

ACCESS: From U.S 12 at milepost 104 +.4 (30 miles east of Kooskia, 70 miles west of Lolo Pass), turn south into the campground.

FACILITIES: 7 sites; all sites are level, quite spacious and well separated; parking pads are medium-length, gravel straight-ins; adequate space for medium to large tents in most sites; fire rings with steel grates; firewood is available for gathering in the area; water at faucets and fountains; vault facilities; gravel driveway; nearest reliable source of limited to adequate supplies is in Kooskia.

SEASON & FEES: $5.00; May to October; 14 day limit.

NATURAL FEATURES: Located on a small flat along the north bank of the Lochsa River, a few miles east of the Lochsa's confluence with the Clearwater River; sites are moderately sheltered/shaded and have a river view; a few camp spots are streamside; the river flows through a fairly densely forested narrow valley in this section; several small sandy beaches along the river within a half-dozen miles east and west of here.

ATTRACTIONS: Lochsa Historic Ranger Station and Visitor Center, 17 miles west, has displays and self-guided tours; fishing and rafting on the several rivers in the area; mini-amphitheater (a large fire ring encircled by several benches).

NOTES: Even though Apgar is somewhat small, it is, nevertheless, one of the nicer campgrounds along this route. There are some really beautiful views of the river from most of the sites. It tends to be less crowded than Wild Goose Campground, a similar, but slightly smaller, National Forest campground 9 miles west.

Least attractive of all the campgrounds along this hwy. Some of the trees were kind of scruffy looking.

Idaho 22

WILDERNESS GATEWAY
Clearwater National Forest

LOCATION: Idaho Panhandle east of Kooskia.

ACCESS: From U.S. 12 at milepost 122 +.8 (48 miles east of Kooskia, 52 miles west of Lolo Pass), turn south, cross the Lochsa River bridge, and follow a paved access road 0.2 mile to the campground.

FACILITIES: 89 sites in 4 loops; sites are generally large and private; parking pads are level, paved, short to medium in length; many pads are double-wide; sites have some possibilities for pitching small to medium tents, but are probably better suited for smaller camping vehicles; several handicapped access units; most spots have fireplaces, some have barbecue grills; firewood is available for collecting nearby; water at faucet-fountains throughout; restroom (H) plus auxiliary vault facilities; holding tank disposal station; paved roadways; campgound host; nearest reliable source of limited to adequate supplies is in Kooskia.

SEASON & FEES: $5.00; May to October; 14 day limit.

NATURAL FEATURES: Located on a large flat along the Lochsa River, in a moderately wide spot in a valley bordered by timbered ridges; pine mixed with an abundance of small hardwoods and large ferns in the camp area.

ATTRACTIONS: Lochsa Historic Ranger Station, 1 mile west, has displays and self-guided tours; amphitheater and children's play area in the campground; river trail; campground serves as a major staging area for wilderness trips.

NOTES: This is probably one of the best campgrounds on this highway, and yet it is usually not crowded. Please note that supplies and services on this section of U.S. 12 are quite scarce. It might be a good idea to fill up with gas and groceries in Lewiston, Idaho, or Missoula, Montana prior to venturing out onto what is one of the most wildly beautiful highways in this region.

JERRY JOHNSON
Clearwater National Forest

LOCATION: Idaho Panhandle east of Lewiston near Lolo Pass.

ACCESS: From U.S. 12 at milepost 150 +.3 (24 miles west of Lolo Pass, 76 miles east of Kooskia), turn north into the campground.

FACILITIES: 15 sites; sites are medium to large, moderately well-spaced, and separated by some low brush between sites; paved parking pads; adequate tent space in most sites; fireplaces; lots of firewood is available for collecting; water at two hand pumps; vault facilities; paved driveway; nearest reliable source of limited to adequate supplies is in Kooskia, or Lolo, Montana, 60 miles east; complete services are available in Lewiston, 150 miles west, or Missoula, Montana, 70 miles east.

SEASON & FEES: $4.00; May to mid-September; 14 day limit.

NATURAL FEATURES: Located on a fairly level portion of a hillside above the Lochsa River; campground has moderate forestation without much underbrush; relatively low timbered ridges flank the campground north and south.

ATTRACTIONS: Catch and release fishing in the Lochsa River, (a foot trail leads from the campground across the highway and down a steep bank to the water's edge); 4-wheel-drive trail leads north from the campground into the nearby primitive areas.

NOTES: This spot is perhaps not as well maintained as some of the other campgrounds along Highway 12, but it also tends to be less crowded. It may also be slightly more comfortable than some of the other camping areas near here, since it is positioned somewhat above the cold and dampness of the river level.

Pretty campground. You couldn't see river from sites. Not very close to river.

WENDOVER
Clearwater National Forest

LOCATION: Idaho Panhandle east of Lewiston near Lolo Pass.

ACCESS: From U.S. 12 at milepost 158 +.2 (16 miles west of Lolo Pass, 84 miles east of Kooskia), turn south into the campground. (Note that the campground sign is on the north side of the highway, directly opposite the campground entrance.)

FACILITIES: 28 sites in two loops (however, only the west loop, with 15 sites, has been in recent operation); campsites are quite level, with fairly large, paved straight-in parking pads; most sites are quite suitable for tents: all sites have fireplaces, some also have barbecue grills; firewood is available for gathering in the area; water at a centrally located hand pump in each loop; vault facilities; paved driveways; campground host; nearest reliable sources of supplies--Lolo, Montana 52 miles east, or Kooskia, Idaho, 84 miles west.

SEASON & FEES: $4.00; May to mid-September; 14 day limit.

NATURAL FEATURES: Located on the north bank of the Lochsa (Lock-Saw) River, part of the National Wild and Scenic River System; moderate forestation in the campground, dense forest throughout the region; a small creek trickles down through the campground between the two loops; large gravel and sand beach areas along the river just to the west of the campground.

ATTRACTIONS: Fishing in the river and adjacent side streams; numerous primitive roads and foot trails in the region.

NOTES: Wendover is nearly a twin of White House campground, 0.3 mile east. Wendover, however, has fewer sites with a river view. It also has a slightly more "open" environment.

Very pretty, about half the sites are on the river, Flies were pesky. Site 13 is the best one.

WHITE HOUSE
Clearwater National Forest

LOCATION: Idaho Panhandle east of Lewiston near Lolo Pass.

ACCESS: From U.S. 12 at milepost 158 +.5 (16 miles west of Lolo Pass, 158 miles east of Lewiston) turn south off the highway into the campground. (Note that the entrance road is difficult to see until you're almost past it. The campground sign is on the north side of the highway directly opposite the entrance.)

FACILITIES: 14 sites; campsites are large, level and reasonably well-distanced from each other; large, paved parking pads; nice, level tent spaces; fireplaces; firewood is available for collecting in the area; water at a centrally located hand pump; vault facilities; wide, paved driveway, with a narrow turnaround at the east end; campground host in summer; minimal supplies at a resort, 3 miles west; limited to adequate supplies are available in Kooskia, 85 miles west, and Lolo, Montana, 51 miles east.

SEASON & FEES: $4.00; May to September; 14 day limit.

NATURAL FEATURES: Located on the north bank of the Lochsa (Lock-Saw) River, part of the National Wild and Scenic River System; quite a few camp spots have river frontage, and most at least have a river view; mostly tall pine combined with tall grass and hardwoods within the campground; campsites are moderately sheltered/shaded; dense conifer forest throughout this region.

ATTRACTIONS: Fairly good fishing in the Lochsa River; many 4 wheel drive and foot trails in the area.

NOTES: The size of this campground is quite large in proportion to the relatively small number of sites. Even though it's close to the highway, dense vegetation between most of the camp units and the road helps to muffle traffic noise a little. This camp is very similar to Wendover Campground, 0.3 mile west.

not very nice. Couldn't see river from sites.

POWELL
Clearwater National Forest

LOCATION: Idaho Panhandle east of Lewiston near Lolo Pass.

ACCESS: From U.S 12 at milepost 161 +.8 (12 miles west of Lolo Pass, 87 miles east of Kooskia), turn south off the highway onto a paved road which leads 0.2 mile to the campground.

FACILITIES: 39 sites in 3 loops; sites are medium-sized, with dense vegetation providing excellent separation between most sites; very level, wide, paved or gravel parking pads, with plenty of space for larger vehicles; fireplaces; firewood is available for gathering in the area; water at faucet-fountain combinations at several locations; central restroom with auxiliary vaults; all driveways are paved; campground host; ranger station just east of the campground; minimal supplies at a nearby lodge; nearest reliable source of limited to adequate supplies and services is in Kooskia and Lolo, Montana, 49 miles east.

SEASON & FEES: $4.00; May to October; 14 day limit.

NATURAL FEATURES: Located on the densely forested north bank of the Lochsa (Lock-Saw) River, part of the National Wild and Scenic River System; the river can be heard but not actually viewed from the campsites, except from a half dozen spots in the A Loop; large, open, grassy recreation area in the center of the B Loop; tall, densely timbered peaks north and south.

ATTRACTIONS: Good views of the Lochsa River and the mountains of the nearby Idaho wilderness; fishing.

NOTES: Particularly considering its relatively remote location, this an absolutely dandy campground--one of the nicest National Forest camping areas along U.S. 12 in this region. Please note that supplies and services are hard to come by on the 130-mile stretch of U.S. 12 between Kooskia, Idaho, and Lolo, Montana.

41

TWIN CREEK
Salmon National Forest

LOCATION: Eastern Idaho near the Montana border.

ACCESS: From U.S. Highway 93 at milepost 342 + .4 (8.6 miles south of Lost Trail Pass and the Idaho/Montana border, 5 miles north of Gibbonsville), turn west; proceed 0.3 mile on a gravel road up to the campground.

FACILITIES: 44 sites in 2 loops; sites are quite spacious, with generally good separation; parking pads are gravel; most pads are medium to long straight-ins; many may require additional leveling; some nice large tent spots, perhaps a bit sloped; barbecue grills and fire rings; firewood is available for gathering; water at several faucet-fountains; vault facilities (H); gravel driveways; gas and groceries in Gibbonsville; adequate supplies and services are available in Salmon, Idaho, 38 miles south.

SEASON & FEES: $4.00; May to mid-September.

NATURAL FEATURES: Located along a forested, sloping gulch high in the Bitterroot Range of the Rocky Mountains; Twin Creek, a clear mountain stream, tumbles past the sites, through a wide ravine, and into the North Fork of the Salmon River; most campsites are surrounded by dense, tall timber with hanging moss, plus hardwoods and second growth pine; a few sites are in more open forest; typically showery.

ATTRACTIONS: Fishing in the North Fork of the Salmon River and at Allan Lake (accessible by a 10-mile-long foot trail); hiking; river rafting at North Fork, 16 miles south on Highway 93; superscenic (though twisty) drive along Highway 93 between Lost Trail Pass and Salmon.

NOTES: The dense forest here provides a really nice, sheltered setting for a campground. This spot is historically significant because of the Lewis & Clark Expedition's camp near here on September 2, 1805.

EVERGREEN
Payette National Forest

LOCATION: Western Idaho between Council and New Meadows.

ACCESS: From U.S. Highway 95 at milepost 149 (13 miles north of Council, 10 miles south of New Meadows), turn east, cross a bridge over the Weiser River, and into the campground.

FACILITIES: 12 sites in 3 loops; sites are well spaced, with a good amount of vegetation separating them; parking pads are gravel; most parking pads are fairly long straight-ins; many may require additional leveling; a few sites are designated for tents--up on a hill where the terrain is more level and cleared; fireplaces and some barbecue grills; firewood is available for gathering in the area; water at several faucets; vault facilities; gravel driveways; minimal supplies at Pine Ridge, 3 miles north; limited to adequate supplies are available in New Meadows and Council.

SEASON & FEES: $3.00; May to October; 16 day limit.

NATURAL FEATURES: Located on a slope in a densely forested canyon along the Weiser River; the river flows swiftly by the campground, and a number of sites are right above the river's edge; tall timber and brush separate the sites nicely; campground elevation is 3800'; to the east are the West Mountains, where peaks rise to 8000'.

ATTRACTIONS: Fishing; hiking; berry-picking in season; boating on nearby Lost Valley Reservoir, accessible about 8 miles north; adjacent day use area has large tables and a campfire circle.

NOTES: Another popular local camping area is near Lost Valley Reservoir. Two campgrounds there, Cold Springs and Slaughter Gulch, have facilities similar to those at Evergreen. They're accessible from Highway 95 milepost 152 +.5. Drive west on a steep gravel access road 3 and 5 miles, respectively.

PONDEROSA
State Park

LOCATION: Western Idaho north of Boise.

ACCESS: From Idaho State Highway 55 at milepost 144 in mid-town McCall, follow the well-marked route through town and northeast on a paved access road for 1.6 miles to the campground entrance.

FACILITIES: 170 sites, including 108 with partial hookups, in 3 loops; most of the sites are level, average or better in size, and most have good separation; parking aprons are paved or oiled gravel; many parking spots are spacious enough to accommodate large rv's; good to excellent tent-pitching spots; fireplaces; b-y-o firewood is recommended; water at many sites as well as at centrally located faucets; restrooms with showers; holding tank disposal station; paved driveways; resident ranger-manager; adequate supplies and services are available in McCall.

SEASON & FEES: $7.00 for a standard site, $9.00 for a partial-hookup site, $4.00 for an extra vehicle; May to September, with limited camping in winter; 10 day limit; reservations accepted.

NATURAL FEATURES: Located on a forested peninsula on Payette Lake, a glacially-formed natural lake fed by the Payette River; campground vegetation is primarily very tall conifers of many varieties and some additional medium-height vegetation; within the boundaries of the park can be found quite a variety of terrain, from marshes to sage flats to steep rocky cliffs; elevation 5000'.

ATTRACTIONS: Boating; sailing; fishing; swimming beach; nature trails; visitor center; campfire programs; children's playground; ice skating, sledding and cross-country skiing; old mining towns in the surrounding area.

NOTES: Ponderosa is located on the shores of a beautiful mountain lake in a high mountain valley. This facility has excellent camping and other recreational opportunities. Reservations might be a good idea for summer weekends.

RAINBOW POINT
Boise National Forest

LOCATION: Western Idaho north of Boise.

ACCESS: From Idaho State Highway 55 at milepost 131+.3 in midtown Donnelly, turn west onto the Cascade Reservoir Loop Road (watch for a "Rainbow Point Campgrounds" sign); drive west across the Payette River on this winding paved access road for 4 miles to a "T" intersection (at Tamarack Falls); turn south (left) onto West Mountain Road; proceed 0.8 mile (gravel) and turn east (left) into the campground.

FACILITIES: 13 sites; sites are mostly level, medium to large, with good to excellent separation; parking pads are oiled gravel, a few may require additional leveling; some sites have pull-through parking pads spacious enough to accommodate large rv's; several very good tent spots in fairly dense vegetation; fireplaces; some firewood is available for gathering in the area; water at several faucets; vault facilities; gravel driveways; minimal supplies in Donnelly; adequate supplies and services are available in McCall, 18 miles north, or Cascade, 20 miles south.

SEASON & FEES: $4.00; June to October; 16 day limit.

NATURAL FEATURES: Located on the densely forested northwest shore of Cascade Reservoir in Long Valley at 4800'; the reservoir was formed by the bridling of the Payette River; the West Mountains, with peaks loftier than 7000,' rise just to the west.

ATTRACTIONS: Fishing (reportedly some of the best fishing in Idaho); boating; boat launch.

NOTES: Views east across Cascade Reservoir and Long Valley are quite impressive. 'Next door' to Rainbow Point is another national forest campground, Amanita, with 10 units and similar facilities. A number of Amanita's sites are lakeside. Campsites at both of these campgrounds are more sheltered than those at several Bureau of Reclamation campgrounds farther south on the west shore.

WEST MOUNTAIN
Bureau of Reclamation Recreation Area

LOCATION: Western Idaho north of Boise.

ACCESS: From Idaho State Highway 55 at milepost 131+.3 in midtown Donnelly, turn west onto the Cascade Reservoir Loop Road (watch for a "Rainbow Point Campgrounds" sign); drive west across the Payette River on this winding paved access road for 4 miles to a "T" intersection (at Tamarack Falls); turn south (left) onto West Mountain Road; proceed 1.5 miles (gravel) south and turn east (left) into the North Unit; continue 1.5 miles further and turn east (left) into the South Unit.

FACILITIES: 56 level sites, including 30 in the North Unit and 26 in the South Unit; sites are medium to large with nominal separation; parking pads are paved and spacious enough to accommodate very large rv's; lawns are perfect for tents; fire rings and/or barbecue grills at each site; firewood is occasionally for sale, some may be available for gathering locally; water at several faucet-fountains; vault facilities in the north unit, restrooms with showers in the south unit; holding tank disposal station nearby; paved driveways; campground host; adequate supplies and services are available in McCall, 20 miles north, and Cascade, 22 miles south.

SEASON & FEES: $4.00; May to September; 14 day limit.

NATURAL FEATURES: Located in Long Valley in an open meadow on the west shore of Cascade Reservoir, which was formed by the damming of the Payette River; the West Mountains, with peaks above 7000', rise within view to the west; vegetation in the campground consists of mown grass with a few large trees.

ATTRACTIONS: Fishing (reportedly there is excellent fishing in Cascade Reservoir); boating.

NOTES: It is a bit of a surprise to find such a nice facility this far off the beaten path. There are terrific views of the lake to the east and of the forested ridges to the west!

BUTTERCUP
Bureau of Reclamation Recreation Area

LOCATION: Western Idaho north of Boise.

ACCESS: From Idaho State Highway 55 at milepost 131+.3 in midtown Donnelly, turn west onto the Cascade Reservoir Loop Road (watch for a "Rainbow Point Campgrounds" sign); drive west across the Payette River on this winding paved access road for 4 miles to a "T" intersection (at Tamarack Falls); turn south (left) onto West Mountain Road; proceed 2.5 miles (gravel) south and turn east (left) into the campground.

FACILITIES: 27 level sites; sites are average to large with nominal separation; parking pads are paved, mostly straight-ins, and spacious enough to accommodate very large rv's; lawns are nicely landscaped and perfect for tents; barbecue grills; firewood is often available for sale, and some may be available for gathering in the area; water at several faucet-fountains; vault facilities; holding tank disposal station 0.4 mile south on West Mountain Road; paved driveways; campground host; camper supplies in Tamarack Falls; adequate supplies and services are available in McCall, 20 miles north, and Cascade, 22 miles south.

SEASON & FEES: $4.00; May to September; 14 day limit.

NATURAL FEATURES: Located in Long Valley on the grassy lakeshore of a small peninsula which extends from this point eastward into Cascade Reservoir, formed by the damming of the Payette River; campground vegetation consists of gently rolling grassy slopes dotted with newly planted fir trees; altitude is 4800'.

ATTRACTIONS: Great lake views; boating; boat ramp at Rainbow Point; reportedly some of the best lake fishing in the state; Long Valley Museum in Donnelly.

NOTES: Buttercup Campground is very new--first opened in 1986. Views of the lake are perhaps a little better here than at other points on the west shore.

47

POISON CREEK
Bureau of Reclamation Recreation Area

LOCATION: Western Idaho north of Boise.

ACCESS: From Idaho State Highway 55 at milepost 131+.3 in midtown Donnelly, turn west onto the Cascade Reservoir Loop Road (watch for a sign "Rainbow Point Campgrounds"); drive west across the Payette River on this winding paved access road for 4 miles to a "T" intersection (at Tamarack Falls); turn south (left) onto West Mountain Road (gravel); proceed 3.7 miles, then turn east (left) into the campground.

FACILITIES: 18 level sites plus parking for an additional 19 walk-in sites; parking pads are gravel, mostly large straight-ins; barbecue grills; b-y-o firewood is recommended; central restrooms (H); water at several faucets; holding tank disposal station 0.6 miles north; gravel driveways; adequate supplies and services are available in McCall, 22 miles north, and Cascade, 24 miles south.

SEASON & FEES: $4.00; June to October; 14 day limit.

NATURAL FEATURES: Located in Long Valley on the west shore of Cascade Reservoir; some sites are lakeside and a number of other sites are situated in a stand of trees a few yards west of the lake; the West Mountains are visible to the west; campground vegetation consists of grass and a few more trees than at the several campgrounds just to the north.

ATTRACTIONS: Boating (boat docks at this campground and boat ramps at the northern end of the lake); fishing (said to be some of the best in Idaho); open grassy area adjacent for recreational activities.

NOTES: This and other west shore campgrounds are also accessible from the south at the town of Cascade. At last report, the scenic drive was fantastic, but a 15-mile section of West Mountain Road was extremely rough. Poison Creek's name belies its attractiveness. It's one of the nicest of the 6 campgrounds along this shore.

MANN CREEK RESERVOIR
Bureau of Reclamation Camp

LOCATION: Western Idaho northwest of Boise.

ACCESS: From U.S. Highway 95 at milepost 95 +.2 (13 miles north of Weiser, 19 miles south of Cambridge), turn west onto Mann Creek Road; drive west (paved for 1 mile), north and west again, past the dam; continue north along the east shore of the reservoir; turn west (left) onto a gravel access road; proceed 0.1 mile to the campground. (Campground is at the far end of the reservoir in a grove of trees, a total of 3 miles from U.S. 95.)

FACILITIES: 10 level sites; parking pads are average-sized, gravel straight-ins or pull-alongs; 5 sites are semi-walk-ins, with sheltered tables; barbecue grills and some fire rings; limited firewood is available for gathering in the area, so b-y-o is suggested; water at a hand pump; vault facilities (H); gravel driveways; camper supplies at a small store on Highway 95, south of Mann Creek Road; limited supplies in Midvale, 10 miles north; adequate supplies are available in Weiser.

SEASON & FEES: No fee; open all year.

NATURAL FEATURES: Located at the far north end of Mann Creek Reservoir, where Mann Creek rushes past the campground and flows into the lake; 5 sites are on a lawn near a stand of hardwoods; 5, more open, sites are bordered by boulders and bunchgrass; the Hitt Mountains rise to about 7000' just north of here.

ATTRACTIONS: Boating; fishing; boat ramp 1 mile south of the campground; picnic area at the dam; foot trail leads along the creek; phenomenally scenic view from a rest area on U.S. 95, near milepost 101.

NOTES: The campground is *really* a pleasant surprise for this part of the country! There is a nice view of the lake through the trees from several of the sites.

SWINGING BRIDGE
Boise National Forest

LOCATION: Western Idaho north of Boise.

ACCESS: From Idaho State Highway 55 at a point 2 miles north of the Boise/Valley County Line, 30 miles south of Cascade, turn west at either of 2 entrances (south or north end) of the campground.

FACILITIES: 12 sites; units are medium to large with average to good separation; parking pads are paved, medium straight-ins or pull-alongs; some additional leveling may be necessary (though pads and tent areas are well leveled, considering the steep slope); both barbecue grills and elaborate fire rings at each site; some firewood is available for gathering in the vicinity; water at a hand pump; vault facilities; paved driveways (maneuvering may be a little difficult for large vehicles); minimal supplies in Banks, 8 miles south; complete supplies and services are available in Boise, 40 miles south.

SEASON & FEES: $4.00; June to October; 16 day limit.

NATURAL FEATURES: Located on a densely forested hillside across the highway from the North Fork of the Payette River which flows through a deep and narrow canyon here between the West Mountains to the west and the Salmon River Mountains to the east; a small rivulet runs through the campground on its way to the North Fork; campground vegetation consists of a fairly dense stand of very tall conifers with some underbrush.

ATTRACTIONS: Fishing in the North Fork; remnants of a hand-cable suspension bridge span the river 0.5 mile to the south; foot trails in the camp area have steps built into the side of the slope; this section of Highway 55 is designated as part of the Payette River Scenic Route.

NOTES: These campsites are nicely situated on a forested hillside sheltered by tall timber. Though some of the sites are rather close to the highway, the dense forest serves as a barrier to traffic noise as well as a pleasing atmosphere.

BANKS
Boise National Forest

LOCATION: Western Idaho north of Boise.

ACCESS: From Idaho State Highway 55 at milepost 77 +.9 (1 mile south of Banks, 14 miles north of Horseshoe Bend), turn east into the upper section, or pull off the highway on the west for access to the lower section.

FACILITIES: 9 sites; 4 sites in the lower section are walk-ins, built on a rocky bluff along the river, where parking is very limited and only smaller tents could easily fit into the small spaces; the upper section has some pads long enough for medium vehicles, and is better than the lower section for larger tents; barbecue grills and also a couple of fire rings; not much firewood is available for gathering in the vicinity, so b-y-o is recommended; water at several faucets; vault facilities; paved driveway to the upper sites; minimal supplies 2 miles south or 1 mile north on Highway 55; complete supplies and services are available in Boise, 37 miles south.

SEASON & FEES: $3.00; June to October; 16 day limit.

NATURAL FEATURES: Located on the east bank of the Payette River, in a steep-walled and rugged canyon situated between the West Mountains and Boise Ridge; 1 mile downstream from where the North Fork flows into the Payette River; sites in the lower section are right along the river; sites in the upper section are on a hill overlooking the river; campground vegetation consists of tall grass and a few trees clinging to a rocky slope in the lower section, open conifer forest in the upper section.

ATTRACTIONS: River rafting; fishing; large, sandy river bar (subject to change); terrific scenery; a drive east from milepost 78 +.9 toward Lowman is a real experience!

NOTES: The fact that room was found for campsites along this stretch is amazing, considering the steep, rocky walls of the canyon. The sound of the rushing river almost drowns out road noise.

HOT SPRINGS
Boise National Forest

LOCATION: Western Idaho northeast of Boise.

ACCESS: From Idaho State Highway 55 at milepost 79 (0.1 mile north of Banks, 37 miles south of Cascade), turn east onto the Banks-Lowman Road (paved); proceed 13.7 miles east; turn north (left) into the campground.

FACILITIES: 12 sites; units are medium to large with minimal to average separation; parking pads are gravel and level; many pads are spacious enough for larger rv's; large tents will easily be accommodated in most of the sites; barbecue grills; limited firewood is available for gathering in the vicinity; water at hand pumps; vault facilities; gravel driveways; minimal supplies in Garden Valley, 3 miles west; nearest source of complete supplies and services is Boise, 50 miles south.

SEASON & FEES: $4.00; June to October; 16 day limit.

NATURAL FEATURES: Located in an open forest area in a valley along the South Fork of the Payette River; some sites are fairly private because of the surrounding tall conifers; other sites are in more open grassy areas; a tall forested ridge borders the campground on the north and the South Fork borders the campground across the highway to the south; the Hot Springs are accessible from the campground via a trail down to the river; the Salmon River Mountains lie just to the north and the Boise Mountains are to the south.

ATTRACTIONS: The Hot Springs are the main attraction here; fishing; hiking; river-floating; the drive from here to Lowman offers some spectacular views of this wild area.

NOTES: This camp is conveniently located just a few miles from the heart of the river-running country near Banks. The road from Banks to Hot Springs Campground follows along a narrow, tree-dotted valley and then a wide, fertile valley. A long section of the gravel road from Lowman to Hot Springs Campground is narrow, steep and winding.

PINE FLATS
Boise National Forest

LOCATION: Western Idaho northeast of Boise.

ACCESS: From Idaho State Highway 21 at midtown Lowman, (70 miles northeast of Boise, 58 miles west of Stanley), turn west onto the Lowman-Banks Road; proceed west for 5 miles (paved for 1.1 miles, then the road becomes a steep but good gravel road); turn south (left) onto a steep dirt access road leading 0.3 mile down into the camping area.

FACILITIES: 29 sites; sites are medium to large with average to excellent separation; parking pads are gravel/dirt; some pads are long enough to accommodate larger rv's, but many may require additional leveling; (sites are quite well leveled for parking and tents, considering the steep slope); many large tent areas; fireplaces and barbecue grills at each site; firewood is available for gathering in the area; water at hand pumps; vault facilities; dirt/gravel driveways (maneuvering larger vehicles is likely to be a challenge); minimal supplies in Lowman; nearest source of complete supplies and services is Boise.

SEASON & FEES: $4.00; June to September; 16 day limit.

NATURAL FEATURES: Located on a forested bluff 75' above the South Fork of the Payette River, which flows between two crests of mountain peaks through a very narrow canyon with steep, rocky walls; sites are stretched out along the bluff and many have views of the river below; campground vegetation consists of moderately dense stands of conifers, grass and some underbrush.

ATTRACTIONS: River running; fishing; hiking; the drive west toward Banks is along a narrow, steep, twisty road which passes through some fantastic mountain scenery.

NOTES: Access to the wild South Fork of the Payette River here is not easy, but it is possible. The forested setting is inviting. The campground's location off the main road provides it with somewhat of a secluded atmosphere.

MOUNTAIN VIEW
Boise National Forest

LOCATION: Western Idaho northeast of Boise.

ACCESS: From Idaho State Highway 21 at milepost 73 +.2 (0.5 mile east of Lowman, 58 miles west of Stanley), turn south into the campground.

FACILITIES: 14 level sites; sites are medium to large with mostly average separation; parking pads are level and paved; some pads are large enough to accommodate large rv's; some very large, level areas for good-sized tents; fire rings in addition to barbecue grills; firewood is available for gathering in the area; water at a hand pump; vault facilities; paved driveways vary from wide to narrow, with a turnaround loop at the west end of the campground; minimal supplies in Lowman; limited supplies in Stanley; nearest complete source of supplies and services is Boise, 75 miles south.

SEASON & FEES: $4.00; May to September; 16 day limit.

NATURAL FEATURES: Located on a forested flat that extends east and west slightly above the South Fork of the Payette River; a number of the sites are riverside, with views of the tree-lined canyon; Deadwood Ridge is to the north and the Boise Mountains lie to the south; the campground has moderately dense stands of tall conifers, moderate underbrush, and tall grass for a forest floor.

ATTRACTIONS: River running; the river is easily accessible at this point; fishing; hiking; a number of forest roads and trails lead off into the mountain areas from near here; Lowman Ranger Station is located just west of the campground.

NOTES: Mountain View Campground is situated in a very alluring river valley setting. A number of really fine sites are situated right along the river. This facility is one of the nicest campgrounds along the South Fork of the Payette River.

KIRKHAM HOT SPRINGS
Boise National Forest

LOCATION: Western Idaho northeast of Boise.

ACCESS: From Idaho State Highway 21 at milepost 77 (4 miles east of Lowman, 54 miles west of Stanley), turn south, drive across a bridge over the South Fork of the Payette River and turn west (right) into the campground.

FACILITIES: 17 sites in 2 loops; sites are mostly level, average in size, with minimal to good separation; parking pads are level and paved, and some are large enough to accommodate large rv's; barbecue grills; some firewood is available for gathering in the area; NO DRINKING WATER; pack-it-in/pack-it-out system of trash removal; vault facilities; paved driveways; minimal supplies in Lowman; limited supplies in Stanley; nearest source of complete supplies and services is Boise, 80 miles southwest.

SEASON & FEES: No fee; 16 day limit.

NATURAL FEATURES: Located on a flat that extends east to west along the South Fork of the Payette River; the forested loop has medium-sized trees, moderate underbrush and tall grass for a forest floor; the more open loop has very few trees and tall grass; the ridge to the north across the river and highway is heavily forested; Kirkham Hot Springs are a series of rivulets bubbling out of the talus of a rock wall.

ATTRACTIONS: The main attraction in this area is the hot springs, which are accessible by a foot trail from the west end of the campground; hiking; fishing.

NOTES: Ths sites at Kirkham Hot Springs Campground are more open than at the other campgrounds along this stretch. The South Fork of the Payette River passes through some very scenic canyon areas in this section. The drive along Highway 21, in both directions, offers outstanding mountain scenery.

HELENDE
Boise National Forest

LOCATION: Western Idaho northeast of Boise.

ACCESS: From Idaho State Highway 21 at milepost 81 +.5 (8 miles east of Lowman, 50 miles west of Stanley), turn south onto a paved access road; proceed south for about 100 yards to the campground.

FACILITIES: 10 sites; sites are spacious and have average or better separation; parking pads are paved; some pads are small and some are ample enough for medium-sized rv's; most sites have level grassy or brushy areas to readily accommodate large tents; fire rings and barbecue grills at each site; firewood is available for gathering in the area; water at a single hand pump; vault facilities; paved driveways; minimal supplies in Lowman; limited supplies in Stanley; nearest complete supplies and services are in Boise, 85 miles southwest.

SEASON & FEES: $4.00; May to September; 16 day limit.

NATURAL FEATURES: Located on a grassy flat above the South Fork of the Payette River at 4000' of altitude; the Boise Mountains lie to the south and the Sawtooth Mountains are to the east; campground vegetation consists of a moderately dense conifer forest over an extensive grass and brush floor.

ATTRACTIONS: River running; fishing; Kirkham Hot Springs is 4 miles west on Highway 21; several forest roads and foot trails lead off into the mountains from near this point; Sawtooth National Recreation Area is east of here.

NOTES: Though the campsites are not actually on the riverbank, the atmosphere created by the nearby river is apparent. The campground is shielded from the highway and traffic noise by a substantial grove of trees.

TEN MILE
Boise National Forest

LOCATION: Central Idaho northeast of Boise.

ACCESS: From Idaho State Highway 21 at milepost 47 +.8 (9 miles north of Idaho City, 25 miles south of Lowman), turn right or left into the campground. (Campsites are located on both sides of the highway.)

FACILITIES: 14 sites; sites are average-sized and fairly well separated; parking pads are gravel, small to medium, and many may require additional leveling; the forest floor is rather rocky, so tent-pitching may require extra preparation; fire facilities; firewood is available for gathering in the area; water at a hand pump; vault facilities; gravel driveways; limited supplies in Idaho City; complete supplies and services are available in Boise, 50 miles south.

SEASON & FEES: $3.00; June to September; 16 day limit.

NATURAL FEATURES: Located in a very narrow, steep-walled canyon, where Ten Mile Creek flows into Mores Creek which flows south into the Boise River; tall trees and some creekside brush separate most sites nicely; a number of campsites right along the swiftly flowing creek.

ATTRACTIONS: Fishing; hiking in the vicinity; Idaho City has an information center and an historic mining town exhibit; the drive along Highway 21 is steep and twisty, but does offer some nice scenery; Sawtooth National Recreation Area is located 60 miles east.

NOTES: Because these campsites are built in a very narrow valley (this territory is almost strictly vertical), many of the sites are rather close to the highway. Ten Mile Campground is probably the best of four campgrounds along this stretch. Others are: Hayfork at milepost 48 +.9, Bad Bear at milepost 48, and Grayback Gulch at milepost 36 +.6. All have very similar facilities and a typical mountain-forest environment. This segment of Highway 21 is a lot more serpentine than it looks on most maps.

STANLEY LAKE
Sawtooth National Recreation Area

LOCATION: Central Idaho west of Stanley.

ACCESS: From Idaho State Highway 21 at milepost 125 +.9 (5 miles west of Stanley, 9 miles east of the western boundary of the Sawtooth National Recreation Area), turn southwest onto a good, wide gravel access road; proceed 3 miles to the camping areas.

FACILITIES: 33 sites in 4 loops; sites vary considerably in size, levelness and separation; parking pads are gravel, medium to large, some are straight-ins and a few are pull-throughs; some good tent spots, though many are sloped; fireplaces; firewood is usually available for gathering in the area; water at several hand pumps; vault facilities; gravel driveways; limited supplies in Stanley; adequate supplies and services are available in Ketchum, 65 miles southeast.

SEASON & FEES: $5.00; June to October; 10 day limit.

NATURAL FEATURES: Located on the northwest shore of beautiful Stanley Lake which is 1 mile long, 0.5 mile wide and 100 feet deep; the dramatic relief of the Sawtooth Range is visible across Stanley Lake, including 9860' McGown Peak, just a few miles to the south; campground vegetation is predominantly light to moderate forest with light underbrush.

ATTRACTIONS: Super scenery; boating; boat ramp; designated swimming beach; hiking trails including Alpine Lake and Summit Trails which lead off into the Sawtooth Wilderness Area; snowmobiling; cross-country skiing.

NOTES: Quite a varied selection of sites: Inlet Loop A has 6 lakeside sites, Inlet Loop B has 6 creekside sites, Stanley Lake Loop has 15 sites on a sloping bluff overlooking the lake, and Lakeview has 6 mostly level sites with very good lakeviews. Stanley Lake offers some magnificent scenery, as the campground and the lake are situated right up against the sheer, jagged, rock-faced Sawtooth Range.

SALMON RIVER
Sawtooth National Recreation Area

LOCATION: Central Idaho between Stanley and Challis.

ACCESS: From Highway 75 at milepost 193 +7 (4 miles east of Stanley, 51 miles west of Challis), turn right or left into the campground. (Campsites are both north and south of the highway.)

FACILITIES: 32 sites in 4 loops (2 on each side of the highway); sites are medium to large, with generally good separation; parking pads are gravel, most are medium to long straight-ins, and well-leveled, considering the slight slope of the hillside; good tent spots; fireplaces; ample firewood is available for gathering in the vicinity; water at hand pumps; vault facilities; gravel driveways; limited supplies in Stanley; nearest sources of adequate supplies and services are Ketchum, 65 miles south, and Salmon, 110 miles northeast.

SEASON & FEES: $4.00; mid-June to September; 10 day limit.

NATURAL FEATURES: Located on the gently sloping north bank of the Salmon River, where the river is fairly wide, shallow and slow-moving; two groves of trees above the highway and two groves below the highway provide shelter and separation for all but a few sites; a number of sites are right at the river's edge; a timbered ridge flanks the river on the south; the river's north boundary is a sage and grass covered hillside; tall mountain peaks beyond the canyon walls.

ATTRACTIONS: River rafting; fishing; the superscenic drive along Highway 75 to the west offers fantastic views of the Sawtooth Range, as the Salmon River Canyon opens into a wider valley; Stanley Museum is 4 miles west.

NOTES: This campground is the westernmost, and also the largest, of a half-dozen campgrounds located in the beautiful Salmon River Canyon in this section of the Sawtooth NRA.

RIVERSIDE
Sawtooth National Recreation Area

LOCATION: Central Idaho between Stanley and Challis.

ACCESS: From Idaho State Highway 75 at milepost 195 +.5 (5.1 miles east of Stanley, 50 miles west of Challis), turn right or left into the campground. (Campsites are both north and south of the highway.)

FACILITIES: 8 sites between the highway and the river; 10 more sites on a hillside across the highway from the river; those on the river's edge are a bit close together and also close to the highway; those above the highway are more roomy; parking pads are gravel, most are small to medium straight-ins; additional leveling may be required; fireplaces; firewood is available for gathering in the area; water at hand pumps; vault facilities; gravel driveways; limited supplies in Stanley; adequate supplies and services are available in Ketchum, 65 miles south.

SEASON & FEES: $4.00; mid-June to September; 10 day limit.

NATURAL FEATURES: Located along the forested bank of the 'Wild and Scenic' Salmon River, where the river is fairly wide, shallow and slow-moving; most sites are nicely sheltered; White Cloud Peaks tower to greater than 11,000' to the south, and the Salmon River Mountains lie to the north.

ATTRACTIONS: River rafting; fishing; hiking; Casino Creek Trail leads up into the White Cloud Peaks and to a number of mountain lakes; Sunbeam Hot Springs is 6 miles east; Stanley Museum is 5 miles west; the Redfish Lake area, an exceptionally scenic (and popular) part of Sawtooth NRA, is 11 miles southwest.

NOTES: Though this campground is built on a slope and rather close to the highway, river access is excellent here, and the setting is beautiful. Riverside Campground is located just east of some of the most spectacular scenery in Idaho.

MORMON BEND
Sawtooth National Recreation Area

LOCATION: Central Idaho between Stanley and Challis.

ACCESS: From Idaho State Highway 75 at mileposts 195 +.9 and 196 +.1 (there are 2 entrances) (5.5 miles east of Stanley, 50 miles west of Challis), turn south into the campground.

FACILITIES: 17 sites; sites are mostly level, with average or better separation; parking pads are gravel, some are spacious enough to accommodate large rv's; good tent-pitching opportunities; fireplaces; firewood is available for gathering in the area; water at hand pumps; vault facilities; gravel driveways; limited supplies in Stanley; nearest source of adequate supplies and services is Ketchum, 65 miles south.

SEASON & FEES: $4.00; mid-June to September; 10 day limit.

NATURAL FEATURES: Located on a grassy riverbank in the timbered Salmon River Canyon; the Salmon is considered a 'Wild and Scenic River' along this stretch; White Cloud Peaks rise to over 11,000' south of here, and the Salmon River Mountains are to the north; campsites at the eastern end, in a section dotted with clusters of trees, are more open; sites at the western end are more forested, but closer to the highway; a number of sites are riverside.

ATTRACTIONS: River rafting; fishing; hiking; Casino Creek Trail leads up into the White Cloud Peaks and to a number of mountain lakes; Sunbeam Hot Springs is 5 miles east; Stanley Museum is 6 miles west; the Redfish Lake area, also part of Sawtooth NRA, is 12 miles southwest.

NOTES: This campground is located in a prime position for those who wish to float the river, or use it as a base camp for exploration of the miles and miles of beautiful country in and around the Sawtooth National Recreation Area.

BASIN CREEK
Sawtooth National Recreation Area

LOCATION: Central Idaho between Stanley and Challis.

ACCESS: From Idaho State Highway 75 at milepost 197 +.5 (8 miles east of Stanley, 47 miles west of Challis), turn north into the campground.

FACILITIES: 15 sites; sites are level, good-sized, with minimal separation for the most part; parking pads are gravel, mostly straight-ins, spacious enough to accommodate medium to large rv's; good tent-pitching opportunities; fireplaces; firewood is available for gathering in the vicinity; water at a hand pump; vault facilities; gravel driveways; minimal supplies at Sunbeam, 4 miles east; limited supplies in Stanley; adequate supplies and services are available in Ketchum, 70 miles south.

SEASON & FEES: $4.00; mid-June to September; 10 day limit.

NATURAL FEATURES: Located on an open grassy flat along Basin Creek where it flows into the Salmon River; the Salmon River Canyon, in this stretch, has steep timbered ridges on the south bank and steep rocky ridges on the north bank; campground vegetation consists of grass, dotted with a few small pines and some creekside brush.

ATTRACTIONS: River rafting on the 'Wild and Scenic' Salmon River; fishing; Basin Creek Road (gravel) leads off into the Salmon River Mountains and to a number of hiking trailheads; Sunbeam Hot Springs is 4 miles east; Yankee Fork Road leads north from Highway 75 (at Sunbeam) to the Custer Museum and historically significant mine diggings.

NOTES: Of the several good campgrounds along this stretch of the river, this one is the most open. If maneuvering a vehicle is a consideration, this 'delta-like' area would be ideal.

UPPER O'BRIEN/LOWER O'BRIEN
Sawtooth National Recreation Area

LOCATION: Central Idaho between Stanley and Challis.

ACCESS: From Idaho State Highway 75 at milepost 204 +.5 (15 miles east of Stanley, 40 miles west of Challis), turn south onto a gravel access road which leads down a short but steep hill and east across a wooden bridge over the Salmon River; Upper O'Brien Campground is located directly on the east side of the bridge; Lower O'Brien Campground is 0.2 mile farther east along the south bank of the river.

FACILITIES: 8 sites in Upper O'Brien and 12 in Lower O'Brien; parking pads are gravel, most are straight-ins, a few are pull-throughs; many may require additional leveling; good tent-pitching opportunities beneath tall trees; fireplaces or fire rings at each site; firewood is available for gathering in the vicinity; water at hand pumps; vault facilities; gravel driveways; minimal supplies in Sunbeam, 3 miles west; limited supplies in Stanley; nearest source of adequate supplies and services is Ketchum, 70 miles south.

SEASON & FEES: $4.00; June to September; 10 day limit.

NATURAL FEATURES: Located in the steep-walled narrow Salmon River Canyon, with towering, forested peaks to the north and south; all units are situated on a slight slope along the riverbank; open forest of tall timber, light underbrush and a carpet of pine needles.

ATTRACTIONS: Fishing; river floating; hiking trail leads south along Warm Springs Creek into the White Cloud Peaks; Sunbeam Hot Springs, 3 miles east; Yankee Fork Road leads north from Highway 75 (at Sunbeam) to the Custer Museum, and a backcountry rich in mining history.

NOTES: Lower O'Brien Campground has sites closer to the river, while Upper O'Brien's sites are on a short bluff above it. Right on the eastern edge of some superscenic country!

HOLMAN CREEK
Sawtooth National Recreation Area

LOCATION: Central Idaho between Challis and Stanley.

ACCESS: From Idaho State Highway 75 at milepost 214 +.8 (25 miles east of Stanley, 30 miles southwest of Challis), turn south onto a gravel access road; campsites start about 75 yards south of the highway.

FACILITIES: 13 sites in a single row at the base of a timbered slope; sites are well-distanced from one another, but with little visual separation; parking pads are level, gravel, short to medium straight-ins; tent-pitching areas are fairly level and good-sized; fireplaces; very little firewood is available in the immediate area for gathering, so b-y-o is suggested; water at a hand pump; vault facilities; gravel driveways; minimal supplies and services in Clayton, 8 miles east; minimal to limited supplies in Stanley and Challis; nearest sources of adequate supplies are Salmon, 90 miles east, or Ketchum, 80 miles south.

SEASON & FEES: $3.00; open all year, subject to weather conditions, with no water in winter.

NATURAL FEATURES: Located just inside the eastern border of Challis National Forest; Holman Creek flows into the Salmon River here, where the valley is narrower and more heavily forested than farther east; forested White Cloud Peaks to the south; peaks of the Salmon River Range to the north; conifers dot the hillside which borders the sites on the south; sparse grass and sagebrush cover the flat between the campground and the river.

ATTRACTIONS: Fishing; river floating; access to the Salmon River, across the highway, is a little easier here than farther to the east; hiking; the Sawtooth National Recreation Area is located 25 miles west.

NOTES: This campground is perhaps a happy compromise: more forested than other campgrounds to the east, yet lower in altitude (and therefore less snowbound) than campgrounds to the west.

MOUNTAIN VIEW & CHINOOK BAY
Sawtooth National Recreation Area

LOCATION: Central Idaho south of Stanley.

ACCESS: From Idaho State Highway 75 at milepost 185 (4.4 miles southeast of Stanley, 57 miles north of Ketchum), turn southwest onto the Redfish Lake Recreation Area Road (paved); proceed 0.1 mile southwest to Chinook Bay Campground and 0.3 mile to Mountain View Campground; turn right into either of the two camping areas.

FACILITIES: 20 sites, including 13 sites at Chinook Bay and 7 sites at Mountain View; sites are well-spaced with some separation; parking pads are gravel, level, and most would accommodate medium-sized rv's; fireplaces; firewood is usually available for gathering in the area; water at several faucets; vault facilities; gravel driveways; camper supplies at a lodge on Redfish Lake, 4 miles west; limited supplies in Stanley; adequate supplies and services are available in Ketchum.

SEASON & FEES: $6.00; May to September; 10 day limit.

NATURAL FEATURES: Located in an open forest on the shores of Little Redfish Lake, a small, clear mountain lake nestled at the foot of the dramatically jagged peaks of the Sawtooth Range; the Salmon River flows along next to Highway 75 within a mile of this camping area; campground vegetation consists of tall conifers, a grassy forest floor and very little underbrush.

ATTRACTIONS: Hiking, fishing; float boating; nearby Redfish Lake Rock Shelter holds archeological artifacts dating back nearly 11,000 years; visitor center at Redfish Lake.

NOTES: Scenery is magnificent here viewed from the shores of this beautiful mountain lake surrounded by towering forested peaks. There is less traffic and congestion here than at campgrounds nearer to the more popular Redfish Lake, 4 miles west.

POINT
Sawtooth National Recreation Area

LOCATION: Central Idaho south of Stanley.

ACCESS: From Idaho State Highway 75 at milepost 185 (4.4 miles southeast of Stanley, 57 miles north of Ketchum), turn southwest onto the Redfish Lake Recreation Area Road (paved); proceed 1.8 miles to a fork in the road; turn right at the fork and continue 1 mile around the north side of the lake, past the visitor center and lodge, to the campground.

FACILITIES: 17 sites in 3 loops; 2 loops are close to the beach and a third is above them on a short bluff; sites are rather small but well-spaced; parking aprons are gravel, mostly level, and fairly small; tent-camping only is permitted; water at several faucets; restrooms; holding tank disposal station near the lodge; fireplaces; firewood is usually available for gathering in the vicinity; gravel driveways; camper supplies and laundry at the lodge a few yards east of the campground; limited supplies in Stanley; adequate supplies and services are available in Ketchum.

SEASON & FEES: $6.00; June to September; 10 day limit.

NATURAL FEATURES: Located on a flat point of land extending south into Redfish Lake; shelter/separation is provided at some sites by medium-sized trees and a little underbrush; Redfish Lake is a superscenic lake located at the base of the towering Sawtooth Mountains; great views from most sites.

ATTRACTIONS: Hiking (trails lead into the Sawtooth Wilderness Area); fishing; boating (marina); swimming (probably the most popular swimming beach on the lake); visitor center.

NOTES: This is a favorite spot for water sports enthusiasts. Adjacent to Point Campground is a large and popular day use area with picnicking and swimming facilities. Fantastic vistas through the trees of Redfish Lake and the surrounding mountains!

OUTLET
Sawtooth National Recreation Area

LOCATION: Central Idaho south of Stanley.

ACCESS: From Idaho State Highway 75 at milepost 185 (4.4 miles southeast of Stanley, 57 miles north of Ketchum), turn southwest onto the Redfish Lake Recreation Area Road (paved); proceed 2 miles (past the righthand turnoff to the lodge and visitor center) on a curvy paved road; turn northwest (right) at the campground entrance and proceed down into the campground.

FACILITIES: 46 sites; sites are mostly small to medium with average separation; parking pads are gravel, mostly small to medium straight-ins, with a few larger pull-throughs; tent spots tend to be rather small; barbecue grills; firewood is usually available for gathering in the area; water at faucets throughout; vault facilities; holding tank disposal station near the lodge; paved driveways; camper supplies at the lodge; limited supplies in Stanley; adequate supplies and services are available in Ketchum.

SEASON & FEES: $6.00; May to September; 10 day limit.

NATURAL FEATURES: Located on a forested flat close to the northeast shore of Redfish Lake, a beautiful mountain lake nestled at the foot of some dramatically rugged peaks of the Sawtooth Range; tall timber and very little underbrush provides some privacy between sites.

ATTRACTIONS: Hiking (Marshall Lake and Baron Creek Trailheads nearby); fishing; boating (ramps nearby at Sandy Beach); visitor center on Redfish Lake's north shore.

NOTES: There is a commanding view from near here of this superscenic mountain lake and the rock face of the Sawtooth Mountains which encompass it. Neighboring Point Campground cannot accommodate trailers, so Outlet Campground is often occupied to capacity early in the day during the peak of the season.

GLACIER VIEW
Sawtooth National Recreation Area

LOCATION: Central Idaho south of Stanley.

ACCESS: From Idaho State Highway 75 at milepost 185 (4.4 miles southeast of Stanley, 57 miles north of Ketchum), turn southwest onto the Redfish Lake Recreation Area access road (paved); proceed 2 miles (past the righthand turnoff to the lodge and visitor center) on a curvy paved road; turn southwest (left) and proceed up into the campground.

FACILITIES: 17 fairly level sites; sites are spacious with average to very good separation; parking pads are paved and mostly level; many pads are long enough to accommodate very large rv's; most sites have large, level tent-pitching areas; fireplaces; firewood is usually available for gathering in the area; water at faucets throughout; vault facilities; holding tank disposal station near the lodge; paved driveways; camper supplies at the lodge; limited supplies in Stanley; adequate supplies and services are available in Ketchum.

SEASON & FEES: $6.00; May to September; 10 day limit.

NATURAL FEATURES: Located on a forested hilltop across the main roadway from beautiful Redfish Lake (and Outlet Campground) at the base of the Sawtooth Range; striking views of steep, rocky slopes; campground vegetation consists of light to moderately dense stands of conifers, grass and light underbrush.

ATTRACTIONS: Hiking (Marshall Lake and Baron Creek Trailheads are located nearby); fishing; boating (boat ramp and beach nearby at Sandy Beach); visitor center on Redfish Lake's north shore.

NOTES: Glacier-clad mountains can be glimpsed through the trees from some really nice sites in this relatively tranquil forest setting. Glacier View Campground is a bit more spacious and often less congested than some of the more popular campgrounds nearer to the lake shore.

MOUNT HEYBURN
Sawtooth National Recreation Area

LOCATION: Central Idaho south of Stanley.

ACCESS: From Idaho State Highway 75 at milepost 185 (4.4 miles southeast of Stanley, 57 miles north of Ketchum), turn southwest onto the Redfish Lake Recreation Area Road (paved); proceed 3.5 miles (past the righthand turnoff to the lodge and visitor center) on a curvy paved road; turn southwest (left) into the campground.

FACILITIES: 42 sites; sites are level, medium to large, with average to good separation; some parking pads are paved, most are straight-ins, with a few long pull-throughs for very large rv's; most sites have good, large, level tent-pitching spots; fireplaces; firewood is usually available for gathering in the vicinity; water at faucets throughout; vault facilities; holding tank disposal station near the lodge; fairly wide, paved driveways; camper supplies and laundry at the lodge; limited supplies in Stanley; adequate supplies and services are available in Ketchum.

SEASON & FEES: $6.00; June to September; 10 day limit.

NATURAL FEATURES: Located on a forested hill above Redfish Lake; Redfish Lake is a beautiful mountain lake at 6500' of altitude, snuggled-in among the jagged peaks of the Sawtooth Range; campground vegetation consists of moderately dense stands of tall conifers with light underbrush.

ATTRACTIONS: Hiking (trailhead to the Sawtooth Wilderness Area); boating; boat ramp and beach at nearby Sandy Beach; fishing; cross-country skiing; snowmobiling.

NOTES: Mount Heyburn Campground has a bit quieter atmosphere than some of the more centrally located campgrounds on Redfish Lake. Some sites are situated right up against the mountains; others offer lake views through the trees. Additional similar sites are located at nearby Sockeye Campground, if Mount Heyburn is crowded.

SMOKEY BEAR
Sawtooth National Recreation Area

LOCATION: Central Idaho northwest of Ketchum.

ACCESS: From Idaho State Highway 75 at a point 10 miles south of Stanley and 51 miles north of Ketchum, turn west at a sign for "Alturas Lake"; proceed west and south (past Perkins Lake on the right) for 3.5 miles; turn southeast (left) into the campground.

FACILITIES: 12 sites in 2 loops; sites are medium to large, with moderate to good separation; parking pads are gravel and mostly level; some pads are medium straight-ins and some are pull-throughs large enough for medium-sized rv's; some good tent-pitching opportunities; fireplaces; firewood is available for gathering in the area; water at several faucets; vault facilities; gravel driveways with a turnaround loop at the eastern end of the campground; limited supplies in Stanley; adequate supplies and services are available in Ketchum.

SEASON & FEES: $5.00; June to September; 10 day limit.

NATURAL FEATURES: Located on an open sage flat along the north shore of Alturas Lake, in the broad Salmon River Valley; peaks of the Sawtooth Range rise sharply from the lake's western shore to above 10,000'; campground vegetation includes grass and some thin pines between sites; campground elevation is 7000'.

ATTRACTIONS: Boating; boat ramp and floating dock at the eastern end of the campground; beach access; hiking; a nearby ghost town, Sawtooth City, is accessible by forest road; the ultra-wide vistas of the Sawtooth Range and Salmon River Valley are really spectacular from Galena Summit Overlook, near here on Highway 75.

NOTES: Smokey Bear Campground is the easternmost campground on Alturas Lake. The superscenic lake and surrounding mountains are visible from virtually all sites.

ALTURAS INLET
Sawtooth National Recreation Area

LOCATION: Central Idaho northwest of Ketchum.

ACCESS: From Idaho State Highway 75 at a point 10 miles south of Stanley and 51 miles north of Ketchum, turn west at a sign for "Alturas Lake"; proceed west and south (past Perkins Lake on the right) for 5 miles; turn southeast (left) into the campground.

FACILITIES: 29 level sites; sites are medium to large, with mostly good to excellent separation; parking pads are gravel, level and most are straight-ins large enough for medium-sized rv's; many good tent-pitching opportunites; fireplaces; firewood is available for gathering in the area; water at several faucets; vault facilities; gravel driveways; limited supplies in Stanley; adequate supplies and services are available in Ketchum.

SEASON & FEES: $5.00; June to September; 10 day limit.

NATURAL FEATURES: Located on a forested flat along the west shore of Alturas Lake, where Alturas Lake Creek flows into the lake; this lovely mountain lake is 2 miles long, 0.5 mile wide and 300' deep; campground vegetation consists of tall pines, tall grass and very little underbrush.

ATTRACTIONS: Boating; sailing, water-skiing, fishing, (boat ramp at Smokey Bear Campground, 2 miles east); hiking; an old ghost town, Sawtooth City, is accessible by forest road from near here; the drive along Highway 75, the Sawtooth Scenic Drive, follows the Salmon River Valley past a point very near the headwaters of the legendary 420-mile-long Salmon River.

NOTES: Alturas Inlet Campground is located in a pocket at the west end of the lake and up against the Sawtooth Mountain Range. Alturas Lake is a liquid sapphire surrounded by emerald-mantled mountain slopes. Very nice indeed.

EASLEY
Sawtooth National Recreation Area

LOCATION: Central Idaho northwest of Ketchum.

ACCESS: From Idaho State Highway 75 at a point 14 miles north of Ketchum and 47 miles south of Stanley, turn southwest onto a gravel access road; proceed 0.2 mile and turn northwest (right) into the campground.

FACILITIES: 17 level sites in 2 loops; units are well-spaced with average to good separation; parking pads are gravel, level, and mostly short straight-ins, though some are quite wide; some good, level, grassy tent-pitching spaces; fireplaces; limited firewood is available for gathering in the area; water at faucets; vault facilities; gravel driveway with a turnaround loop at the end; camper supplies at Easley Hot Springs (store adjacent to the hot springs), 0.1 mile southwest; adequate supplies and services are available in Ketchum.

SEASON & FEES: $3.00; June to September; 10 day limit.

NATURAL FEATURES: Located in a broad sweeping mountain meadow near the headwaters of the Wood River; the Boulder Mountains rise to the east; foothills of the Sawtooth Range are immediately to the west; a few sites are within a few yards of the Wood River; campground vegetation consists of some tall grass and a few medium-sized trees.

ATTRACTIONS: Great scenery on the drive along the Sawtooth Scenic Route (Highway 75) north from here toward Stanley; "hot water plunge" at the private resort just to the southwest (across the wooden bridge); stream fishing; hiking in the nearby mountain areas; adjacent group camping area available by reservation.

NOTES: The super scenery in this valley overshadows the somewhat ordinary facilities at the campground itself.

WOOD RIVER
Sawtooth National Recreation Area

LOCATION: Central Idaho northwest of Ketchum.

ACCESS: From Idaho State Highway 75 at a point 10 miles northwest of Ketchum and 51 miles south of Stanley, turn south (this stretch of the highway actually lies in an east/west directrion) into the campground.

FACILITIES: 32 sites in 3 loops; sites are average to large with mostly good separation; most parking pads are paved, level, medium-sized straight-ins, with a few longer pull-throughs; some good tent-pitching opportunities; fireplaces; firewood is available for gathering in the vicinity; water at faucets throughout; restrooms supplemented by vault facilities; paved driveways; campground host; adequate supplies and services are available in Ketchum.

SEASON & FEES: $5.00; June to September; 10 day limit.

NATURAL FEATURES: Located on a forested flat along the Wood River; the Boulder Mountains rise to the east; foothills of the Sawtooth Range are immediately to the west; campground vegetation consists of moderately dense stands of conifers, grass and considerable underbrush.

ATTRACTIONS: Great scenery in the Wood River Valley and along the Sawtooth Scenic Route (Highway 75) especially northward toward Galena Summit Overlook and Stanley; amphitheater for campfire programs; self-guided nature trail from near the day use area; nearby on Highway 75, a jeep trail leads up to Boulder Basin, a 'high-in-the-sky' deserted mining camp; stream fishing; hiking.

NOTES: The rushing Wood River provides an ambient quality which helps to create what might be called a 'cordial' atmosphere at this very inviting campground. Some sites are forested, some are in the open, and some are creekside. All sites are really nice!

NORTH FORK
Sawtooth National Recreation Area

LOCATION: Central Idaho north of Ketchum.

ACCESS: From Idaho State Highway 75 at a point 8 miles north of Ketchum and 53 miles south of Stanley, turn west into the campground (there are 2 entrances fairly close together).

FACILITIES: 26 sites in 2 forested loops; sites are average or better in size, with fairly good separation; most parking pads are level, gravel/dirt (may be muddy or rutty in wet weather); some pull-throughs are long enough to accommodate medium-sized trailers; some good tent-pitching possibilities; fireplaces; firewood is available for gathering in the vicinity; water at several faucets; vault facilities; gravel driveways; adequate supplies and services are available in Ketchum.

SEASON & FEES: $4.00; June to September; 16 day limit.

NATURAL FEATURES: Located where the North Fork flows into the Wood River; the Boulder Mountains rise to the east and the foothills of the Sawtooth Range are immediately to the west; an open meadow bordered by an aspen grove is located across the highway to the east; several riverside sites; campsites are within a fairly dense conifer forest with considerable underbrush.

ATTRACTIONS: The Sawtooth Scenic Route follows Highway 75 along the Wood River in this section and offers fantastic scenery, especially when you reach Galena Summit Overlook, north of here; stream fishing; hiking in the nearby mountains; skiing and snowmobiling; the Sawtooth National Recreation Area Headquarters is located directly across the highway.

NOTES: This campground is a step down from nearby Wood River Campground (see separate listing) as far as 'best' in this region north of Ketchum and ski-famous Sun Valley. It's slightly handier to town, though.

74

EAST FORK
Bureau of Land Management Camp

LOCATION: Central Idaho between Challis and Stanley.

ACCESS: From Idaho State Highway 75 at milepost 227 (17 miles southwest of the intersection of Highways 75 and 93 near Challis, 38 miles northeast of Stanley), turn northwest into the campground.

FACILITIES: 10 level sites; units are rather small and close together; parking pads are gravel pull-throughs or pull-alongs, large enough to accommodate medium-sized vehicles; tent spots are level and grassy, but rather small; several tables have cement foundations and sun shelters; fireplaces; very limited firewood is available in the area, so b-y-o is recommended; water at faucets; vault facilities; gravel driveway; minimal supplies in Clayton, 4 miles west; minimal to limited supplies in Challis, 20 miles north, or Stanley.

SEASON & FEES: $3.00; open all year, with no water or fee in winter.

NATURAL FEATURES: Located in the Salmon River Valley on a rather barren bluff overlooking the Salmon River, where the East Fork of the Salmon enters the Salmon; steep canyon wall across the river; some brush and small trees along the river, but vegetation in the campground itself consists of sparse grass with only a few seedlings planted for future shelter; typically breezy; the Salmon River Range rises to almost 10,000' to the north.

ATTRACTIONS: Fishing; river floating; a foot trail leads from the campsites down to the river's edge; access from the west, along either Highway 75 or Highway 21, is through the Sawtooth National Recreation Area, with the spectacular scenery of the rugged Sawtooth Range.

NOTES: The facilities at this campground are some of the best in this stretch of Highway 75. The campsites and the surrounding barren terrain are, however, quite exposed to the effects of the prevailing winds and the summer sun.

BAYHORSE
Bureau of Land Management Camp

LOCATION: Central Idaho between Challis and Stanley.

ACCESS: From Idaho State Highway 75 at milepost 237 (7 miles southwest of the intersection of Highway 75 and U.S. 93 near Challis, 48 miles northeast of Stanley), turn northwest into the campground.

FACILITIES: 12 sites in 3 loops; sites are well-spaced, but with virtually no visual separation; parking pads are level, gravel, short to medium straight-ins; tent sites are level, grassy and quite sizeable; barbecue grills at each site, plus some additional fire rings; very limited firewood is available for gathering, so b-y-o is recommended; water at a single hand pump; vault facilities; gravel driveways; minimal to limited supplies in Challis, 10 miles north, or Stanley; adequate supplies and services are available in Salmon, 70 miles northeast. (You may want to stock up before coming through this stretch.)

SEASON & FEES: $3.00; open all year, with no water or fee in winter; 16 day limit.

NATURAL FEATURES: Located at 5500' on a grassy, sage flat along the Salmon River, just below the level of the highway; the Salmon River Mountains rise to almost 10,000' just to the west, and the White Cloud Peaks tower to over 11,000' to the southwest; campground vegetation consists of sparse grass, with some brush and trees along the river.

ATTRACTIONS: Fishing; good river access; a small wooden footbridge spans an irrigation canal which flows between the campsites and the river; nearby Bayhorse Creek Road follows the creek for 7 miles to Bayhorse Lake, at almost 8600'; hiking.

NOTES: This campground is located in a fairly dry river valley flanked by high, dry hills and distant timbered mountains. Shelter is very limited, and, though the river is close at hand, there's a thirsty look about the locale.

SPRING GULCH
Bureau of Land Management Camp

LOCATION: Central Idaho between Salmon and Challis.

ACCESS: From U.S. Highway 93 at milepost 256 +.7 (10 miles northeast of Challis, 50 miles south of Salmon), turn northwest into the campground. (The campground entrance is just 100 yards west of the Salmon River Bridge.)

FACILITIES: 12 level sites in 2 loops; sites are fairly well spaced, with average separation in the loop closer to the highway, minimal separation between other sites; most units have level, gravel, pull-along parking aprons; larger vehicles could be accommodated; small to medium, level, grassy tent areas; some sites have barbecue grills, others have stone fire rings; limited firewood is available for gathering in the vicinity; water at a hand pump; vault facilities; driveway (a bit rutty) has a dirt and gravel surface; minimal to limited supplies in Challis; adequate supplies and services are available in Salmon.

SEASON & FEES: No fee; open all year.

NATURAL FEATURES: Located on a bluff slightly above the Salmon River; the river valley is flanked by dry barren mountains on either side; forested peaks of the Salmon River Mountains, rising to almost 10,000', are visible to the west; campground vegetation consists of patches of tall grass, some eye-level brush and a few tall cottonwood trees.

ATTRACTIONS: Limited access to the river at this point; a "carry-in" boat launch; river floating; good stream fishing here and on nearby Morgan Creek.

NOTES: In addition to Spring Gulch, there are 2 other small BLM recreation sites in the vicinity: Cottonwood (5 miles east), and Morgan Creek (5 miles west and 4 miles north off Highway 93 on Morgan Creek Road). Of the trio, Spring Gulch has the most complete facilities and is the most easily accessible.

MACKAY RESERVOIR
Bureau of Land Management Recreation Area

LOCATION: South-central Idaho northwest of Arco.

ACCESS: From U. S. Highway 93 Alternate at milepost 113 +.6 (4.8 miles north of the town of Mackay, 46 miles south of Challis), turn west into the campground.

FACILITIES: 58 sites in 2 loops; Loop A is on a sage slope overlooking the lake; Loop B is closer to the shore; Loop A has short to medium straight-ins with good distance between sites; Loop B has pull-alongs or long, level, parallel pull-throughs quite close together; parking pads are gravel; some large tent sites in Loop A, but they may be a bit slopey; most sites have barbecue grills, some have fireplaces; a few sites have sun/wind shelters; water at faucets throughout; vault facilities; holding tank disposal station; gravel driveways; limited supplies are available in Mackay, Challis and Arco.

SEASON & FEES: $3.00; May to October; 16 day limit.

NATURAL FEATURES: Located on the east/northeast shore of Mackay Reservoir, formed by the damming of the Big Lost River; the area surrounding the reservoir is quite arid, with only a few poplars planted in the campground area; sage and grass-covered hills surround the lake; dry rocky peaks of the Big Lost River Range rise to the east; the White Knob Mountains are visible to the southwest.

ATTRACTIONS: Boating; fishing; 4-wheel-drive trails lead from near here up into the Challis National Forest; the heavily timbered and jagged-peaked Sawtooth National Recreation Area is about 70 highway miles to the west.

NOTES: Considering the semi-arid conditions and the fairly constant breeze/wind/gale that persists here, this is a fine campground. The lake is large enough to offer good water recreational opportunities in an otherwise lakeless part of Idaho.

CRATERS OF THE MOON
National Monument

LOCATION: Central Idaho west of Arco.

ACCESS: From U.S. 20/26 at milepost 229 +.4 (18 miles west of Arco, 24 miles east of Carey), turn south into Craters of the Moon National Monument; proceed 0.3 mile to the entrance station; continue 0.1 mile further and turn right into the campground.

FACILITIES: 52 sites; sites are small to medium with minimal to average separation; parking areas are cinder-covered straight-ins and pull-alongs, many are long enough to accommodate medium to large rv's; some additional leveling may be necessary; nice, medium to large, barren tent areas; barbecue grills (charcoal fires only); water at faucets throughout; restrooms; paved driveways; resident manager; limited supplies and services are available in Arco, 18 miles east.

SEASON & FEES: $5.00 for a site, plus $3.00 for the park entrance fee; May to October; 14 day limit.

NATURAL FEATURES: Located on a rocky hill with many sites in among a number of knolls and dips and rock pockets; 'Craters of the Moon', so-named because of the moonscape terrain, encompasses an 83-square-mile volcanic area with lava flows, cinder cones and other unusual geological features; campground vegetation consists mostly of mesquite, sage and other brushy plants.

ATTRACTIONS: Within the park is a 7-mile loop drive with side spurs; foot trails lead to fascinating features including the Craters of the Moon Wilderness Area; ranger-directed hikes in season; geological and historic exhibits at the visitor center; naturalist programs on summer evenings.

NOTES: The volcanic features in this park are truly fascinating. The campground terrain is unique, and it's not uncommon for campers (particularly younger ones) to vividly imagine that they've been transported to another planet!

79

BRUNEAU DUNES
State Park

LOCATION: Southern Idaho south of Mountain Home.

ACCESS: From Idaho State Highway 78 at milepost 84 +.3 (2 miles east of the intersection of Idaho State Highways 51 and 78, 14 miles west of the hamlet of Hammett), turn south onto a paved access road; proceed south for 1 mile to the park entrance; continue 1.7 miles to the campground turnoff.

FACILITIES: 48 sites, including many with partial hookups; sites are average-sized with minimal separation; parking pads are gravel, fairly level, medium to large straight-ins; excellent tent-pitching opportunities; many sites have sun/wind shelters; water at faucets throughout; restroom with solar-heated showers; fireplaces; b-y-o firewood; resident ranger-manager; paved driveways; adequate to complete supplies and services are available in Mountain Home, 17 miles north.

SEASON & FEES: $7.00 for a standard site, $9.00 for a partial-hookup site, reduced fees in winter; open all year; 10 day limit.

NATURAL FEATURES: Located on a tree-dotted, mown grassy slope surrounded by treeless sage hills; tiny Bruneau Lake is within the park; largest single sand dune in North America rises 470' above the level of the lake; typically breezy; temperatures can reach 110° F in summer; less than 10 inches of rainfall per year.

ATTRACTIONS: Sand dune exploration, limited to foot traffic; hiking; trails lead through marshes, desert prairie and sand dunes; motorless boating on Bruneau Lake; visitor center with interpretive displays; Silver City, an 1864 ghost town, located nearby; C.J. Strike Reservoir, 2 miles west at the intersection of Idaho State Highways 51 and 78.

NOTES: Bruneau Dunes is situated in a distinctively different environment. The terrain surrounding the park is barren, but the campground itself is rather inviting.

THREE ISLAND CROSSING
State Park

LOCATION: Southwest Idaho between Boise and Twin Falls.

ACCESS: From Interstate 84 exit 120 (eastbound) or exit 121 (westbound) at Glenns Ferry; drive 1 mile on Business Route 84 into mid-town Glenns Ferry; turn south onto Commercial Street; proceed to a "T" intersection; turn west (right); continue west to the park, on the left. (The well-signed route totals 2.6 miles from I-84 to the park.)

FACILITIES: 50 sites, many with partial hookups; sites are level and medium-sized, with minimal separation; parking pads are paved, and typically spacious enough to accommodate large rv's; good tent-pitching opportunities on mown lawns; fireplaces; b-y-o firewood; restrooms (H) with showers; holding tank disposal station; paved driveways; limited supplies and services in Glenns Ferry.

SEASON & FEES: $7.00 for a standard site, $9.00 for a partial-hookup site; open all year, with limited facilities in winter; 15 day limit.

NATURAL FEATURES: Located on a bluff above the Snake River; in summer, the green mown lawn, with a few tall hardwoods planted for limited separation/shelter, stands in sharp contrast to the surrounding sage flat.

ATTRACTIONS: An interpretive center has displays and historical information; boat launches nearby; adjacent day use area with a Conestoga wagon, picnic facility, covered shelter, nature trail and beach; the park maintains an unusual exhibit--a small herd of buffalo and longhorn cattle.

NOTES: Three Island Crossing is the site where Oregon Trail travelers crossed the Snake River. (Wagon tracks are still visible.) This campground is, at times, bothered by disagreeable odors, if the wind is from the wrong direction. Many campers (and mid-summer insects) are not noticeably distressed. The park is a veritable oasis on the southern Idaho plains.

DEVIL'S GARDEN
Massacre Rocks State Park

LOCATION: Southeast Idaho southwest of Pocatello.

ACCESS: From Interstate 86 exit 28, (43 miles east of Burley, 12 miles west of American Falls), proceed east on the north frontage road for 0.8 mile; turn left into the park; the campground is just beyond the Visitor Center. (Exit is signed for "Massacre Rocks State Park".)

FACILITIES: 52 sites, all with partial hookups; sites are small to average in size, and have minimal separation; parking pads are gravel, and vary from short straight-ins to long pull-throughs; additional leveling may be required; tent-pitching could be a challenge; framed and leveled, gravel table pads; fireplaces; b-y-o firewood; restrooms with showers; gravel driveways; holding tank disposal station; limited to adequate supplies in American Falls; complete supplies and services are available in Pocatello, 36 miles east.

SEASON & FEES: $9.00 for a site, $2.00 for an extra vehicle; open all year, with limited facilities in winter; 15 day limit.

NATURAL FEATURES: Located on a hill overlooking the Snake River; the terrain is quite rocky, with some tall grass and short junipers; the most impressive attraction here is "Devil's Garden", a unique geological formation that features jagged lava rocks jutting up from the arid plains.

ATTRACTIONS: Boat launch; visitor center provides exhibits and information; campfire programs during the summer season; "Meadows" self-guided nature trail leads down to the river; Oregon Trail pioneers inscribed their names on Register Rock, 2 miles south.

NOTES: The unusual terrain and arid conditions of the campground stand in contrast to the impressive Snake River, which is quite near the camp area. From some sites atop the hill the views are outstanding--across the plains and across the river to a prominent rock escarpment.

TWIN SPRINGS
Curlew National Grassland

LOCATION: Southern Idaho southwest of Pocatello.

ACCESS: From Idaho State Highway 37 at milepost 32 +.5 (36 miles south of Interstate 86 exit 36, 10 miles north of Holbrook), turn west onto a gravel access road; continue 0.1 mile across a sage flat to the campground.

FACILITIES: 5 fairly level sites; sites are good-sized with average separation; parking aprons are gravel, and sizable enough for large vehicles; small to medium tents could be pitched among the tall sage and boulders; several sun/wind shelters; most sites have steel fire rings; very little firewood is available for gathering in the vicinity, so b-y-o is recommended; water at a hand pump; vault facilities; pack-it-in/pack-it-out trash removal system; gravel driveway; minimal supplies in Rockland, 23 miles north; limited to adequate supplies and services are available in Malad City, 32 miles east.

SEASON & FEES: No fee; open all year.

NATURAL FEATURES: Located in a dry valley between 2 barren ridges; the treeless setting has only sparse grass and some massive sagebrush for vegetation; a tiny rivulet trickles through an otherwise harsh habitat; the barren Blue Spring Hills rise to the east.

ATTRACTIONS: Twin Springs is an historically significant campground because it was a very important water stop for goldrush travelers about 1849; Hudspeth's Trail is still visible on the ridge above the camp to the west.

NOTES: Though the campground itself is certainly not one of the best, it does have the necessary requirements, and it is the one and only public camp for many miles. We have included it mostly because of its historical importance and its unusual physical features.

HENRY'S LAKE
State Park

LOCATION: Eastern Idaho west of Yellowstone National Park.

ACCESS: From U.S. 20 at milepost 401 (16 miles west of West Yellowstone, Montana, 41 miles north of Ashton), turn west onto a paved, 2-lane road; drive 2 miles across an immense sage flat; turn north (right) into the campground.

FACILITIES: 32 sites; sites are of average size for a state park campground, with minimal separation; fairly well leveled, paved parking pads, many spacious enough to accomodate very large rv's; grassy areas will accomodate tents nicely; fireplaces; firewood is usually for sale, or b-y-o; water at several faucets; restrooms with solar-heated showers; holding tank disposal station near the park entrance; paved driveways; resident ranger-manager; minimal supplies at Mack's Inn, 9 miles south; limited to adequate supplies and services are available in West Yellowstone.

SEASON & FEES: $7.00 for a site, $2.00 for an extra vehicle; May to late-September; 15 day limit.

NATURAL FEATURES: Located on a grassy slope above Henry's Lake, a 586-acre natural lake enlarged by a dam on the Snake River; the lake lies in a great basin with distant mountains in all directions; altitude is 6470'.

ATTRACTIONS: Boating; boat launches at and near the campground; fishing; nature trail starts at the east end of the campground; trail around the lake; Harriman State Park, 22 miles south, has a visitor center and a number of organized activities.

NOTES: The lake and surrounding sage flat are ringed by towering forested peaks. Insects can occasionally be bothersome, but are usually kept at bay by a good breeze during daylight hours. The grounds are mowed and well-maintained. Spectacular sunsets are common in the area.

BIG SPRINGS
Targhee National Forest

LOCATION: Eastern Idaho west of Yellowstone National Park.

ACCESS: From U.S. Highway 20 at milepost 392 +.6 at the south edge of the settlement of Mack's Inn, (25 miles southwest of West Yellowstone, Montana, 32 miles north of Ashton), turn southeast onto Big Springs Road (paved); proceed southeast then northeast for 4.7 miles, and turn east (right) into the campground.

FACILITIES: 17 sites; sites are level, average to large, with mostly average separation; parking pads are medium to long straight-ins or pull-alongs; some pads are gravel, others are paved; large, level tent spots; fire facilities include fireplaces, fire rings or barbecue grills; firewood is usually available for gathering in the area; water at several faucets; vault facilities; paved driveways; minimal supplies in Mack's Inn; adequate supplies and services are available in West Yellowstone.

SEASON & FEES: $4.00; May to September; 16 day limit.

NATURAL FEATURES: Located on a lightly forested flat near Big Springs, a principal source for Henry's Fork of the Snake River; tall grass and a few scattered pines separate the sites; Big Springs has a constant temperature of 52° F; 120 million gallons of water flow through here daily; the peaks of the Rocky Mountains and Continental Divide rise within a few miles to the east.

ATTRACTIONS: Big Springs; the river is a spawning ground for trout (the fish and their fry feast on swarms of mosquitoes); historically significant John Sack's Cabin is adjacent to the Springs; interpretive trail; Big Springs Water Trail and boat ramp, 1 mile southwest.

NOTES: Though the campground setting itself is rather nondescript, the nearby phenomenon, and the campground's proximity to Yellowstone Park, are factors making a stay here worth considering. But bring the bug stuff.

FLAT ROCK
Targhee National Forest

LOCATION: Eastern Idaho northeast of Idaho Falls.

ACCESS: From U.S. Highway 20 at mileposts 392 and 392 +.5 (2 entrances) on the south edge of Mack's Inn, (25 miles southwest of West Yellowstone, Montana, 32 miles north of Ashton), turn west into the campground.

FACILITIES: 34 sites in 2 loops; units are mostly medium to large; sites in Loop B are more level and have a little better separation than those in Loop A; parking pads are gravel, many are large enough to accommodate medium-sized vehicles; some leveled, framed, gravel tent pads; water at several faucets; restrooms with supplemental vault facilities; holding tank disposal station nearby; fireplaces and barbecue grills; firewood is available for gathering in the area; gravel driveways; minimal supplies and services are available in Mack's Inn; limited to adequate supplies and services are available in Ashton and West Yellowstone.

SEASON & FEES: $5.00; May to September; 16 day limit.

NATURAL FEATURES: Located just a few miles downstream from Big Springs, the origin of Henry's Fork of the Snake River; sites in Loop A are located very near the highway on a fairly open hillside in a terraced arrangement; sites in Loop B are located on a forested flat where sites are more level and have better shelter from tall conifers and considerable underbrush; tall peaks of the Rocky Mountains rise to the north and east.

ATTRACTIONS: Fishing in Henry's Fork; hiking to nearby Coffeepot Rapids; boating and fishing on nearby Island Park Reservoir; Yellowstone National Park is 30 miles northeast.

NOTES: Flatrock Campground seems to be a fairly well-designed facility, except, perhaps, for the sites closest to the busy Yellowstone Highway. It's a nice place--good fishin' around here, too.

UPPER COFFEEPOT
Targhee National Forest

LOCATION: Eastern Idaho northeast of Idaho Falls.

ACCESS: From U.S. Highway 20 at milepost 392+.3 (0.2 mile south of Mack's Inn, 25 miles southwest of West Yellowstone, Montana, 32 miles north of Ashton), turn west onto a gravel forest road; proceed west and south for 1 mile to a fork in the road; bear right and continue 0.5 mile west; turn right into the campground.

FACILITIES: 14 sites; sites are mostly medium-sized, fairly level, with minimal to average separation; parking pads are gravel, mostly level, and some are long enough to accommodate medium-sized vehicles; some nice grassy spots for tents in among the new growth of pines; fireplaces; firewood is available for gathering in the area; water at several faucets; vault facilities; gravel driveways with large turnaround loops at both ends; limited supplies and services in Mack's Inn; limited to adequate supplies and services are available in Ashton, 33 miles south, and West Yellowstone, Montana, 24 miles northeast.

SEASON & FEES: $5.00; May to September; 16 day limit.

NATURAL FEATURES: Located on the grassy riverbank of Henry's Fork of the Snake River, which is, at this point, a wide, crystal-clear stream meandering through an open forest; elevation 6300'; tall mountain peaks rise to the north and east.

ATTRACTIONS: Trout fishing on Henry's Fork is widely acclaimed; hiking trail leads to Coffeepot Rapids from the south end of the campground; Harriman State Park, 15 miles south; boating on nearby Island Park Reservoir.

NOTES: Upper Coffeepot Campground is situated on a quiet stretch of a lazy river. It's removed from the noise of the main highway, but handily located close to several other popular recreational areas and activities.

McCREA BRIDGE
Targhee National Forest

LOCATION: Eastern Idaho west of Yellowstone National Park.

ACCESS: From U.S. Highway 20 at milepost 389 +.2 (28 miles north of Ashton, 29 miles southwest of West Yellowstone, Montana), turn west onto Fremont County Road A2; proceed 2.1 miles west; turn south (left) into the campground.

FACILITIES: 24 sites in 2 loops; sites are average to large, with minimal to fair separation; parking pads are gravel, mostly medium-sized, straight-ins or pull-throughs; many may need some additional leveling; some large grassy tent spots; barbecue grills; some firewood is available for gathering in the vicinity; water at several faucets; vault facilities; gravel driveways; minimal to limited supplies and services in Mack's Inn and Island Park, 3 miles north and south, respectively; limited to adequate supplies are available in Ashton and West Yellowstone.

SEASON & FEES: $6.00; May to October; 16 day limit.

NATURAL FEATURES: Located on the grassy east bank of Henry's Fork of the Snake River near the inlet to Island Park Reservoir; rolling, grassy hillsides with a few thin pines around the perimeter of the campground; reasonable distance between most sites, but only a little tall grass for separation; views of distant forested ridges and mountains from several sites; river views from most sites.

ATTRACTIONS: Fishing; boating; 2 boat ramps are nearby; Yellowstone National Park is less than an hour's drive east.

NOTES: Since it's right along the river, McCrea Bridge Campground is very popular with Island Park recreationists. Another nearby nice, but less crowded, campground is Buttermilk, 3 miles south, on the shore of the reservoir. There's usually room at Buttermilk, even when McCrea Bridge is full.

BUTTERMILK
Targhee National Forest

LOCATION: Eastern Idaho west of Yellowstone National Park.

ACCESS: From U. S. Highway 20 at milepost 389 +.2 (28 miles north of Ashton, 29 miles southwest of West Yellowstone, Montana), turn west onto Fremont County Road A2; proceed west 1.8 miles; turn south (left) onto Forest Road 126; continue south and east for 2.6 miles (still paved); turn south (right) onto Meadow Drive; continue 0.2 mile south to the campground.

FACILITIES: 60 sites in 4 loops; most sites are average to large with good separation; most parking pads are level pull-throughs, spacious enough to accommodate larger rv's; some may need additional leveling; many large, grassy tent spots; most sites have fire rings, a few have barbecue grills; some firewood is available for gathering in the vicinity; water at several faucets; vault facilities; gravel driveways; campground host; minimal to limited supplies in the Mack's Inn/Island Park area; limited to adequate supplies are available in Ashton and West Yellowstone.

SEASON & FEES: $5.00; May to October; 16 day limit; operated by a concessionaire.

NATURAL FEATURES: Located along the north shore of Island Park Reservoir, a man-made lake created by Island Park Dam across Henry's Fork of the Snake River; a few sites are on a hillside, most are on a grassy flat; light to moderately dense pine throughout most of the campground, with just a few sites out in the open; distant timbered ridges are visible to the east and north.

ATTRACTIONS: Boating; fishing; floating docks and boat ramps are nearby; Yellowstone National Park is less than an hour's drive east of here.

NOTES: Island Park is a popular recreation area, but there is usually space for one more camper in Buttermilk Campground.

BUFFALO
Targhee National Forest

LOCATION: Eastern Idaho northeast of Idaho Falls.

ACCESS: From U.S. Highway 20 at milepost 387 +.4 (1 mile north of Island Park, 27 miles north of Ashton, 30 miles southwest of West Yellowstone, Montana), turn east into the campground.

FACILITIES: 127 level sites in 7 loops; sites are generally well-spaced, with minimal to good separation; parking pads are gravel in Loops A and B, paved in Loops C through G; some parking pads are large enough to accommodate the largest rv's; some good, large, level tent-pitching areas; fireplaces and barbecue grills; firewood is available for gathering in the vicinity, or is often for sale; water at faucets throughout; restrooms with supplemental vault facilities; holding tank disposal station; gravel driveways in Loops A and B; paved driveways in Loops C through G; minimal supplies in Island Park; limited to adequate supplies and services are available in Ashton.

SEASON & FEES: $5.00; May to September; 16 day limit; operated by concessionaire.

NATURAL FEATURES: Located on a fairly open forested flat along the north bank of the wide and slow-moving Buffalo River before it flows into Henry's Fork of the Snake River; campground vegetation consists of tall grass and some new-growth timber in some loops, and denser forest in other loops; Island Park Reservoir, formed on Henry's Fork, is located nearby; the Rockies rise to the north and east.

ATTRACTIONS: Fishing; boating and fishing on nearby Island Park Reservoir; Harriman State Park is 8 miles south; Yellowstone National Park is less than an hour's drive northeast.

NOTES: This is a BIG campground. Oddly enough, irrespective of its proximity to Yellowstone and the Island Park area, it doesn't swell to capacity very often.

RIVERSIDE
Targhee National Forest

LOCATION: Eastern Idaho northeast of Idaho Falls.

ACCESS: From U.S. 20 at milepost 375 +.5 (7.5 miles south of Island Park, 15 miles north of Ashton, 42 miles southwest of West Yellowstone, Montana), turn east onto a paved access road; drive 0.7 mile to the campground.

FACILITIES: 57 sites in 2 loops, plus a riverside strip of sites; parking pads are gravel, and many pull-through or straight-in spaces are spacious enough to accommodate very large rv's; some leveling may be necessary in those sites; both barbecue grills and fire rings in each site; some firewood is available for gathering in the vicinity; water at a number of faucets; vault facilities; driveway is mostly paved, but some sections are oiled gravel; campground host during the summer; minimal to limited supplies in Island Park; limited to adequate services and supplies are available in Ashton.

SEASON & FEES: $5.00; May to October; 16 day limit.

NATURAL FEATURES: Henry's Fork of the Snake River flows right by the campground; a number of sites are along the riverbank, and they tend to be more open than the sites away from the river on a forested slope; a short, rocky ridge is just across the river, and there's a mid-stream island for added interest; though mountains are not visible from the campground itself, the Rockies rise just to the east.

ATTRACTIONS: Fishing; boating; Island Park Reservoir, just 8 miles north, also offers most water recreational opportunities; Harriman State Park, with a visitor center and numerous organized activities, is 5 miles north.

NOTES: Henry's Fork provides some of the West's best fly fishing. If you're into angling, it usually is worthwhile to stop at one of the local sport shops to find out which pattern is currently hot on the river.

WARM RIVER
Targhee National Forest

LOCATION: Far eastern Idaho northeast of Idaho Falls.

ACCESS: From the intersection of U.S. Highway 20 at milepost 360 +.6 and Idaho State Highway 47 in Ashton, proceed east/northeast on Highway 47 for 8.9 miles; drive east (right) across the Warm River Bridge and turn south (right) onto Fish Creek Road; continue 0.2 mile on a paved road and turn south (right) into the campground.

FACILITIES: 20 level sites, including 6 sites designated for tents; sites are average or better in size with moderate to good separation; parking pads are paved, level and several are long enough for large rv's; barbecue grills; firewood is available for gathering in the vicinity; water at several faucets; vault facilities; paved driveways; limited to adequate supplies and services are available in Ashton.

SEASON & FEES: $5.00 for a standard site, $3.00 for a tent site; April to November; 16 day limit.

NATURAL FEATURES: Located at 5200' in a narrow forested canyon along both grassy banks of the Warm River, which flows westward into Henry's Fork of the Snake River; mostly open grassy areas, with some trees for shelter, especially toward the eastern end of the campground; the Teton Mountains rise abruptly to heights greater than 13,000', a few miles to the east.

ATTRACTIONS: Stream fishing; an old wooden bridge spans the river between sites; picnic shelter at the day use area; grand views along the highway to the north toward deep, steep Bear Gulch, and Upper and Lower Mesa Falls.

NOTES: There are 2 small campgrounds, called Grandview and Pole Bridge, near Lower Mesa Falls, north of here. They offer super scenery but their facilities are definitely second-best to those at Warm River. Warm River Campground is nestled in a beautiful canyon near a superscenic mountain drive.

FALLS
Caribou/Targhee National Forest

LOCATION: Eastern Idaho east of Idaho Falls.

ACCESS: From U.S. Highway 26 at milepost 373 +.6 (4 miles west of Swan Valley, 40 miles east of Idaho Falls), turn south onto a gravel road which crosses a bridge and follows the south bank of the Snake River; proceed east for 1.2 miles; take a left fork; continue 1.2 miles east along the river; turn left into the campground.

FACILITIES: 24 level sites; sites are spacious, with very good separation; parking pads are gravel, mostly small to medium straight-ins; some very nice, large, grassy tent spots; fireplaces or fire rings at each site; firewood is available for gathering in the area; water at faucets throughout; vault facilities; gravel driveways; campground host during the season; minimal supplies in Swan Valley; complete supplies and services are available in Idaho Falls.

SEASON & FEES: $3.00; May to October; 16 day limit.

NATURAL FEATURES: Located on the south bank of the Snake River, just below the confluence of Fall Creek with the Snake; the river follows several channels along this section, thus forming a number of islands in the river; tall cottonwoods, light underbrush, and tall grass are the predominant vegetation in the campground; low ridges with light vegetation border the river on the north and south banks; a picturesque waterfall is visible from the south bank of the river, just west of the campground.

ATTRACTIONS: Fishing; river floating (boat ramp nearby off Highway 26 at Spring Creek); Fall Creek Trail leads south along the creek and up into the Caribou Range.

NOTES: Falls Campground is not heavily used. It's tucked away in a very pleasant and secluded spot, and is yet only 2.4 miles from a main thoroughfare. The countryside in this section of the Snake River Valley is a pastoral picture.

PINE CREEK
Targhee National Forest

LOCATION: Far eastern Idaho near the Wyoming border.

ACCESS: From Idaho State Highway 31 at a point 15 miles east of Swan Valley, and 6 miles west of Victor, turn south into the campground.

FACILITIES: 11 sites; sites are medium to large and fairly well separated; parking pads are gravel, mostly straight-ins; parking is level, and adequate for medium or large vehicles; smaller tents could be pitched in tall grass, beneath the trees; barbecue grills; firewood is available for gathering in the area; water at several faucets; vault facilities; gravel driveways; turnaround loop at the west end of the campground; limited supplies in Victor; nearest source of adequate supplies and services is Jackson, Wyoming, 27 miles east.

SEASON & FEES: $5.00 for a site, 2 vehicles permitted per site; June to October; 16 day limit.

NATURAL FEATURES: Located at 6600' in the Teton Mountains, just 0.2 mile east of Pine Creek Pass; sites are sheltered and situated in a stand of pines along Pine Creek; Pierre's Hole, a vast, forested valley, is an impressive feature of the landscape.

ATTRACTIONS: Fishing in the creek; short hiking trails; perhaps the most extraordinary attraction is the *magnificent* panoramic view from nearby hilltops.

NOTES: The campground is situated in a beautiful mountain setting with a small rivulet trickling past the sites. Highway access to the area is quite steep--as much as a 10 % grade. The scenery along Highway 31 west of here is lovely, as the highway winds through fertile Swan Valley and up the west slopes of the Tetons. Views from the east slopes will not soon be forgotten!

MIKE HARRIS
Targhee National Forest

LOCATION: Far eastern Idaho near the Wyoming border.

ACCESS: From Idaho State Highway 31 at a point 4 miles east of Victor and 19 miles west of Jackson, Wyoming, turn south onto a gravel access road; proceed 0.4 mile to the campground.

FACILITIES: 11 sites; sites are fairly good-sized with good separation; parking pads are level, gravel, and adequate in size for medium to large vehicles; some good tent spots; sites have gravel table pads which have been leveled and framed; barbecue grills; firewood is available for gathering in the area; water at several faucets and a hand pump; vault facilities; gravel driveways; limited supplies in Victor; nearest source of adequate supplies and services is Jackson.

SEASON & FEES: $5.00; May to October; 16 day limit.

NATURAL FEATURES: Located on the east slope of the Teton Range of the Rocky Mountains; sites are situated in a stand of tall conifers on a hillside overlooking Trail Creek; campground vegetation consists of fairly dense timber, low-level brush and a forest floor of tall grass and pine needles.

ATTRACTIONS: Stream fishing; hiking; the highway leading to this spot from both east and west is superscenic; Jackson Hole, visible off to the east, became renowned as the scene of a big fur rendezvous held annually during much of the 19th century; historical museum in Jackson.

NOTES: Without the Forest Service campground sign on the highway, a casual passerby would probably never know that there was this *neat* little campground tucked away up on a pine-covered hillside, just off the highway, near what seems to be the top of the world. About 1.5 miles east of this campground, in Wyoming, is another 11-unit forest camp, Trail Creek.

PALISADES CREEK
Targhee National Forest

LOCATION: Eastern Idaho east of Idaho Falls.

ACCESS: From U.S. Highway 26 at milepost 384 +.1 (1 mile north of Palisades, 7 miles south of Swan Valley), turn east onto Forest Road 255; proceed 2.1 miles east to the campground.

FACILITIES: 7 sites; sites are larger than average and fairly well separated; parking pads are gravel, mostly level, small to medium, pull-throughs or straight-ins; some good areas for large tents; barbecue grills and fire rings; firewood is available for gathering in the area; water at several faucets; vault facilities; gravel driveways; minimal supplies in Palisades and Swan Valley; nearest sources of adequate to complete supplies are Idaho Falls, or Jackson, Wyoming, about 50 miles west and east, respectively.

SEASON & FEES: $3.00; May to September; 16 day limit.

NATURAL FEATURES: Located on a flat in a narrow canyon along small Palisades Creek, which flows westward into the Snake River; bridge over the creek; some sites are on each side of the creek; a rocky "palisades" escarpment borders the campground on the south; vegetation in the campground consists of medium-height conifers, hardwoods, some underbrush and grass; limited view to the south of the mountains.

ATTRACTIONS: Hiking; trailhead for Upper Palisades Lake (7 miles east) and Lower Palisades Lake (4 miles east); facilities for horseback travel on this trail and at the campground; for boating and fishing, Palisades Reservoir is about 6 miles south (located along Highway 26 at milepost 388).

NOTES: Most of these secluded sites are creekside. The setting is very pleasant. Palisades Creek Campground serves well and often as a jumping-off point for nearby backcountry trails.

CALAMITY
Targhee National Forest

LOCATION: Southeast Idaho east of Idaho Falls.

ACCESS: From U. S. Highway 26 at milepost 388 (11 miles southeast of Swan Valley, 17 miles northwest of Alpine, Wyoming), turn west onto a paved access road; proceed for 1 mile over the dam and then left around the west lakeshore. (Sites are right and left of the entrance.)

FACILITIES: 43 sites in 2 sections, including 27 sites along the lake and 16 sites on a hillside above the lake; parking pads are gravel; most are straight-ins; many pads will need additional leveling; a few very long, pull-through, tableless sites are located in the upper section (good for self-contained units); most tent spots are small and sloped; barbecue grills plus a few stone fire rings; firewood is available for gathering; water at several faucets; vault facilities; sanitary disposal station below the dam; gravel driveways; campground host; minimal supplies in Palisades, 4 miles north, or Alpine; adequate supplies and services are available in Jackson, Wyoming, 53 miles east.

SEASON & FEES: $3.00 for a site in the upper section, $5.00 for a lakeside site.

NATURAL FEATURES: Located on the northwest shore of Palisades Reservoir, just south of the Palisades Dam; fairly dense vegetation in the campground consists of conifers, bushes, grass and a few hardwoods; forested mountains and slopes ring the lake.

ATTRACTIONS: Boating and fishing on the lake and also below the dam in the Snake River.

NOTES: Calamity Campground is densely forested. A more open area for self-contained camping, just below the dam at a Bureau of Reclamation facility, has about a dozen semi-designated sites on the east bank of the Snake River. It has faucets, vault facilities and no fee. Across from there, on the west riverbank, near the power plant, are day use shelters and a restroom.

ALPINE
Targhee National Forest

LOCATION: Far eastern Idaho on the Wyoming border.

ACCESS: From U.S. 26 at Idaho milepost 402 +.8 and Wyoming milepost 0 (2.5 miles north of the intersection of U.S. Highways 26 and 89 near Alpine, Wyoming, 26 miles south of Swan Valley), turn southwest into the campground.

FACILITIES: 22 sites; sites are average or better in size, with typically good separation; parking pads are gravel straight-ins or pull-throughs; some spaces are built for double occupancy and have very large parking spaces; some table/tent areas are situated on a slope with a terraced arrangement of rails and steps; fireplaces; firewood is available for gathering in the area; water at several faucets; vault facilities; campground host; gravel driveways; minimal supplies in Alpine, 3 miles south; nearest source of adequate supplies and services is Jackson, Wyoming, 50 miles northeast.

SEASON & FEES: $4.00 for a single unit, $6.00 for a double unit; May to September; 16 day limit.

NATURAL FEATURES: Located in an open forest area at the south end of Palisades Reservoir, a large mountain lake formed by the damming of the Snake River; vegetation in the campground consists of tall grass, some brush, conifers, and a few hardwoods; most sites are nicely sheltered; a few are fairly open.

ATTRACTIONS: Fishing; boating; some orv travel in the vicinity; nice views through the trees of the lake and surrounding forested peaks of the Caribou Range.

NOTES: This campground is located within an easy drive of the very popular Snake River Canyon, just east of here, toward Jackson. River rafters, at times, swarm into Canyon campgrounds, bringing them to overflowing during the peak of the rafting season. Alpine Campground is a good camping facility outside of the mainstream of river activity.

PINE BAR & TINCUP
Caribou National Forest

LOCATION: Southeast corner of Idaho east of Pocatello.

ACCESS: From Idaho State Highway 34 at milepost 104 (10 miles west of Freedom, Wyoming, 45 miles east of Soda Springs), turn south into Pine Bar Campground; on the same road, except 6 miles east, at milepost 110 +.4, turn south into Tincup Campground.

FACILITIES: 9 sites, including 5 sites at Pine Bar and 4 sites at Tincup; sites at Pine Bar are small to medium, with gravel straight-in parking pads that may require some additional leveling; sites at Tincup are level and better-separated by vegetaton, but slightly smaller and closer together; mostly small to medium tent spots in both areas; fire rings; firewood is available for gathering in the area; water at a single hand pump at each campground; vault facilities; gravel driveways; minimal supplies in Freedom; limited to adequate supplies and services are available in Afton, Wyoming, 20 miles south.

SEASON & FEES: No fee; May to October; 14 day limit.

NATURAL FEATURES: Both small campgrounds are located along Tincup Creek which flows eastward to the Salt River; sites at Pinebar are on a grassy hilltop overlooking the creek, in an open forest; sites at Tincup are in a grassy creekbed, with more dense vegetation, and situated slightly farther from the highway; rolling, piney hillsides are the prevailing landscape to the west of Pinebar, while flat farmland lies to the east of Tincup.

ATTRACTIONS: Stream fishing (especially near Tincup); Pinebar is near a trailhead leading south along Lau Creek.

NOTES: A number of similarities led us to list these 2 small campgrounds together. Because they are located along the same highway and the same creek and have the same facilities, it's almost as if they are 2 distinctively different loops of the same campground.

EMIGRATION
Caribou National Forest

LOCATION: Southeast corner of Idaho west of Montpelier.

ACCESS: From Idaho State Highway 36 at milepost 23 +.1 (17 miles west of Montpelier, 28 miles northeast of Preston), turn south, and proceed 0.2 mile on a paved access road to the campground.

FACILITIES: 26 sites in 2 loops; sites are medium to large and fairly well separated; parking pads are paved, most are medium straight-ins which may require some additional leveling; some good-sized tent spots in dense vegetation; fireplaces or fire rings, plus a few barbecue grills; firewood is available for gathering in the area; water at faucets throughout; 2 restrooms with service sinks; paved driveways; minimal supplies in Ovid, 11 miles east; adequate supplies and services are available in Montpelier.

SEASON & FEES: $4.00; June to September; 14 day limit.

NATURAL FEATURES: Located high in the Wasatch Range just 1 mile east of a 7424' mountain pass; a small rivulet flows through the campground; tall pine, medium aspen and some underbrush are the predominant vegetation on this heavily forested slope.

ATTRACTIONS: The drive along the highway offers superscenic views of the northern end of the Wasatch Range; Highline Trail passes along the south and western edges of the campground.

NOTES: Emigration Campground is far enough from the highway to avoid most traffic noise. Sites are nicely separated to provide campers with relative privacy. Emigration appears to have been recently improved. Overall, it's one of the nicest campgrounds in this area of Idaho.

PORCUPINE
Caribou National Forest

LOCATION: Far southeast Idaho northwest of Bear Lake.

ACCESS: From U.S. Highway 89 at milepost 9 (11 miles south of Ovid, 6.5 miles north of Fish Haven), turn west onto St. Charles Canyon Road (which dead-ends at Minnetonka Caves); continue west for 7.5 miles; turn south (left) into the campground.

FACILITIES: 12 sites; sites are medium to large with average or better separation; parking pads are paved, mostly medium to long straight-ins; some may require additional leveling; some nice large tent spots on a grassy slope; fire rings; limited firewood is available for gathering in the area; water at several faucets (check for potability before using); restrooms; paved driveways; minimal supplies on Highway 89 in St. Charles and Fish Haven; adequate supplies and services are available in Montpelier, 30 miles northeast.

SEASON & FEES: $4.00; June to September; 14 day limit.

NATURAL FEATURES: Located in a narrow canyon along St. Charles Creek with rocky ridges rising across the canyon to the north; campsites are in a string along the slope of the creek; vegetation in the campground consists of medium-dense, tall conifers, hardwoods, and grass.

ATTRACTIONS: Minnetonka Caves is the main attraction in the area; tours of these limestone caves are conducted on summer weekends; foot trails follow the creek and lead off into the hills; Bear Lake, which straddles the Idaho-Utah border just 10 miles east has boating and fishing.

NOTES: Another national forest campground along this same creek is St. Charles, 4 miles east of here, and only 3.1 miles from Highway 89. It has 6 sites and facilities similar to those at Porcupine. Note that some recently distributed literature indicates this canyon is located in Caribou National Forest, while other sources say Cache.

CLOVERLEAF
Caribou National Forest

LOCATION: Far southeast Idaho northwest of Bear Lake.

ACCESS: From U.S. Highway 89 at milepost 9 (11 miles south of Ovid, 6.5 miles north of Fish Haven), turn west onto St. Charles Canyon Road (which dead-ends at Minnetonka Caves); continue west for 8.9 miles; turn left (south) into the campground.

FACILITIES: 18 sites in a complex loop on a forested slope; size of the paved, mostly straight-in, parking pads varies from small to large; spots for tents are rather slopey and snug for the most part; fire rings at some sites and barbecue grills at others; firewood is available for gathering in the area; water at several faucets; restrooms; paved driveways; minimal supplies on Highway 89 in St. Charles and Fish Haven; adequate supplies and services are available in Montpelier, 30 miles northeast.

SEASON & FEES: $4.00; June to September; 14 day limit.

NATURAL FEATURES: Located in the narrow St. Charles Canyon along St. Charles Creek near the entrance to Minnetonka Caves; sunlight filters down through the tall conifers and medium-height aspen; some sites are fairly grassy and open; many sites are engulfed by vegetation.

ATTRACTIONS: Minnetonka Caves is the main attraction in the area--guided tours of these limestone caves are conducted during the summer; foot trails follow the creek and lead to the Caves; boating and fishing on Bear Lake, 15 miles east.

NOTES: Sites here at Cloverleaf have certain advantages over sites at other area campgrounds. They are within walking distance of the caves and are a bit farther from the roadway than sites at Porcupine and St. Charles, two campgrounds which you'll pass on the way to Cloverleaf and the Minnetonka Caves. (Minnetonka is an Indian word meaning "falling water".)

Oregon

Oregon has a reputation to live up to.

From the earliest days of the exploration of the Great American West, Oregon has been sought as the promised land, the fertile, lush, green, territory by the western sea.

Today, Oregon's parks and forests are the promised lands of many recreationists. While much of the highly prized land in the western half of the state has been agriculturalized and populated, thousands of square miles remain in the public domain.

Oregon was one of the early leaders in the establishment of an extensive network of state parks to preserve its natural inheritance. Its state park system is now the envy of dozens of other states.

A trip along the Oregon Coast takes top priority on most visitors' intineraries, and here is where the state park concept has been most completely implemented. While there are a few national forest and county campgrounds along the 300-mile seacoast, numerous state parks provide most of the coastal recreation access.

If you've never been to Oregon, there are a few other practical items which may be of interest to you: self-service gas has been outlawed; a "bottle law" requires a deposit on most beverage containers, so you may have empties clinking and clanking around in the camper between pit stops; Oregon is one of very few states which does not impose a sales tax; and the controversial non-resident surcharge in state park campgrounds was recently rescinded.

Whether it's along the coast, in the Cascades, or on the eastern plains, your next Oregon campground will be accompanied by outstanding scenery and a lot of history.

Oregon lives up to its reputation.

FORT STEVENS
State Park

LOCATION: Northwest corner of Oregon near Astoria.

ACCESS: From U.S. 101 at a point 5 miles west of Astoria, near the community of Warrenton, turn west onto Harbor Drive or north onto Main Street; continue through midtown Warrenton, then northwest on Warrenton Drive for 2.3 miles to the park entrance.(There are quite a few 'Fort Stevens State Park' signs throughout this area to help point the way.)

FACILITIES: 600 sites, most having either partial or full hookups, in 15 loops; all sites are of standard size for an Oregon park, with very level, paved, medium to large, straight-in or pull-through parking pads; medium to large grassy tent spaces; fire rings; firewood for sale or b-y-o; water at sites and at several faucets in each loop; central restrooms with showers; several waste water basins in each loop; all loop drives are paved; adequate supplies in Warrenton; complete supplies and services are available in Astoria.

SEASON & FEES: $8.00 for a standard site, $9.00 for a partial-hookup site, $10.00 for a full-hookup site, $1.00 for a hiker/biker site, $3.00 for an extra vehicle; reduced fees October to April; open all year; 10 day limit.

NATURAL FEATURES: Located in a very forested setting, with dense hardwoods, pine, and shrubbery between campsites in most loops; some loops are more open; Pacific Ocean; Coffenbury Lake.

ATTRACTIONS: Fort Stevens Historical Center; ocean beaches; fishing, boating at Coffenbury Lake; several miles of paved bicycle and hiking trails.

NOTES: This is a *very* popular campground--the largest in the Oregon State Park system. The park itself has a tri-faceted personality: salt water, fresh water and historical. Evergreen-fringed Coffenbury Lake is a pleasantly scenic inland surprise.

OSWALD WEST
State Park

LOCATION: Northern Oregon coast north of Manzanita.

ACCESS: From U.S. 101 at milepost 39 +.4 (10 miles south of Cannon Beach, 4 miles north of Manzanita), turn west off the highway into the large campground parking lot.

FACILITIES: 36 walk-in sites; accessible only via a rather steep trail which leads from the parking lot down into the forest; most sites are reasonably level and large enough for a medium-sized tent; most sites are well separated by vegetation; fireplaces; firewood is usually for sale or b-y-o; water at several faucets; central restroom; hand trucks are available for transporting camping gear up and down on the trail; limited supplies are available in Manzanita.

SEASON & FEES: $8.00; April to October; 10 day limit.

NATURAL FEATURES: Located on a heavily forested hillside a few hundred yards from the Pacific Ocean; a small creek, crossed by a footbridge, gurgles past the campground on its way to the sea.

ATTRACTIONS: Trails to the beach; Oregon Coast Trail extends north and south from here for a total of 64 miles along the Pacific Ocean; nice views of the Cape Falcon area from the beach.

NOTES: Although close to the highway, the atmosphere here is surprisingly quiet and non-distractive, due, in part, to the baffling effect of the dense vegetation. The campground designers utilized the natural surroundings well, allowing the campsites to choose themselves, as it were. A unique spot.

NEHALEM BAY
State Park

LOCATION: Northern Oregon Coast south of Manzanita.

ACCESS: From U.S. 101, at a point 0.6 mile southeast of Manzanita and 0.8 mile west of Nehalem, turn south onto the paved park access road (prominently signed); proceed 1.6 miles to the park entrance; turn northwest (right) opposite the small airstrip, then proceed 0.4 mile to the campground.

FACILITIES: 292 sites with partial hookups, in 6 loops; most units have fairly large, level, paved parking pads, and level, grassy tent sites; special areas for hiker-biker and equestrian camping; fire rings; firewood is usually for sale, or b-y-o; water at each site; several restrooms with showers; holding tank disposal station; paved loop driveways; campground host; limited supplies in Manzanita and Nehalem.

SEASON & FEES: $9.00 for a partial-hookup site, $3.00 for an extra vehicle; mid-April to November; 10 day limit.

NATURAL FEATURES: Located on a 4-mile-long spit which separates Nehalem Bay from the Pacific Ocean; the campground has been planted with (well maintained) grass and short evergreens, but is still quite "open"; a beach extends the full length of the spit.

ATTRACTIONS: Several trails (some paved) to the Pacific Ocean Beach; beachcombing; clamming and crabbing in the bay; boat launch nearby; special parking area for horse trailers.

NOTES: This campground is unique for two reasons: special facilities are provided for horseback riders; and this is one of the few state parks in Oregon which is conveniently accessible by air. Since the small airport is only a few hundred yards from the entrance, many campers fly in.

BARVIEW JETTY
Tillamook County Park

LOCATION: Northern Oregon Coast north of Tillamook.

ACCESS: From U.S. 101 in the hamlet of Barview (2 miles north of Garibaldi, 3 miles south of Rockaway), turn west, proceed across the railroad tracks and into the park.

FACILITIES: 156 sites, including 31 `trailer' sites with full hookups, in two sections; the standard campsites are in a sand/grass loop, and most sites will accommodate tents; a few sites are close to the beach; the hookup area is in somewhat of a 'parking lot' arrangement; sand/gravel parking pads; fire rings; b-y-o firewood; water at several faucets; central restrooms with showers; holding tank disposal station; paved driveways; limited supplies in Garibaldi and Rockaway; fairly complete supplies and services are available in Tillamook, 11 miles south.

SEASON & FEES: $6.00 for a standard site, $9.00 for a full-hookup site; open all year.

NATURAL FEATURES: Located on a long windswept flat near a Pacific Ocean beach; a rock jetty extends several hundred yards into the ocean; lots of tall conifers plus smaller hardwoods in most of the campground; the hookup area is more open, but has trees every few sites.

ATTRACTIONS: Beachcombing; fishing; large sandy children's play area.

NOTES: This campground, which stretches for about a half mile along the shore, looks a lot like a typical coastal Oregon state park. The facilities are perhaps a little more rustic, however. For about the same amount of money, you might consider Nehalem Bay State Park, a dozen miles north.

KILCHIS
Tillamook County Park

LOCATION: Northern Oregon coastal area northeast of Tillamook.

ACCESS: From U.S. 101 at milepost 63 +.1 (3 miles north of Tillamook, 2 miles south of Bay City), turn east/southeast onto Alderbrook Road and proceed 1 mile to a "T" intersection; turn right onto Kilchis River Road and continue 4 miles to the park entrance.

FACILITIES: 30 sites in 1 large loop; sites are small to medium with minimal to fair separation; most sites are quite level, with grass/dirt/gravel parking pads and large grassy tent spots; stone fire rings; some firewood is available for collecting, b-y-o is suggested; water at several faucets; restrooms; paved loop drive; adequate to complete supplies and services are available in Tillamook.

SEASON & FEES: $5.00; April to October.

NATURAL FEATURES: Located in a deep, narrow valley on a large flat overlooking the Kilchis River; the campsites are situated around the heavily wooded perimeter of the park, and encircle a large, open recreation area; vegetation consists primarily of tall conifers and maple, plus other low-level hardwoods; the campground is several miles inland from the ocean.

ATTRACTIONS: Huge recreation area in the center of the park/campground: facilities include volleyball courts, horseshoe pits, and a large children's playground.

NOTES: The environment here differs from most of the other campgrounds along the coast, since it isn't right on the sea, but rather is in the coastal mountains. Very popular with the locals, the campground is also a favorite spot of parents with children. The park is named after Chief Kilchis, a cooperative Indian leader who maintained the peace in the county during the early days of settlement.

CAPE LOOKOUT
State Park

LOCATION: Northern Oregon coast southwest of Tillamook.

ACCESS: From mid-town Tillamook, turn west onto Third Street and follow the signs along a series of roads to Cape Lookout. [Note that 2 miles outside of Tillamook, you'll need to follow the Tillamook River in a southwesterly direction (rather than stay on the Three Capes Scenic Route). The park is 11.5 miles from Tillamook.]

FACILITIES: 250 sites, including 53 with full hookups; most sites are closely spaced and semi-private; most parking spaces are level, paved and of medium length; some long, designated trailer sites; large grassy tent areas; fireplaces; firewood for sale, or b-y-o; water at faucets throughout; central restrooms with showers; waste water basins; holding tank disposal station; paved driveways; park host; limited supplies in Netarts, 5 miles north; adequate supplies and services are available in Tillamook.

SEASON & FEES: $8.00 for a standard site, $10.00 for a full-hookup site; reduced fees October to April; no extra vehicles allowed in the campsite; open all year; reservations accepted; 10 day limit.

NATURAL FEATURES: Located in a moderately forested area, with some separation provided between sites; excellent Pacific Ocean beach just over the hill from the campground; Cape Lookout is on a rugged peninsula which extends nearly 2 miles into the sea.

ATTRACTIONS: Beachcombing; hiking trail leads to the tip of Cape Lookout; amphitheater for evening programs.

NOTES: This campground is located in one of Oregon's more primitive ocean shore areas. It is, however, one of the most popular spots along the coast. Reservations are recommended for summer weekends, or for late arrivals during the week.

DEVIL'S LAKE
State Park

LOCATION: Central Oregon coast at Lincoln City.

ACCESS: From U.S. 101 in Lincoln City, turn east onto North 6th Drive and proceed 0.1 mile to the park entrance.

FACILITIES: 100 sites, including 32 with full hookups; most sites are of average size for an Oregon coastal park; a substantial amount of vegetation provides separation between most campsites; short, level, paved parking pads; many hookup units can accommodate larger rv's; medium-sized, grassy tent areas; hiker-biker camp near the entrance; fireplaces; b-y-o firewood is recommended; water at faucets throughout the campground; restrooms (H) with solar showers; adequate to complete supplies and services are available in Lincoln City.

SEASON & FEES: $8.00 for a standard site, $10.00 for a full-hookup site, $3.00 for an extra vehicle; mid-April to late October; reservations accepted; 10 day limit.

NATURAL FEATURES: Located a few yards from Devil's Lake, a fairly good-sized body of freshwater connected to the Pacific Ocean by what the locals claim to be the world's shortest river; densely forested within the campground.

ATTRACTIONS: Fishing; large dock facility; paved boat ramp nearby; wide, paved walkways from the campground to the lake; Pacific Ocean beach, within walking distance, across the main highway.

NOTES: This campground is surprisingly close to the tourist center of Lincoln City. Its popularity stems in large measure from its proximity to the Portland area--Devil's Lake is the most easily accessible of the Oregon coastal parks from that metropolis. Reservations are decidedly recommended for Friday and Saturday nights in summer.

BEVERLY BEACH
State Park

LOCATION: Central Oregon coast north of Newport.

ACCESS: From U.S. 101 near milepost 134 (7 miles north of Newport, 18 miles south of Lincoln City), turn east into the park entrance.

FACILITIES: 279 sites, including 75 with partial hookups and 52 with full hookups, in 8 loops; site size is typical for an Oregon state park; a substantial amount of low-level vegetation within the campground provides site separation; parking spaces are paved, mostly level and vary in length, with some able to accommodate the longest rv combinations; framed tent pads in some sites; hiker-biker campsites; fireplaces or fire rings; firewood for sale, or b-y-o; water at faucets throughout; central restrooms (H) with showers; waste water receptacles in several locations; holding tank disposal station; park host; complete supplies and services are available in Newport.

SEASON & FEES: $8.00 for a standard site, $9.00 for a partial-hookup site; $10.00 for a full-hookup site, $3.00 for an extra vehicle; reduced fees October to April; open all year; reservations accepted; 10 day limit.

NATURAL FEATURES: Located in a heavily forested area a short distance from the ocean; a small creek flows past the campground, and a rail fence meanders through several loops; very long wide Pacific Ocean beach within walking distance.

ATTRACTIONS: Trail to the beach; whale watching (contact the park host for information); beachcombing, particularly good during the winter.

NOTES: This campground has almost a rain forest atmosphere, particularly in the easternmost loops. It is one of only a handful of coastal state parks which are open all year. Reservations are highly recommended for summer weekends.

SOUTH BEACH
State Park

LOCATION: Central Oregon coast south of Newport.

ACCESS: From U.S. 101 just south of the Yaquina Bay bridge (2 miles south of Newport, 14 miles north of Waldport), turn west into the park entrance.

FACILITIES: 254 sites, all with partial hookups, in 6 loops; sites are medium-sized with average separation at most sites; paved, medium to long, level parking pads; grassy tent spots; small hiker-biker camping area; fire rings; firewood is usually for sale, or b-y-o; water at each site; large restrooms (H) with showers in each loop; holding tank disposal station; paved driveways; park host; limited supplies on U.S. 101 near the campground; complete supplies and services are available in Newport.

SEASON & FEES: $9.00 for a partial-hookup site, $3.00 for an extra vehicle; Mid-April to late-October; reservations accepted; 10 day limit.

NATURAL FEATURES: Located a short distance from the Pacific Ocean; short evergreens within the campground provide a moderate amount of separation between campsites; broad sandy beach with dunes; typically windy.

ATTRACTIONS: Paved trails to the beach (0.2 to 0.4 mile long); beachcombing; long, sweeping views of the Pacific Ocean.

NOTES: This campground is surprisingly different from nearby Beverly Beach, its counterpart just to the north of Newport. Whereas Beverly Beach has a pleasant, very lush, 'rain forest' atmosphere, South Beach is definitely 'coastal' in character. Either would make a good choice. It might be helpful to have a tarp or awning when camping at South Beach, since there is only a modicum of natural protection from the elements here.

114

BEACHSIDE
State Park

LOCATION: Central Oregon Coast south of Waldport.

ACCESS: From U.S. 101 near milepost 159 (3 miles south of Waldport, 5 miles north of Yachats), turn west into the campground.

FACILITIES: 80 sites, including 20 with partial hookups; sites are mostly average-sized for an Oregon State Park, with mostly better than average separation; paved, level, short to medium, straight-in parking pads; level, medium-sized grassy tent spaces; fire rings; firewood usually for sale, or b-y-o; water at faucets in several locations; central restrooms with solar showers; waste water receptacles; paved driveways; camp host; adequate supplies and services are available in Waldport.

SEASON & FEES: $8.00 for a standard site, $9.00 for a partial-hookup site, no extra vehicles permitted at the site; mid-April to late-October; reservations accepted; 10 day limit.

NATURAL FEATURES: Located along a small narrow Pacific Ocean beach; the hookup units are closest to the ocean; the standard sites are right along the main highway, but still have an ocean/beach view; quite a bit of vegetation separates the campsites; lots of shade (if you should need it); large, open grass-covered recreation areas; a short bluff/dune separates the campground from the beach proper.

ATTRACTIONS: Beachcombing; fishing; short trails to the beach; day use area.

NOTES: This comparatively small park is certainly appropriately named--it's right on the beach. Interestingly, this park hasn't been mentioned in the section which covers this region in recent editions of the state's "Official Oregon State Travel Guide". *only one campsite had ocean view*

115

TILLICUM BEACH
Siuslaw National Forest

LOCATION: Central Oregon Coast south of Waldport.

ACCESS: From U.S. 101 at milepost 160 + .5 (4 miles south of Waldport, 30 miles north of Florence), turn west into the campground entrance.

FACILITIES: 57 sites; sites are medium to large with average to excellent separation; most sites have paved, straight-in parking pads, a few have pull-throughs; many sites may require some additional leveling; adequate tent-pitching spots; fireplaces; b-y-o firewood; restrooms; paved driveways; campground host; adequate supplies and services are available in Waldport.

SEASON & FEES: $6.00 for a standard site, $8.00 for a 'premium site'; open all year; 10 day limit.

NATURAL FEATURES: Located on the side of a bluff at the ocean's edge; very dense high brush and a few tall conifers provide a significant amount of separation between most sites; a rail fence borders the campground on the ocean side.

ATTRACTIONS: Tremendous ocean views; beach-combing, particularly during the winter; amphitheater; Siuslaw National Forest Visitor Center at Cape Perpetua, 7 miles south.

NOTES: This is about the only national forest campground in Oregon which provides campers with beachfront property. The Forest Service, it seems, has capitalized on this and charges an extra $2.00 for the so-called "premium" sites--those with a more commanding view of the sea. Some campers have questioned this approach to the establishment of fees, saying that it arbitrarily places a value on the scenery which is owned by all visitors.

Sites seemed close together. Cramped looking. Reminded me of Kalaloch. 10/14 - Half the campground was closed off & the rest was full.

116

CAPE PERPETUA
Siuslaw National Forest

LOCATION: Central Oregon Coast south of Waldport.

ACCESS: From U.S. 101 at milepost 167 + .3 (11 miles south of Waldport, 23 miles north of Florence), turn east onto the campground access road, then proceed 0.1 mile to the entrance. (Note that the access road is just a few yards north of the Cape Perpetua Visitor Center.)

FACILITIES: 37 sites; sites are mostly average in size with medium to good separation; parking pads are paved; pads vary considerably in size and proximity to each other, but most are in the small to medium range; sites are basically level, but a bit of extra leveling may be required in some spots; many good tent spots; fireplaces; some firewood is available for gathering in the vicinity; water at faucets throughout; restrooms; holding tank disposal station; paved driveways; campground host; limited supplies in Yachats, 3 miles north; adequate supplies and services are available in Waldport.

SEASON & FEES: $6.00; May to mid-September; 10 day limit.

NATURAL FEATURES: Located along Cape Creek in a long, narrow valley in a very lush coastal forest environment; nearly all campsites are creekside; the Pacific Ocean is located just to the west.

ATTRACTIONS: Within a short walk of fascinating tidal pools along the ocean shore; a nature trail leads off into the forest from the east end of the campground; Cape Perpetua Visitor Center, with it informative forestry exibits and an ageless film, "Forces of Nature"; small amphitheater.

NOTES: The campground is certainly in a very attractive setting. But the tidal pools, with their variety of ocean life, and the Visitor Center, seem to be the main attractions here. Even if you're not planning on staying at the campground, it's definitely worth a stop.

ROCK CREEK
Siuslaw National Forest

LOCATION: Central Oregon Coast north of Florence.

ACCESS: From U.S. 101 at milepost 174 + .2 (15 miles north of Florence, 18 miles south of Waldport), turn east onto a paved campground access road, and proceed 0.2 mile to the campground entrance.

FACILITIES: 16 sites; sites are medium-sized, with adequate separation; parking pads are paved, level, and fairly short but wide; fireplaces; firewood is available for gathering in the area; water at several faucets; restrooms; paved driveways; limited supplies in Yachats, 10 miles north; adequate supplies and services are available in Florence.

SEASON & FEES: $5.00; May to mid-September; 10 day limit.

NATURAL FEATURES: Located along the bank of Rock Creek in a densely forested narrow valley; nearly all campsites are creekside; the campground setting stands in vivid contrast to the windswept ocean bluffs and beaches a few yards to the west.

ATTRACTIONS: Some really majestic oceanic scenery is just a short walk from any of the campsites--follow the creek to the beach; one of the most photogenic landmarks on the Pacific Coast--the lighthouse at Heceta Head--is located just a few miles south of here.

NOTES: Although it is one of the smaller campgrounds on the Oregon Coast, and has limited facilities, Rock Creek is certainly worth considering for a stay. Many campers are attracted by the quiet forest atmosphere of this camp. Since it is located somewhat away from the main highway, there is less traffic noise here than in many other coastal campgrounds. More complete camping facilities, including showers, are available at Washburne State Park, 2 miles south.

CARL G. WASHBURNE
State Park

LOCATION: Central Oregon Coast north of Florence.

ACCESS: From U.S. 101 near milepost 176 (13 miles north of Florence, 20 miles south of Waldport), turn east into the park entrance.

FACILITIES: 66 sites, including 58 with full hookups; sites are average-sized, for a state park, with fairly good separation; most sites have long, level, paved parking pads and small to medium-sized tent areas; 8 walk-in tent sites; fireplaces; firewood for sale, or b-y-o; water at most sites; restrooms with solar showers; waste water receptacles; paved, rather narrow driveways; campground host; limited supplies in Yachats, 12 miles north; adequate supplies and services are available in Florence.

SEASON & FEES: $8.00 for a standard site, $10.00 for a full-hookup site, $3.00 for an extra vehicle; mid-April to October; 10 day limit.

NATURAL FEATURES: Located in very heavily vegetated surroundings; on somewhat more hilly terrain than many of the other state park campgrounds along the coast; an expansive Pacific Ocean beach is just across the main highway.

ATTRACTIONS: Beachcombing; China Creek Trail; extensive nature exhibits; picturesque Heceta Head lighthouse is 2 miles south.

NOTES: This campground seems to be especially suitable for trailer campers. Most of the sites offer spacious parking pads coupled with a considerable amount of privacy. Because of the frequent vehicular traffic here at Washburne State Park, tent campers might want to consider staying at a Siuslaw National Forest Campground, Rock Creek, two miles north.

ALDER DUNE
Siuslaw National Forest

LOCATION: Central Oregon Coast north of Florence.

ACCESS: From U.S. 101 at milepost 183 + .5 (7 miles north of Florence, 26 miles south of Waldport), turn west onto the paved campground access road, and proceed 0.2 mile to the campground.

FACILITIES: 40 sites; most campsites are large and private, with long, straight-in or pull-through, paved parking pads; about half the spots will require some additional leveling; small to medium-sized tent areas; fireplaces; a minimal amount of firewood is available for gathering; water at faucets throughout the campground; restrooms; paved driveways; campground host; limited supplies on the main highway, 1 mile south; adequate supplies and services are available in Florence.

SEASON & FEES: $6.00; May to late-September; 10 day limit.

NATURAL FEATURES: Located in a lightly forested, hilly area, with some pine and tall hardwoods; several small ponds are within or near the campground; sand dunes.

ATTRACTIONS: Several self-guiding nature trails; beach access trails; Oregon Dunes National Recreation Area is a few miles south of here; boating, boat ramp and fishing at Sutton Lake, about 1 mile south.

NOTES: This campground is just far enough off the main highway that traffic noise shouldn't be much of a problem. It usually is quite quiet here. The design of the loops and facilities isn't typical of Forest Service campgrounds. Rather nicely done. This recreation area doesn't have the appearance of being overused.

SUTTON
Siuslaw National Forest

LOCATION: Central Oregon Coast north of Florence.

ACCESS: From U.S. 101 at milepost 185 + .4 (5 miles north of Florence, 28 miles south of Waldport), turn west onto a good paved road and proceed 0.8 mile to the campground.

FACILITIES: 80 sites in quite a maze of loops; most sites are medium to large, level and well separated; most parking pads are paved or packed-gravel straight-ins, some are long pull-throughs; fireplaces; some firewood is available for gathering; water at faucets throughout the campground; restrooms; all driveways are paved; campground host; adequate supplies and services are available in Florence.

SEASON & FEES: $6.00; open all year; 10 day limit.

NATURAL FEATURES: Located in a heavily vegetated area near the Pacific Ocean beach; a creek flows past the north edge of the campground.

ATTRACTIONS: Trail to the beach (about 0.7 mile); nature trail, along which you can observe the insect-eating Darlingtonia plant in its natural setting; boat launch at Sutton Lake, across the main highway; Oregon Dunes National Recreation Area is nearby; Siuslaw Pioneer Museum in Florence.

NOTES: Sutton, which is also called Sutton Creek in some Forest Service literature, appears to be a fairly new campground. It doesn't seem to receive as much use as some of the other campgrounds in this area. If you prefer a spot which offers an opportunity to stay some distance away from the main highway, along with campsites which afford a substantial amount of privacy, this might be a good place to check.

JESSIE M. HONEYMAN
State Park

LOCATION: Central Oregon Coast south of Florence.

ACCESS: From U.S. 101 near milepost 193 (3 miles south of Florence, 18 miles north of Reedsport), turn west into the park entrance; proceed 0.1 mile to a "Y" intersection, then turn south (left) toward the campground.

FACILITIES: 382 sites, including 75 with partial hookups and 66 with full hookups; sites and parking spaces are reasonably level and vary in size from small to a generous medium; all parking pads are paved; hiker-biker campsites; group camping facilities; fireplaces or fire rings; firewood is usually for sale, or b-y-o; restrooms (H) with showers; paved driveways; resident manager; holding tank disposal station; restaurant in the park near the day use area; adequate supplies and services are available in Florence.

SEASON & FEES: $8.00 for a standard site, $9.00 for a partial-hookup site, $10.00 for a full-hookup site, $3.00 for an extra vehicle; reduced fees October to April; open all year; reservations accepted.

NATURAL FEATURES: Located in a grove of tall conifers mixed with low-level hardwoods; sand dunes; Cleawox and Woahink Lakes; bordered on the west by Oregon Dunes National Recreational Area; the park is noted for its wild rhododendrons.

ATTRACTIONS: Paved walkways to the dunes area; fishing; swimming; boat launches; day use area with kitchen shelters; Siuslaw Pioneer Museum in Florence.

NOTES: The campground is a favorite spot for off road vehicle (orv) enthusiasts. Cleawox Lake is a small, tree-trimmed gem on the edge of the dunes. (The best time for picture-taking at the lake is early morning, just as the sun is rising.)

LAGOON & WAXMYRTLE
Oregon Dunes National Recreation Area

LOCATION: Central Oregon Coast south of Florence.

ACCESS: From U.S. 101 near milepost 198 (7 miles south of Florence, 14 miles north of Reedsport), turn west onto the (paved) campground access road, and proceed 0.8 mile to the campgrounds; Lagoon is to the north (right), Waxmyrtle is to the south (left).

FACILITIES: 40 sites at Lagoon, 56 sites at Waxmyrtle; all parking pads are paved; most pads are straight-ins at Lagoon; straight-ins and many pull-throughs at Waxmyrtle; plenty of level tent space in most sites; fireplaces; some firewood is available for collecting; water at several faucets; restrooms; paved driveways; campground host; adequate supplies and services are available in Florence.

SEASON & FEES: $6.00; open all year, with either Lagoon or Waxmyrtle open in winter; 10 day limit.

NATURAL FEATURES: Located on opposite sides of the Siltcoos River, in a semi-open forest setting with a substantial amount of lower-level vegetation; Waxmyrtle is somewhat more open than Lagoon; beaches 1 mile west are barren, wide, windswept and dune-covered.

ATTRACTIONS: These campgrounds serve as a staging area for off road vehicle (orv) enthusiasts; "River of No Return" nature trail leads off from Lagoon; "Stagecoach" nature trail starts at Waxmyrtle; amphitheater in Lagoon.

NOTES: Lagoon and Waxmyrtle are so similar and so close to each other that they are really more like two loops of the same campground. A large camping area for off road vehicles, called Driftwood II, is located within the primary dune area less than a mile west (just continue straight ahead on the access road, past Lagoon/Waxmyrtle). Also, a small 14 unit campground with limited facilities, Tyee, is located on the east side of U.S. 101 near milepost 197, just north of here.

123

TAHKENITCH
Oregon Dunes National Recreation Area

LOCATION: Central Oregon Coast north of Reedsport.

ACCESS: From U.S. 101 at milepost 203 +.3 (8 miles north of Reedsport, 13 miles south of Florence), turn west into the campground.

FACILITIES: 34 sites; most sites have level, paved, straight-in parking pads, although some may require additional leveling; a few sites have pull-through parking spaces; small to medium-sized, level tent areas; there are a couple of walk-in sites suitable for small tents; fireplaces; firewood is available for gathering; water at faucets throughout the campground; restrooms; paved loop road; adequate supplies and services are available in Reedsport.

SEASON & FEES: $6.00; open all year; 10 day limit.

NATURAL FEATURES: Located in a heavily forested area, with some "open" campsites; Tahkenitch Lake, one of the larger lakes in this section of the coast, is a short distance from here, on the east side of the highway.

ATTRACTIONS: Tahkenitch Trail leads through dense forest to the open dunes area along the coast; fishing and boating at Tahkenitch Lake; Three-Mile Lake, a little less than 3 miles south, is a favorite hike-in fishing spot; like most lakes in the NRA, Tahkenitch and Three-Mile are stocked with species that include trout, perch, and crappie.

NOTES: Tahkenitch is quite different from the other Oregon Dunes National Recreation Area campgrounds in this region. It really looks more like a state park campground. Although it's close to the main highway, the area's dense vegetation dampens the traffic sounds to a very reasonable level. Another NRA campground near here which might be worth considering is Carter Lake, 4.5 miles north, on the west side of the highway.

WINDY COVE
Douglas County Park

LOCATION: Central Oregon Coast south of Reedsport.

ACCESS: From U.S. 101 at milepost 215 +.8 at the south end of the small community of Winchester Bay (4 miles south of Reedsport, 23 miles north of Coos Bay), turn southwest onto Douglas County Highway 251 and proceed 0.2 mile to the campground. (Note that there are signs indicating "Windy Cove Park" at the intersection of U.S.101 and Highway 251.)

FACILITIES: 92 sites, including 64 with full hookups, in 3 areas: 2 loops with hookups, and a third area for tent camping; sites are small to medium in size, with little or no separation; parking areas are paved in the hookup sections and oiled gravel in the tent section; no fire facilities; water at each hookup site or from several faucets; restrooms with showers; paved driveways; resident manager; limited supplies in Winchester Bay; adequate supplies and services are available in Reedsport.

SEASON & FEES: $7.35 for a standard site, $9.45 for a hookup site, $1.00 for an extra vehicle; open all year.

NATURAL FEATURES: Located harborside on an open flat, with sandy/grassy areas in and around the campsites; forested hillside to the east, behind the camping area.

ATTRACTIONS: Beach and dune access (most of the beach south of here is closed to vehicles); county fishing and crabbing dock; unique county park, "Children's Fort" across the road; and, of course, just watching the activity of a small harbor is interesting in itself.

NOTES: Windy Cove has a unique waterfront setting. Major improvements were recently made to this campground. There's also inexpensive camping for self-contained units in the landscaped parking lot near the harbormaster's office, directly across the highway from Windy Cove.

UMPQUA LIGHTHOUSE
State Park

LOCATION: Southern Oregon Coast south of Reedsport.

ACCESS: From U.S. 101 at milepost 216 +.7 (5 miles south of Reedsport, 22 miles north of Coos Bay), turn west and continue 0.1 mile up a long hill, then south (left) down a short hill into the park entrance.

FACILITIES: 63 sites, including 22 with full hookups; most hookup units are near the campground entrance in a side-by-side 'parking lot' arrangement, and have long, level, paved, straight-in parking pads; the main part of the campground is located a short distance beyond the hookup area; most sites here are level, with medium to long, paved pads and good-sized, grass tent areas; site spacing is fairly close throughout the campground; hiker-biker campsites, (access is near the campground entrance); fire rings; firewood is usually for sale, or b-y-o; water at faucets throughout; restrooms with showers; waste water disposal basins; limited supplies in Winchester Bay, 1 mile north; adequate supplies and services are available in Reedsport.

SEASON & FEES: $8.00 for a standard site, $10.00 for a full-hookup site, $3.00 for an extra vehicle, additional charges for extra people; mid-April to October.

NATURAL FEATURES: Located on a moderately forested hill above a small gem of a lake--Lake Marie; the hiker-biker campsites are in the forest down near the lake.

ATTRACTIONS: Umpqua Lighthouse and Visitor Center, 0.5 mile; adjacent to Oregon Dunes National Recreation Area; trails to Lake Marie.

NOTES: Although this campground doesn't have direct beach access or ocean views, it certainly is worth considering as a stopover location. (There are, however, some magnificent sea vistas from several viewpoints in the surrounding area.)

WILLIAM M. TUGMAN
State Park

LOCATION: Southern Oregon Coast south of Reedsport.

ACCESS: From U.S. 101 at milepost 221 +.4 (10 miles south of Reedsport, 11 miles north of Coos Bay), turn east and proceed 0.1 mile to the park entrance.

FACILITIES: 115 sites, all with partial-hookups; most sites are quite level, with medium to long, paved, straight-in parking spaces; tent areas are medium to large and have a grass/sand surface; hiker-biker camp in a stand of trees near the entrance; fireplaces; firewood is usually for sale, or b-y-o; water at each site; restrooms with showers; waste water receptacles throughout the campground; holding tank disposal station; paved loop driveways; campground host; limited supplies in Lakeside, 1 mile south; adequate supplies in Reedsport; complete supplies and services are available in the Coos Bay-North Bend area.

SEASON & FEES: $9.00 for a partial-hookup site, $3.00 for an extra vehicle; mid-May to October; 10 day limit.

NATURAL FEATURES: Located among moderately dense medium-height conifers; short evergreens have been planted between sites, but otherwise there's very little low-level vegetation; Eel Lake is just to the north of the campground.

ATTRACTIONS: Beautiful, spacious day use area in the park; children's playground; Eel Lake is just a short walk from the campground on a paved path; displays with information about local flora and fauna; swimming; fishing; boat launch and dock.

NOTES: This is *really* a nice-looking place. The designers of the day use area and the campground seem to have achieved a reasonable balance between forest and open space. The campsites are rather close together, but otherwise it's an excellent facility.

NORTH EEL
Oregon Dunes National Recreation Area

LOCATION: Southern Oregon Coast north of Coos Bay.

ACCESS: From U.S. 101 at milepost 222 +.3 (10 miles north of Coos Bay, 11 miles south of Reedsport), turn west onto the campground access road and proceed 0.1 mile to the campground entrance.

FACILITIES: 53 sites in 2 loops; sites are of average size with standard separation; medium to long, paved/oiled gravel, straight-in or pull-through parking pads; fireplaces; some firewood is available for gathering; water at faucets throughout the campground; restrooms; paved/oiled gravel driveways; campground host; limited supplies in Lakeside, 0.5 mile; adequate supplies in Reedsport; complete supplies and services are available in the Coos Bay-North Bend area.

SEASON & FEES: $6.00 for a single site, double occupancy requires double fees; open all year; 10 day limit.

NATURAL FEATURES: Located in a moderately forested area along Eel Creek; Umpqua Scenic Dunes section of the National Recreation Area lies to the west; some camp units are in the open, others are sheltered by trees.

ATTRACTIONS: Several hiking trails, including one along Eel Creek and another to Umpqua Dunes; no orv sand access from here.

NOTES: This campground experiences somewhat less activity and provides more seclusion than Tugman State Park, 1 mile north. However, Tugman does have showers and other comforts, so take your pick. Two other NRA campgrounds directly south of here, Middle Eel and South Eel, provide camping on weekends only and reserved group camping only, respectively. A third local NRA campground, Spinreel, 2 miles south, serves as a major orv area and tends to be very dusty. NRA sources have indicated that there are tentative plans to renovate Spinreel.

128

BLUEBILL
Oregon Dunes National Recreation Area

LOCATION: South-central Oregon coast north of Coos Bay.

ACCESS: From U.S. 101 at a point 0.7 mile north of the great bridge which spans Coos Bay (4 miles north of midtown Coos Bay, 23 miles south of Reedsport), turn west/southwest onto a causeway that crosses the north end of the bay; proceed 1 mile, then bear northwest just before the Weyerhouser plant and continue another 1.4 miles to the campground on the south (left) side of the road.

FACILITIES: 19 sites; most campsites are level and medium-sized, with straight-in parking pads; several units have pull-through parking spaces; tent areas are of adequate size; fireplaces; minimal firewood is available for gathering in the vicinity, b-y-o is suggested; water at faucets; restrooms; complete supplies and services are available in the Coos Bay-North Bend area.

SEASON & FEES: $6.00; open all year; 10 day limit.

NATURAL FEATURES: Located on the northwest corner of Bluebill Lake in a moderately forested lowland area; Bluebill Lake is small, shallow, and usually dry in summer; there are several other small coastal lakes and ponds in the vicinity.

ATTRACTIONS: Off road vehicle (orv) access to dunes; beach access 1 mile west; Wild Mare horse camp near here; hiking.

NOTES: This one is perhaps a little "iffy". The surroundings are quite nice and there is limited beach access. It's quite popular with orv enthusiasts and tends to be busy in summer, even in mid-week. You may catch an occasional whif of some of the vapors from the Weyerhouser forest products plant near here, however. This is somewhat balanced by the convenience of being close to the services of the largest metropolitan area along the Oregon Coast.

SUNSET BAY
State Park

LOCATION: South-central Oregon Coast southwest of Coos Bay.

ACCESS: From U.S. 101 in midtown Coos Bay, turn west onto Virginia Street; follow a well-signed "Ocean Beaches and Sunset Bay" route for 11 miles west and south to the park.

FACILITIES: 137 level sites, including 29 with full hookups, in 4 loops; sites are average-sized, with minimal to average separation; parking pads are paved, most are straight-ins, some are spacious enough for large rv's; some large grassy areas for tents; fireplaces; firewood is usually for sale, or b-y-o; water at faucets throughout; centrally located restrooms (H) with showers; a telephone is located in Loop A; paved driveways; campground host; complete supplies and services are available in Coos Bay.

SEASON & FEES: $8.00 for a standard site, $10.00 for a full-hookup site; April to October; 10 day limit.

NATURAL FEATURES: Located just east of the Pacific Ocean in a lightly timbered, protected cove; sandstone bluffs shelter Sunset Bay on the north and south; sandy beach at the eastern edge of the Bay; a small creek flows through the campground; most sites have a grassy floor, with small trees and shrubbery for limited separation.

ATTRACTIONS: Fishing; swimming; an adjacent, very well-landscaped day use area has a picnic shelter; a hiking trail to the beach connects with the Oregon Coast Trail; Shore Acres State Park, 1 mile south, has formal gardens and an interpretive center; Cape Arago State Park, 2 miles south, offers great vantage points for wave watching.

NOTES: Sunset Bay has good camping facilities near a terrific ocean beach which stretches for miles. The ocean water is a bit warmer than at other less protected beaches. Ocean views are spectacular along this section of the coast!

BULLARDS BEACH
State Park

LOCATION: Southern Oregon Coast north of Bandon.

ACCESS: From U.S. 101 at the north end of the Coquille River bridge (2 miles north of mid-town Bandon, 20 miles south of Coos Bay), turn west into the park entrance, then north into the campground.

FACILITIES: 192 sites, including 100 with partial hookups and 92 with full hookups; sites are level, somewhat closely spaced, but tend to be longer than the typical state park site; medium to long, paved, straight-in parking pads; fairly large grassy tent areas; hiker-biker sites near the entrance; fire rings; firewood is usually for sale, or b-y-o; water at each site; restrooms (H) with showers; waste water receptacles; holding tank disposal station; paved driveways; campground host; limited to adequate supplies in Bandon; complete supplies and services are available in Coos Bay.

SEASON & FEES: $9.00 for a partial-hookup site, $10.00 for a full-hookup site, $3.00 for an extra vehicle; mid-April to October; 10 day limit.

NATURAL FEATURES: Located along the Coquille River estuary, on the north bank of the river; mature evergreens and shrubbery in and around the camping area provide some shelter/shade and separation between campsites.

ATTRACTIONS: Paved, level walkway (no bikes permitted) leads 1.5 miles through beautifully landscaped natural park lands to the beach; other minor trails in the park; abandoned Coquille River Lighthouse (built in 1896) 2 miles; nice children's playground; boat ramp and dock; salmon fishing, clamming and crabbing; amphitheater.

NOTES: What a showplace! The campground and surrounding park lands are, in many respects, elegant in their simplicity. At the risk of sounding too much like a promotional message, let's say that, while there aren't any 'big' attractions here, there are lots of neat little things to do in this area.

131

CAPE BLANCO
State Park

LOCATION: Southern Oregon Coast north of Port Orford.

ACCESS: From U.S. 101 at milepost 296 +.5 (4.5 miles north of Port Orford, 23 miles south of Bandon), turn west onto the Cape Blanco Road and proceed 5.5 miles to the campground entrance.

FACILITIES: 58 sites, all with partial hookups; sites are quite spacious (by Oregon park standards) with good to excellent separation; paved, medium to long, level, straight-in parking pads; some designated trailer units; medium to large, level, grassy tent areas; hiker-biker campsite near the entrance; fire rings; firewood is usually for sale, or b-y-o; water at each site; central restroom (H) with showers; waste water disposal basins at each site; holding tank disposal station; paved driveways; campground host; limited to adequate supplies are available in Port Orford and Bandon.

SEASON & FEES: $9.00 for a partial-hookup site, $3.00 for an extra vehicle; mid-April to October; 10 day limit.

NATURAL FEATURES: Located on a high windswept bluff overlooking the Pacific Ocean; dense, tall shrubbery between most of the sites; some tall conifers, but many sites have an "open", i.e. unshaded, environment; wide, long, black sand beach.

ATTRACTIONS: A first-rate beach; absolutely superb views; near Port Orford, the oldest townsite on the Oregon coast (established in 1851); Cape Blanco Lighthouse is a half mile northwest of the campground.

NOTES: Cape Blanco is the most westerly park in the contiguous 48 states. The campground has what are probably the most spacious and private sites of any coastal state park. If you're looking for an easily accessible campground that maintains an atmosphere of remoteness and seclusion, this is it.

HUMBUG MOUNTAIN
State Park

LOCATION: Southern Oregon Coast south of Port Orford.

ACCESS: From U.S. Highway 101 at milepost 307 (6 miles south of Port Orford, 22 miles north of Gold Beach), turn east into the campground.

FACILITIES: 107 sites, including 30 with full hookups, in 3 loops; sites are level and somewhat larger than typical state park campsites; small to medium-length, paved parking pads; adequate space for large tents in most sites; hiker-biker camp near the entrance; both barbecue grills and fire rings in most sites; firewood is usually for sale, or b-y-o; water at faucets throughout; restrooms with showers; waste water disposal basins at most sites; holding tank disposal station; paved driveways; campground host; resident ranger-manager; limited to adequate supplies and services are available in Port Orford and Gold Beach.

SEASON & FEES: $8.00 for a standard site, $10.00 for a full-hookup site, $3.00 for an extra vehicle; April to October; 10 day limit.

NATURAL FEATURES: Located at the base of Humbug Mountain on a somewhat open flat in a section of the coast which is generally forested and hilly; Brush Creek flows by between the campground and the highway; campground vegetation consists of large, open grassy areas, dotted with conifers.

ATTRACTIONS: A segment of the Oregon Coast Trail passes through the park; Humbug Mountain Trail leads 3 miles to the summit of 1756' Humbug Mountain; paved, 0.4-mile trail to a Pacific Ocean beach; surf fishing and stream fishing.

NOTES: Nice campground--a lot different from the others on the Oregon Coast. Though there's some shelter from the trees in many sites, the overall character of the campground is one of openness. The only real drawback might be its all-too-close location right along the highway.

133

HARRIS BEACH
State Park

LOCATION: Far southwest corner of Oregon north of Brookings.

ACCESS: From U.S. 101 for at milepost 356 (1 mile north of Brookings),turn west into the park. (The entrance is directly across from an SRA information center and chamber of commerce rest area.)

FACILITIES: 151 sites, including 51 with partial hookups, and 34 with full hookups, in 4 loops; sites vary considerably--small to spacious, forested to open, level to slopey; parking pads are paved; fireplaces; b-y-o firewood is recommended; water at faucets; centrally located restrooms (H) with showers; holding tank disposal station near the entrance; paved driveways; telephones; campground host; adequate supplies and services are available in Brookings.

SEASON & FEES: $8.00 for a standard site, $9.00 for a partial-hookup site, $10.00 for a full-hookup site, $3.00 for an extra vehicle; reduced fees October to April; open all year; reservations recommended in summer; 10 day limit.

NATURAL FEATURES: Located on a bluff 200 feet above a wide, sandy ocean beach--the southernmost public beach in Oregon; vegetation in the campground varies from very little, to dense stands of tall hardwoods and conifers with a considerable amount of underbrush; numerous rock spire formations stand offshore; great ocean views.

ATTRACTIONS: Beachcombing; fishing; swimming; surfbathing; nature trail; bike trail; playground; picnic area; amphitheater for ranger-naturalist programs.

NOTES: The Harris Beach camping area is on an interesting geologic bench, or terrace, which is a classic example of an elevated coastline. This very popular park is one of southern Oregon's nicest beach parks with camping facilities.

✕ LOEB
State Park

LOCATION: Far southwest Oregon northeast of Brookings.

ACCESS: From the intersection of U.S. Highway 101 and Curry County Road 784 in mid-town Brookings, drive north and east on Road 784 (a winding paved road) for 7.5 miles to the park entrance.

FACILITIES: 53 sites, all with partial hookups; sites are mostly level, average-sized, with fair to good separation; parking pads are paved, medium-sized straight-ins; some good-sized areas for tents; fireplaces or fire rings; b-y-o firewood is recommended; water at each site; centrally located restrooms; showers are not available on the grounds, but a receipt from Loeb entitles the camper to a shower at nearby Harris Beach State Park; paved driveways; campground host; adequate supplies and services are available in Brookings.

SEASON & FEES: $9.00 for a partial-hookup site, $3.00 for an extra vehicle; reduced fees October to April; open all year; 10 day limit.

NATURAL FEATURES: Located in the Coast Range on the bank of the Chetco River; campground altitude is near sea level; forested peaks rise to almost 3000' nearby; the deep blue-green (in summer) Chetco River is quite wide at this point; ferns and tall trees, including myrtles, offer shelter and privacy for all sites, a number of which are right on the riverbank.

ATTRACTIONS: Stream fishing; swimming beach; trails in the vicinity lead up into the Kalmiopsis Wilderness a few miles east; unique native azaleas are grown nearby in Azalea State Park; day use area.

NOTES: Loeb Park was dedicated to the preservation of the myrtle forest located within its boundary. The forested atmosphere here in this campground is decidedly different from the beach settings of other nearby state parks.

LAKE SELMAC
Josephine County Park

LOCATION: Southwest Oregon southwest of Grants Pass.

ACCESS: From U.S. Highway 199 at milepost 20 +.8 (22 miles north of the California border, 20 miles southwest of Grants Pass), turn east at a Selmac Lake sign; drive 2 miles (paved) to the park entrance; Loops A, B & C are around the south end of the lake (right) and loops D & E are around the north side of the lake (left).

FACILITIES: Approximately 30 sites, some with partial hookups; Loops A & B have average-sized, mostly level sites with fair separation; Loops C, D & E have smaller sites, with minimal separation; pads in Loops A & B are mostly straight-ins, long enough for medium to large vehicles; maneuvering room is tight in Loops C, D, and E, and pads may need additional leveling; all parking pads are gravel; water at several faucets; fireplaces; b-y-o firewood is recommended; restrooms with showers in Loops A & B, vaults in Loops C, D & E; paved driveways; phone and minimal supplies are available locally; complete supplies and services are available in Grants Pass.

SEASON & FEES: $7.00; April to October.

NATURAL FEATURES: Located in an open forest, surrounding Lake Selmac, in the southern mountains at 1300'; peaks of the Siskiyou Mountains are visible to the east;

ATTRACTIONS: Fishing; swimming beach; boat ramp and dock; open, grassy day use area with playground, barbecue grills, covered tables and a bridge over a creek.

NOTES: The camping facilities here vary considerably-- "comfortable" camping a short distance from the lake, or "roughing it" camping in a tight spot where you can pitch a small tent and throw a line in from your picnic table.

SCHROEDER
Josephine County Park

LOCATION: Southwest Oregon west of Grants Pass.

ACCESS: From U.S. 199 at milepost 3 (3 miles west of Grants Pass, 40 miles northeast of the California border), turn north onto Willow Lane; drive north for 1.2 miles to the park entrance, on the east side of the road.

FACILITIES: Approximately 30 sites, some of which have full hookups; most sites are small to medium, rather close together, with minimal separation; parking pads are paved and fairly level, considering many campsites are situated on a grassy knoll; some really nice, grassy tent spots; fireplaces and/or barbecue grills; b-y-o firewood; water at several faucets; centrally located restrooms with showers; paved driveways; complete supplies and services are available in Grants Pass.

SEASON & FEES: $7.00 for a standard site, $8.00 for a hookup site; open all year; 14 day limit.

NATURAL FEATURES: Located in a grassy park on the south bank of the Rogue River; sites at the north end of the campground are separated by tall hardwoods and shrubbery; other sites are out on an open, grassy lawn; the park is surrounded by rolling, forested hills.

ATTRACTIONS: Rafting on the Wild and Scenic Rogue River; adjacent day use area has lush lawns, formal gardens, a fountain, picnic area, children's playground, and swimming beach.

NOTES: This campground, with its lawns and gardens, looks almost like a private rv park. Its strategic location-- on the outskirts of the sizeable community of Grants Pass-- also accounts for its undeniable popularity.

VALLEY OF THE ROGUE
State Park

LOCATION: Southwest Oregon between Grants Pass and Medford.

ACCESS: From Interstate 5 Exit 45B (10 miles east of Grants Pass, 15 miles west of Medford) turn west (right) onto a frontage road which parallels the Interstate on the south; continue 0.2 mile west to the campground. (Note that I-5 lies in an east-west direction in this area.)

FACILITIES: 174 level sites, including 55 with partial hookups and 97 with full hookups, in 6 loops; most sites are better than average in size, and are very well spaced; all parking pads are paved; many pads in Loops B through F are pull-throughs long enough to accommodate large vehicles and trailers; Loop A has some large, grassy tent spots; fireplaces; firewood is usually for sale, or b-y-o; centrally located restrooms with showers; water at faucets throughout; holding tank disposal station; paved driveways; campground host; complete supplies and services are available in Grants Pass and Medford.

SEASON & FEES: $8.00 for a standard site, $9.00 for a partial-hookup site, $10.00 for a full-hookup site; reduced fees October to April; open all year; 10 day limit.

NATURAL FEATURES: Located along the north bank of the Rogue River between the Coast Range and the southern Cascades; the park grounds include expanses of mown lawns with a variety of trees and bushes for shelter and separation.

ATTRACTIONS: Boat ramp; fishing; children's playground located near Loops B, C & D; amphitheater for evening programs in summer.

NOTES: This campground is in a lovely 'park' setting, between the swiftly flowing river and the swiftly flowing Interstate traffic. Though a few sites do have river frontage, many other sites are within earshot of the highway. Nevertheless, it's still an excellent, handy I-5 stop.

CHAMPOEG
State Park

LOCATION: Northwest Oregon southwest of Portland.

ACCESS: From Interstate 5 Exit 278 drive west on Ehlen Road and Champoeg Road following the "Champoeg" (sham-poo-ee) signs for a total of 6 miles from the Interstate Highway; turn north (right) into the park and drive east 1 mile to the campground.

FACILITIES: 48 level sites, all with water and electric hookups; individual sites are average-sized with minimal separation; parking pads are paved, medium to large enough for very large vehicles; good tent areas on the lawns; separate group area for rv's; fireplaces or fire rings at each site; firewood is usually for sale, or b-y-o; central restrooms with showers; holding tank disposal station near the entrance; paved driveways; adequate supplies and services are available in Aurora, 8 miles east.

SEASON & FEES: $9.00 for a site, $3.00 for an extra vehicle; reduced fees October to April; open all year; 10 day limit.

NATURAL FEATURES: Located on prairie land on the east bank of the Willamette River; Champoeg Creek flows past some of the campsites; one of the oldest groves of white oak trees in Oregon is a prominent feature of the park; the camp area itself is landscaped with mown lawns, bushes and tall oaks which somewhat separate the sites.

ATTRACTIONS: Visitor center; historical museum; 2 extensive day use areas; paved bikeway connects the campground and dayuse areas; a hiking-only trail follows the river.

NOTES: This park is historically significant because it's the site of the 19th century settlement of Champoeg. A city park atmosphere prevails here, even though the spacious grounds are surrounded by miles of fertile farmland. Campsites fill early, and individual sites cannot be reserved.

SILVER FALLS
State Park

LOCATION: Western Oregon east of Salem.

ACCESS: From Oregon State Highway 214 at milepost 25 (9 miles east of the intersection of Oregon State Highways 214 and 22, 16 miles south of Silverton), turn southeast into the campground.

FACILITIES: 105 individual sites, including 53 with electric hookups, plus separate group camping areas; sites are average-sized with minimal to good separation; parking pads are paved, short to medium straight-ins; many good tent spots are located in grassy areas or on a carpet of pine needles; fireplaces; water at faucets throughout; central restrooms with solar showers; holding tank disposal station in the park, at North Falls Group Camp; public telephone at park headquarters; paved driveways; adequate supplies are available in Silverton.

SEASON & FEES: $8.00 for a standard site, $9.00 for a partial-hookup site, $3.00 for an extra vehicle; April to October; 10 day limit.

NATURAL FEATURES: Located in the foothills of the Cascades on the south bank of Silver Creek; campground vegetation is a mixture of conifers and hardwoods, with very little underbrush; there are ten separate falls in the park, including Silver Falls, which is a mile west of the campground;.

ATTRACTIONS: The canyon and falls are accessible by foot trail and bike trail; an extensive day use area nearby has a picnic shelter, swimming beach and playground; the visitor center features nature talks and displays.

NOTES: The drive to Silver Falls State Park winds through hilly, fertile farmland. The campground is located in a sylvan setting with a hushed atmosphere. It's within about an hour's drive of metropolitan Portland, so many, many people like to visit Silver Falls.

FISHERMEN'S BEND
Bureau of Land Management Camp

LOCATION: West-central Oregon east of Salem.

ACCESS: From Oregon State Highway 22 at milepost 28 +.5 (1.5 miles west of Mill City, 30 miles east of Salem), turn south onto a paved access road; drive south, then west for 0.4 mile to the camping area.

FACILITIES: 35 individual sites, including some with electrical hookups, plus several additional group areas; sites are medium to spacious, level, and well separated; parking pads are paved; sites on the interior of the loop are straight-ins with nice tent spots; sites on the exterior of the loop are pull-throughs with electrical hookups; fireplaces; firewood is often for sale, or b-y-o; water at faucets throughout; 2 centrally located restrooms with showers; holding tank disposal station near the entrance; paved driveways; campground host; limited supplies in Mill City; complete supplies and services are available in Salem.

SEASON & FEES: $5.00 for a standard site, $6.00 for a partial-hookup site; open all year; 10 day limit.

NATURAL FEATURES: Located at the west edge of the Cascades and on the eastern edge of the great Willamette Valley; the North Santiam River flows west past here and into the Willamette River; campsites are all situated in densely wooded areas with a considerable amount of leafy vegetation, tall conifers, and hanging moss.

ATTRACTIONS: Boating; paved boat ramp with large parking area; fishing (steelhead and trout); encircling the campground is a self-guiding nature trail connected to a number of additional river access trails; several day use areas with picnic shelters, open grassy areas, ball fields and horseshoe pits.

NOTES: Fishermen's Bend Campground, built in 1963, is one of the nicest BLM campgrounds you'll find anywhere. A 'bend' in the North Santiam River here gives the campground its appropriate name.

Pretty campground. On a hillside, though

AINSWORTH
State Park

LOCATION: Northern Oregon border in the Columbia River Gorge.

ACCESS: From Interstate 84 at exit 35 (9 miles west of Cascade Locks, 18 miles east of Troutdale), turn south, then west, onto the Columbia River Scenic Highway, U.S.30; proceed west 0.5 mile to the campground entrance, on the south side of the highway.

FACILITIES: 45 full-hookup sites in 2 loops; sites are generally medium-sized and quite well separated by vegetation; all parking pads are paved, and many are pull-throughs long enough for very large rv's; some additional leveling may be required; adequate space for a small tent in most sites; fireplaces; b-y-o firewood; water at each site; restrooms with showers; paved driveways; resident ranger-manager; limited supplies in Cascade Locks; adequate supplies and services are available in Troutdale.

SEASON & FEES: $10.00; April to October; 10 day limit.

NATURAL FEATURES: Located on a forested slope near the bank of the Columbia River, although there is no river access from the park; campground vegetation consists of mown grass, medium-height conifers, and tall hardwoods.

ATTRACTIONS: A 2-mile section of the Columbia Gorge Trail links Ainsworth to John Yeon State Park, east of here.

NOTES: This section of the Columbia Gorge contains some of the highest and most spectacular, yet exquisite and graceful, waterfalls you'll find anywhere. Ainsworth's campground has some of the nicer, more private, rv sites in the state park system. Some of the sites are a tad close to the Scenic Route. Some Interstate traffic noise can be heard, as well. Because the Scenic Route is quite narrow, parking and congestion west of here, near the major falls areas, can sometimes be a problem. But it's surely worth the trip.

EAGLE CREEK
Mount Hood National Forest

LOCATION: Northern Oregon border west of Cascade Locks.

ACCESS: From Interstate 84 eastbound, take exit 41 (3 miles west of Cascade Locks, 24 miles east of Troutdale); proceed east 0.2 mile on the off-ramp to the fish hatchery; turn south into the recreation area entrance, then east on a fairly steep,paved road 0.4 mile to the campground. (Note: Exit 41 is an eastbound exit only; if westbound, take exit 44 at Cascade Locks and proceed 3 miles west on a frontage road to the recreation area.)

FACILITIES: 19 sites; most sites are medium-sized and moderately well separated; parking pads are fairly level, paved, medium-length, straight-ins; adequate space for medium-sized tents in most sites; fireplaces, plus a few barbecue grills; a small quantity of firewood is available for gathering in the vicinity, b-y-o is suggested; water at several faucets; restrooms; paved driveway; campground host; limited supplies in Cascade Locks; adequate supplies are available in Troutdale, or Hood River, 23 miles east.

SEASON & FEES: $5.00; mid-May to October; 7 day limit.

NATURAL FEATURES: Located on a densely forested hill overlooking the Columbia River; campground vegetation consists of alder, maple, Douglas fir, and ferns; Eagle Creek enters the Columbia River below the campground, a short distance to the north.

ATTRACTIONS: Shady Glen Interpretive Trail leads off from an associated day use area; suspension bridge over the creek; Eagle Creek Trailhead, 0.5 mile south.

NOTES: The pathways and trails in the area are popular with joggers. (And, considering the 11+ percent grade on some of the trails, they're quite invigorating as well.) A number of the campsites have very impressive views of the Columbia Gorge.

WYETH
Mount Hood National Forest

LOCATION: Northern Oregon border west of Hood River.

ACCESS: From Interstate 84 exit 51 (13 miles west of Hood River, 6 miles east of Cascade Locks), turn south off the Interstate, then head immediately west onto Herman Creek Road; continue west for 0.1 mile to the campground entrance on the south (left) side of the road.

FACILITIES: 14 individual sites, plus 6 group sites; most units are spacious, with wide, long, level, paved, straight-in parking pads; good for tents, but probably better for rv's; a few spots may need a little additional leveling; fire rings, plus barbecue grills at the group sites; some firewood is available for gathering in the area; water at faucets throughout; restroom; paved driveways; limited supplies at Cascade Locks; adequate supplies and services are available in Hood River.

SEASON & FEES: $5.00; mid-May to October; 14 day limit.

NATURAL FEATURES: Great views of the Columbia River Gorge from the campground area; tall pine and spruce forest, along with big leafy hardwoods; very little low-level vegetation other than ferns; set against the south face of the gorge.

ATTRACTIONS: Trailhead parking at the south end of the campground; museum and visitor center in Cascade Locks.

NOTES: An extensive landscaping project recently completed by various government and volunteer groups has turned Wyeth into one of the most attractive campgrounds in this part of the country. The rock work alone is worth a king's ransom. Definitely worth the stop-- even if it's just to take a look.

Nice campground. I don't agree about it being the most attractive campground, though. Just ordinary.

Lots of big trees. Pretty. But right between the freeway + the rail road tracks. No view of river.

Oregon 40

VIENTO
State Park

LOCATION: Northwest Oregon in the Columbia River Gorge.

ACCESS: From Interstate 84 Exit 56 (8 miles west of Hood River, 50 miles east of Portland), take the exit signed for "Viento Park"; drive 0.2 miles east, past the picnic area, to the campground.

FACILITIES: 61 sites, including 58 with partial hookups; sites are average-sized, mostly level, and fairly well separated; parking pads are paved, small to medium straight-ins, and fairly well leveled; grassy areas for tents; fireplaces; b-y-o firewood is recommended; water faucets at most sites; centrally located restrooms with showers; paved driveways; adequate supplies and services are available in Hood River.

SEASON & FEES: $8.00 for a standard site, $9.00 for a partial-hookup site; April to October; 10 day limit.

NATURAL FEATURES: Located on a sheltered hillside along the south bank of the Columbia River; tall pines and bushes provide privacy for most sites; terraced lawns; the views across the Columbia River--to the rock formations and tall bluffs on the north shore--are striking.

ATTRACTIONS: Limited river access; a marina in Hood River provides boating access to the river; hiking trails; picnic area; Old Wagon Road historical area is located to the west; Cascade Locks Marine Park and Bridge of the Gods are located 11 miles west.

NOTES: Viento Campground is situated between the interstate highway and a railroad line, so you may want to consider that the traffic or the trains may at times be a bother. The park grounds are grassy and inviting, and provide a verdant stop for Interstate campers. Views of the Columbia River and Columbia River Gorge along this stretch are fabulous!

145

MEMALOOSE
State Park

LOCATION: Northern Oregon along the Columbia River.

ACCESS: Westbound: from Interstate 84 near milepost 73 (9 miles east of Hood River, 12 miles west of The Dalles), take rest area exit; drive through rest area lot and continue west into the campground. **ALTERNATE ACCESS:** Eastbound: from I-84 exit 76, backtrack on I-84 westbound to the rest area near milepost 73; proceed as above.

FACILITIES: 110 mostly level sites, including 43 with full hookups; most sites are average-sized with fair separation; parking pads are paved, fairly level, and many are spacious enough for very large rv's; some units have gravel tent/table pads; fireplaces; b-y-o firewood is recommended; water at numerous faucets; restrooms with showers; holding tank disposal station; complete supplies and services are available in The Dalles.

SEASON & FEES: $8.00 for a standard site, $10.00 for a full-hookup site, $3.00 for an extra vehicle; April to October; 10 day limit.

NATURAL FEATURES: Located on a mown grassy flat above the Columbia River; assorted conifers, hardwoods, and bushes dot the landscape; vegetation is more abundant here than further east in the drier climate of eastern Oregon; fantastic views of the Columbia River Gorge, and of the mountains and bluffs across on the north shore.

ATTRACTIONS: Grassy area for recreation; river access and boat watching; some hiking in the area; nearby Mayer State Park provides river access with swimming, boat ramp and fishing; Dalles Dam tours and the Fort Dalles historical Museum, 11 miles west in The Dalles.

NOTES: Though this campground is located between the Interstate and the railroad line, many campers apparently aren't disturbed by those distractions. Memaloose is a nicely-maintained facility with convenient access. Views of the Columbia from here are truly impressive.

DESCHUTES RIVER
State Recreation Area

LOCATION: Northern Oregon along the Columbia River.

ACCESS: From Interstate 84 exit 97, (12 miles east of The Dalles, 7 miles west of the junction of U. S. 97 with I-84), turn east onto Oregon State Highway 206; continue for 3.2 miles (Highway 206 parallels I-84), and over the Deschutes River Bridge; turn south (right) into the campground. **ALTERNATE ACCESS:** From I-84 exit 104, (at the intersection of I-84 with U.S 97), turn west onto Oregon State Highway 206; continue 4.5 miles and turn south (left) into the campground.

FACILITIES: 34 sites; most sites are fairly level, average-sized, and fairly well separated; parking pads are small to medium, level, paved straight-ins; gently sloping grass area for tents; fireplaces; b-y-o firewood is recommended; water at several faucets; centrally located restrooms; telephone near the entrance; paved driveways; limited supplies in Celilo Village, 5 miles west; complete supplies and services are available in The Dalles.

SEASON & FEES: $6.00 for a site, $3.00 for an extra vehicle; April to October; 10 day limit.

NATURAL FEATURES: Located along the east bank of the Deschutes River; the Deschutes flows into the Columbia River near this point; fairly steep and rocky canyon walls to the east; rolling, grassy hillsides to the west; campground and adjacent day use area are situated in a grove of tall hardwoods.

ATTRACTIONS: Fishing and river-running on the Deschutes River; Oregon Trail point of interest; The Dalles Dam Visitor Center is 15 miles west; Celilo State Park, 4 miles west, has a boat ramp and swimming beach along the Columbia River.

NOTES: This campground is conveniently located near enough to I-84 to be an easy stop for Interstate campers. A passing train may occasionally disturb the tranquility.

147

TOLL BRIDGE
Hood River County Park

LOCATION: Northwestern Oregon south of Hood River.

ACCESS: From Oregon State Highway 35 at milepost 84 (12 miles south of Hood River, 29 miles northeast of the intersection of Oregon State Highways 35 and 26), proceed 0.4 mile west and south on a paved, 2-lane access road; turn west (right) into the campground. (Look for a "Tollbridge Park Junction" sign on Highway 35.)

FACILITIES: 38 level sites, including 20 with full hookups and 18 specifically designated for tents, in 2 loops; average-sized sites, most with some separation; some parking pads are paved, and some are oiled gravel; many pads are long enough to accomodate large rv's; fireplaces; b-y-o firewood is recommended; water at faucets throughout; restrooms with showers; paved driveways; resident manager; limited supplies in the community of Mt. Hood, 2 miles north; complete supplies and services are available in Hood River.

SEASON & FEES: $6.00 for a standard site, $8.00 for a full-hookup site; April to November.

NATURAL FEATURES: Located on a flat along the East Fork of the Hood River in the forested Hood River Valley; the East Fork rushes-by the campground, just a few yards to the west of many sites; camping area has some grassy areas, and some conifers and hardwoods for separation; timbered ridges border the valley on the east and west; majestic Mount Hood rises a few miles to the west.

ATTRACTIONS: Fishing; hiking trails in the area; adjacent day use area has barbecue grills, kitchen shelter, children's play area, ball diamond and a large expanse of mown lawn.

NOTES: Toll Bridge is situated right along a lovely river and surrounded by the tall peaks of the Cascades. It's located just far enough off the main highway to provide easy access, yet retain its tranquility.

Close to highway. Small campground.

SHERWOOD
Mount Hood National Forest

LOCATION: Northern Oregon south of Hood River.

ACCESS: From Oregon State Highway 35 at milepost 72 +.1 (24 miles south of Hood River, 17 miles northeast of the intersection of Oregon State Highways 35 and 26); turn west (right) into the campground.

FACILITIES: 18 sites; sites are fairly level, somewhat close together and reasonably well separated; parking pads are gravel, small to medium straight-ins; adequate space for smaller tents; fireplaces; firewood available for gathering in the area; water at 2 faucets and 1 hand pump; vault facilities; paved driveways; limited supplies in the community of Mount Hood, 10 miles north; adequate supplies and services are available in Hood River.

SEASON & FEES: $5.00; April to October; 14 day limit.

NATURAL FEATURES: Located in a very forested atmosphere, typical of the Hood River Valley, in the Cascade Mountains; some sites are located right along the East Fork of the Hood River, which flows past here toward the Columbia River, 30 miles north; timbered ridges to the east and west; Mount Hood and the Mount Hood Wilderness Area are located a few miles west.

ATTRACTIONS: Stream fishing; foot bridge over the river; several foot trails lead off from the campground, including trails to Tamanawas Falls and toward the Mount Hood Wilderness; adjacent picnic area has barbecue grills; winter sports area nearby for skiing and snowmobiling.

NOTES: The scenery and overall environment here in the Hood River Valley are great. The rushing East Fork of the Hood River should muffle traffic noise from the nearby highway.

sites are very small. Road through campground is narrow with a lot of overhanging branches.

Oregon 45

ROBINHOOD
Mount Hood National Forest

LOCATION: Northern Oregon south of Hood River.

ACCESS: From Oregon State Highway 35 at milepost 68 +.1 (28 miles south of Hood River, 13 miles northeast of the intersection of Oregon State Highways 35 and 26), turn west (right) into the campground.

FACILITIES: 24 sites; units are fairly level, well spaced, and the dense vegetation provides reasonable privacy; parking pads are gravel, small to medium, and mostly straight-ins; several good, level spaces for tents; fireplaces; firewood is available for gathering in the area; water at several faucets; vault facilities; oiled gravel driveways; limited supplies in the community of Mt. Hood, 14 miles north; adequate supplies and services are available in Hood River.

SEASON & FEES: $5.00; April to October; 14 day limit.

NATURAL FEATURES: Located along the East Fork of the Hood River which joins the Columbia River, 30 miles to the north; smaller creeks flow into the East Fork here as it rushes by the campsites; moderately dense vegetation in the campground consists of conifers, hardwoods, and a considerable amount of underbrush; high, timbered ridges flank the Hood River Valley; the extinct volcano, Mount Hood, rises a few miles west.

ATTRACTIONS: Stream fishing in the East Fork of the Hood River; foot bridge over the East Fork; several foot trails lead off from the campground, including one to Horsethief Meadows; a winter sports area is located nearby for skiing and snowmobiling.

NOTES: Robinhood Campground's forested atmosphere is typical of this section of the Cascade Mountains. While some sites are rather close to highway, some riverside sites are nicely tucked away in the forest.

TOLLGATE
Mount Hood National Forest

LOCATION: Northwest Oregon southeast of Portland.

ACCESS: From U.S. Highway 26 at milepost 44 +.9 (0.4 mile east of Rhododendron, 10 miles west of Government Camp) turn south onto a paved access road; continue 0.1 mile to the campground entrance.

FACILITIES: 15 hilly sites; the sites are fairly good-sized and well separated by forest vegetation; parking pads are gravel, double-wide straight-ins or long pull-throughs; many parking spaces have stone retaining walls; some pads may require additional leveling; some very nice tent spots are sheltered by trees; fireplaces; firewood is available for gathering in the area; water at faucets throughout; vault facilities (H); paved driveways; minimal supplies are available in Rhododendron and Government Camp; complete supplies and services are available in Portland, 40 miles west.

SEASON & FEES: $4.00; May to September; 14 day limit.

NATURAL FEATURES: Located on the west slope of the Cascades on Camp Creek which flows into Zigzag River; campsites are in fairly dense forest, surrounded by tall conifers, bushes, ferns and moss-covered rocks; a few units are right on the bank of the creek; driveway through the camping area is rather narrow, and may prove a bit tight for maneuvering larger vehicles.

ATTRACTIONS: Stream fishing; an extensive day use area has a picnic shelter; a number of forest roads in the area provide access to the nearby mountains; Mount Hood Wilderness is accessible by foot trail from near Rhododendron.

NOTES: Tollgate is located near the historical site of a tollgate on the Barlow Trail. A rail fence borders some really pleasant creekside sites. There are a number of large stone fireplaces and rock retaining walls along parking pads and pathways in the campground.

151

CAMP CREEK
Mount Hood National Forest

LOCATION: Northwest Oregon southeast of Portland.

ACCESS: From U.S. 26 at milepost 47 +.1 (2.5 miles east of Rhododendron, 8 miles west of Government Camp), turn south onto a paved access road; continue 0.2 mile to the campground entrance.

FACILITIES: 24 sites in 2 loops; sites are fairly large and well spaced; parking pads are gravel, double-wide straight-ins, or long pull-throughs; many may need additional leveling; some nicely forested tent spots; fireplaces; firewood is available for gathering in the area; water at hand pumps; vault facilities (H); waste water receptacles; gravel driveways are somewhat narrow for maneuvering larger vehicles; campground host; minimal supplies in Government Camp and Rhododendron; complete supplies and services are available in Portland, 40 miles west.

SEASON & FEES: $5.00 for a single unit, $10.00 for double unit; May to September; 14 day limit.

NATURAL FEATURES: Located on the west slope of the Cascades on a forested hillside along Camp Creek, which flows into Zigzag River; the camp area vegetation is not as dense here as at nearby Tollgate; conifers, ferns and leafy bushes are interspersed with open grassy areas; a number of sites are located right on the creek bank.

ATTRACTIONS: Camp Creek is a refreshing stream which attracts fishermen, hikers and picnickers; a foot trail follows along the creek and a wooden footbridge crosses over it; a number of forest roads in the area provide mountain access; Mount Hood Wilderness is located just to the north of Zigzag River.

NOTES: There are a number of large, old, stone fireplaces and rock retaining walls along the parking pads and pathways in this campground. These were built by CCC crews in the 1930's. One enormous fireplace is located in the site usually occupied by the campground host.

STILL CREEK
Mount Hood National Forest

LOCATION: Northwest Oregon southeast of Portland.

ACCESS: From U.S. 26 at milepost 55 +.5 (0.5 mile south of Government Camp, 60 miles north of Madras), turn west onto a steep paved access road; continue 0.5 mile down to the campground.

FACILITIES: 27 sites; sites are spacious, with some separation from limited underbrush; parking pads are paved, level, and mostly long straight-ins; some very nice tent spots; fireplaces; firewood is available for gathering in the area; water at faucets throughout; vault facilities; waste water receptacles; paved driveways; minimal supplies in Government Camp; complete supplies and services are available in Portland, 55 miles west.

SEASON & FEES: $4.00; May to September; 14 day limit.

NATURAL FEATURES: Located in the heart of the Cascades in a narrow valley along Still Creek, a rivulet which flows into the Zigzag River; the surrounding territory is very densely forested, but the camp area itself is fairly open, with tall conifers and only a little underbrush; Mount Hood, of volcanic origin, rises to over 11,000' just a few miles north.

ATTRACTIONS: Stream fishing in Still Creek and Zigzag River; Trillium Lake, 2 miles south via a gravel forest road, offers motorless boating, fishing, swimming and a sizable day use facility.

NOTES: All the sites at Still Creek Campground are in good locations, but a few top-notch sites are located right along the creek. The atmosphere here is quiet and casual. Sites are far enough from the highway so that the forest vegetation muffles traffic noise, and far enough from the lake so campers are protected from the steady stream of day use traffic.

TRILLIUM LAKE
Mount Hood National Forest

LOCATION: Northwest Oregon between Portland and Madras.

ACCESS: From U.S. 26 at milepost 56 +.8 (1.8 miles south of Government Camp, 59 miles north of Madras), turn west onto a steep access road; proceed 1.5 miles down to the campground entrance.

FACILITIES: 39 sites in 2 loops; most sites are small to medium, generally level and quite well separated; parking pads are paved, medium-sized straight-ins; some pads may require additional leveling; many nice, secluded tent spots; fireplaces; firewood is available for gathering in the vicinity; water at faucets throughout; vault facilities (H); waste water receptacles; paved driveways; minimal supplies in Government Camp; complete supplies and services are available in Portland, 56 miles west.

SEASON & FEES: $6.00; May to September; 14 day limit.

NATURAL FEATURES: Located in the heart of the Cascades on the west shore of Trillium Lake, a small mountain lake completely surrounded by forested slopes; a dense conifer forest provides privacy and shelter for the sites; Mount Hood, the tallest peak in Oregon, is visible across the lake as it rises to over 11,000' just a few miles north.

ATTRACTIONS: Motorless boating; fishing; swimming; a sizable day use facility is adjacent to the camping area; a number of forest roads nearby provide access to the surrounding mountains.

NOTES: Trillium Lake is a mountain-lake gem! Really super scenic sights in this basin! A few campsites are located close enough to the lake to provide lake views through the trees. The campground and adjacent day use facility are typically bustling with activity, though.

FROG LAKE
Mount Hood National Forest

LOCATION: Northwest Oregon between Portland and Madras.

ACCESS: From U.S. 26 at milepost 62 (7 miles south of Government Camp, 53 miles north of Madras), turn east onto a paved access road; proceed 0.5 mile and turn left into the campground.

FACILITIES: 33 sites; sites are mostly average-sized with some separation between interior sites, and good separation between sites around the perimeter; parking pads are gravel, level, and mostly medium-sized straight-ins; some nice, level tent spots; fireplaces; firewood is available for gathering in the area; water at 2 hand pumps; vault facilities (H); paved driveways; limited supplies in Government Camp; adequate supplies and services are available in Madras.

SEASON & FEES: $6.00; May to September; 14 day limit.

NATURAL FEATURES: Located in the heart of the Cascades; Frog Lake is a tiny mountain lake completely surrounded by forested slopes; waters of Frog Lake feed into Frog Creek, which flows eastward to the Deshutes River; the center of the camp area is fairly open with only some tall trees, grass and a little underbrush; sites around the exterior are situated in dense forest; located near the summit of 3950'Wapinitia Pass; Mount Hood rises to over 11,000' just a few miles north.

ATTRACTIONS: Motorless boating; fishing; large day use facility adjacent to the camping area; a foot trail leads toward the Pacific Crest Scenic Trail.

NOTES: Frog Lake Campground is situated far enough from the highway to provide campers with a quiet environment. A few of the sites are located close enough to Frog Lake to provide a lake view through the trees.

CLEAR LAKE
Mount Hood National Forest

LOCATION: Northwest Oregon between Madras and Portland.

ACCESS: From Oregon State Highway 26 at milepost 64 +.5 (10 miles south of Government Camp, 50 miles northwest of Madras) turn west onto a winding, paved access road; continue 1.1 miles down to the campground.

FACILITIES: 26 forested sites; sites are medium to large with mostly average separation; parking pads are gravel pull-ins or pull-throughs; some are spacious enough to accommodate fairly large rv's; parking and tent spaces may need some additional leveling; the most level sites are situated on the hilltop; fireplaces; firewood is available in the area for gathering; water at a hand pump; vault facilities; paved driveways; camper supplies in Government Camp; adequate supplies and services are available in Madras.

SEASON & FEES: $6.00; operated by a concessionaire; May to September.

NATURAL FEATURES: Located in the heart of the Cascades on a slope on the northeast shore of Clear Lake; surrounded by low forested ridges; some lakeside sites; in August, or other low water times, Clear Lake may be speckled with tree stumps; campground vegetation consists of a few large trees, grass and many small scrub pines.

ATTRACTIONS: Windsurfing; boating (boat launch); a number of forest roads nearby provide access to the surrounding mountain areas.

NOTES: Clear Lake Campground provides fine facilities, but the lake itself can be spoiled by the protruding stumps along the edges of this newly enlarged recreational waterway. If the camper can look 'between the tree stumps', he could enjoy a stay here.

DETROIT LAKE
State Park

LOCATION: West-central Oregon between Albany and Bend.

ACCESS: From Oregon State Highway 22 at milepost 48 (1.8 miles west of Detroit, 15 miles east of Mill City), turn south into the campground.

FACILITIES: Over 300 sites, including 106 with full hookups, and 70 with electrical hookups, in 5 loops; sites vary considerably in size from small to medium, and in separation from minimal to average; parking pads are paved and fairly level; most parking pads are straight-ins, but there are some long pull-throughs; fire rings; firewood is usually for sale, or b-y-o; water at faucets throughout; central restrooms with showers; paved driveways; limited supplies are available in Detroit.

SEASON & FEES: $8.00 for a standard site, $9.00 for a partial-hookup site, $10.00 for a full-hookup site; May to September; 10 day limit.

NATURAL FEATURES: Located on Detroit Lake in the North Santiam River Canyon; forested slopes of the Cascades rise all around the lake and are visible from the campground; a number of sites are located within a few yards of the lakeshore; all loops of the campground are situated in open forest, with little or no underbrush to separate the sites.

ATTRACTIONS: Boating; fishing; water-skiing; ranger-naturalist programs on summer evenings; a nice swimming beach is located 0.5 mile west at Mongold Day Use Area; tours at nearby Big Cliffs and Detroit Dams.

NOTES: Campsites at Detroit Lakes are all situated on a narrow strip of land between the lake and the highway. Sites near the entrance and the lake tend to be a bit overused, and other sites are rather close to the highway. You may wish to request a preview before being assigned a site. Scenery in this section of the Cascades is terrific!

157

HOOVER
Willamette National Forest

LOCATION: West-central Oregon between Albany and Bend.

ACCESS: From Oregon State Highway 22 at milepost 53 +.1 (3 miles east of Detroit, 2 miles west of Idanha), turn southwest onto Blowout Road (Forest Road 10); proceed west on Blowout Road for 0.9 mile to the campground.

FACILITIES: 35 level sites; sites are fairly open and spacious, with some separation; parking pads are gravel; most pads are straight-ins, but there are a few larger pull-throughs spacious enough to accomodate larger rv's; some nice tent sites in open forest areas; all sites have fireplaces, some of the multiple sites also have barbecue grills; firewood is usually available for gathering in the vicinity; water at several faucets; central restrooms; waste water receptacles; paved driveways; limited supplies and services are available in Detroit.

SEASON & FEES: $6.00 for a single unit, $12.00 for a multiple unit; May to September; 16 day limit.

NATURAL FEATURES: Located on the west slope of the Cascades at the very eastern edge of Detroit Lake, a reservoir with 32 miles of shoreline; the North Santiam River and Detroit Lake are in the narrow, steep-walled North Santiam Canyon.

ATTRACTIONS: Boating; large boat ramp; fishing; water-skiing; adjacent picnic area; ranger-naturalist programs on summer evenings; tours at nearby Big Cliffs and Detroit Dams; several nearby forest roads lead up into the surrounding mountain areas.

NOTES: Hoover Campground has some terrific campspots--many with river views. Sites are far enough from the highway to provide reasonable solitude. Boating access to Detroit Lake is through a narrow river channel, so Hoover is somewhat removed from the mainstream of boating traffic as well.

RIVERSIDE
Willamette National Forest

LOCATION: West-central Oregon between Albany and Bend.

ACCESS: From Oregon State Highway 22 at milepost 64 +.3 (14 miles east of Detroit, 32 miles west of Sisters), turn southwest into the campground.

FACILITIES: 36 sites; sites are average-sized, mostly level and very well separated; parking pads are gravel; parking is adequate for medium-sized vehicles; some nice, private tent sites surrounded by the dense vegetation; some fireplaces and some fire rings; firewood is available for gathering in the vicinity; water at several faucets; vault facilities; paved driveways; limited supplies and services are available in Idanha, 9 miles northwest.

SEASON & FEES: $5.00; May to September; 16 day limit.

NATURAL FEATURES: Located on the east slope of the Cascades along the rushing Santiam River; sites are in a double row on the east bank of the Santiam River, which flows through a narrows at this point; Mount Jefferson Wilderness is to the east; tall forested peaks are visible to the west; dense campground vegetation is of tall cedars and pine with rhododendron, fern and a pine needle forest floor.

ATTRACTIONS: Stream fishing; Detroit Lakes, 15 miles west, has boating, fishing and swimming; there are a number of nearby forest roads leading up into the surrounding mountains.

NOTES: This densely forested campground offers campers an atmosphere of privacy and seclusion. Many sites are right on the riverbank. Another small campground, Whispering Falls, is located about 7 miles north on Highway 22. It is a bit smaller, but has similar facilities.

BIG LAKE
Willamette National Forest

LOCATION: West-central Oregon northwest of Bend.

ACCESS: From U.S. 20 near milepost 80 (8.5 miles east of the intersection of U.S. 20 with Oregon State Highway 126, 40 miles northwest of Bend), turn south onto Forest Road 2690 (paved); proceed 0.7 mile south to a fork in the road; take the left fork, and continue 2 miles to the campground entrance.

FACILITIES: 41 sites on the north and west shores of the lake; sites are average or better in size, with mostly good separation; north shore units may be a bit roomier; parking pads are gravel; some pads are spacious enough for large vehicles; a few sites may require additional leveling; some very nice, grassy tent spots sheltered/shaded by tall timber; fire rings; limited firewood is available for gathering in the vicinity, b-y-o is suggested; water at several faucets; central restrooms; paved driveways; campground host; limited supplies and services are available in Sisters.

SEASON & FEES: $6.00 for a standard site, $8.00 for a 'premium site'; May to September; 10 day limit.

NATURAL FEATURES: Located in Hidden Valley on a high mesa in the Cascades; all sites are in an open conifer forest, including some right on the shore of beautiful Big Lake; Three Fingered Jack Peak can be seen to the north; Mount Washington Wilderness is located just a few miles from the southern edge of the lake.

ATTRACTIONS: Boating; sailing; water skiing; fishing; swimming; the Pacific Crest Trail passes within 0.5 mile; winter activities in the nearby Santiam Pass area.

NOTES: Though only a few 'premium' sites are right along the lake, most units have views of the picturesque lake and surrounding mountains. The sight of razor-backed Mount Washington, rising from the south shore of Big Lake, is most impressive! Definitely recommended.

COLDWATER COVE
Willamette National Forest

LOCATION: West-central Oregon between Albany and Bend.

ACCESS: From Oregon State Highway 126 at milepost 4 +.6 (4.6 miles south of the intersection of Oregon State Highway 126 with U.S. 20, 15 miles north of the intersection of Oregon State Highways 126 and 242), turn east onto a paved access road; continue 0.5 mile to the campground.

FACILITIES: 34 sites; most sites are small to medium in size, and fairly well separated by forest vegetation; parking pads are paved, most are smaller straight-ins, but there are a few pull-throughs long enough to accomodate medium-sized vehicles; many sites may require additional leveling; mostly small tent spots which may be a bit slopey; fire rings at all sites, additional barbecue grills at some; water at faucets and a hand pump; vault facilities; paved driveways; campground host; minimal supplies at a nearby resort.

SEASON & FEES: $6.00 for a single unit, $12.00 for a multiple site; May to September; 16 day limit.

NATURAL FEATURES: Located on the west slope of the Cascades on a hillside overlooking beautiful blue-green Clear Lake; campground vegetation consists of fairly dense conifers and underbrush; interesting deposits of volcanic rock surround the camp area.

ATTRACTIONS: Fishing; motorless boating; boat ramp; a paved trail (H) leads from the campground down to the lake; the McKenzie River Trail passes by the campground; picnic area on the west shore of Clear Lake.

NOTES: Coldwater Cove is located on the south shore of 140-acre Clear Lake, the headwaters of the McKenzie River. Though only a few of the best sites overlook the lake, all the sites enjoy the tranquility of the forested setting near this picturesque mountain lake.

161

ICE CAP CREEK
Willamette National Forest

LOCATION: Western Oregon east of Albany.

ACCESS: From Oregon State Highway 126 drive south on Highway 126 at milepost 5 +.5 (5.5 miles south of the intersection of Oregon State Highway 126 with U.S. 20, 14.5 miles north of the intersection of Oregon State Highways 126 and 242), turn west onto a paved access road; continue 0.2 mile west to the campground.

FACILITIES: 22 sites; most sites are rather small, with good to excellent separation; parking pads are gravel straight-ins, small to medium in size; some additional leveling may be required; tent spots tend to be a bit small and some are rather slopey or bumpy; fire rings; firewood is available for gathering in the vicinity; water at faucets throughout; centrally located restroom; paved driveways; campground host; limited supplies are available in the town of McKenzie Bridge, 17 miles southwest.

SEASON & FEES: $5.00 for a single unit, $10.00 for a multiple unit; May to September; 16 day limit.

NATURAL FEATURES: Located on the west slope of the Cascades on a forested hillside east of the McKenzie River; tiny Carmen Reservoir is within view; Ice Cap Creek flows through a narrow deep gorge here, and into the McKenzie River; surrounded by dense forest, the campground itself is a bit more open, with tall timber and a pine needle forest floor.

ATTRACTIONS: Fishing; motorless boating on Carmen Reservoir; boat launch; adjacent picnic area; foot trail leads to viewpoints at nearby Koosah Falls and Sahalie Falls; the McKenzie River Trail follows along the west bank of the river.

NOTES: Since Ice Cap Creek Campground is situated away from the main highway, and no motors are allowed on Carmen Reservoir, the only real 'noise' here is the rush of the stream over the falls.

TRAILBRIDGE
Willamette National Forest

LOCATION: Western Oregon northeast of Springfield.

ACCESS: From Oregon State Highway 126 at milepost 10 +.8 (11 miles south of the intersection of Oregon State Highway 126 with U.S. Highway 20, 9 miles north of the intersection of Oregon State Highways 126 and 242), turn west onto Forest Road 730 (paved); drive 0.2 mile, across a McKenzie River Bridge, and turn south (left) at a "T" intersection; proceed 0.5 mile south to the campground.

FACILITIES: 35 fairly level walk-in sites; tables, fireplaces and tent spots for all 35 average-sized camp units are located in one central area with minimal to average separation; parking places are on a gravel drive which completely encircles the units; parking spots have virtually no separation, and may require additional leveling; fire rings; limited firewood is available for gathering in the vicinity; water at several locations; restrooms with supplementary vaults; gravel driveways; limited supplies are available in the community of McKenzie Bridge.

SEASON & FEES: $4.00 for a single unit, $8.00 for a multiple site; mid-May to September; 16 day limit.

NATURAL FEATURES: Located on the west slope of the Cascades along the west shore of Trail Bridge Reservoir, a deep-green 120-acre lake formed on the McKenzie River; the campground is situated in dense forest which is quite clear of underbrush.

ATTRACTIONS: Boating; boat launch; fishing; McKenzie River Trail; a foot trail leads to nearby Smith River Reservoir.

NOTES: This is a really different camp spot with uncommon facilities. Of course, vehicle campers would be welcome to use this campground, but their outdoor 'kitchen' wouldn't be right out the rear door of the camper.

OLLALIE
Willamette National Forest

LOCATION: Western Oregon northeast of Springfield.

ACCESS: From Oregon State Highway 126 at milepost 13 (13 miles south of the intersection of Oregon State Highway 126 with U.S. 20, 7 miles north of the intersection of Oregon State Highways 126 and 242), turn west into the campground.

FACILITIES: 19 sites in 2 tiers; site size varies from small sites along the river to large sites in the upper tier; units have minimal to fair separation; parking pads are gravel straight-ins or pull-throughs; some pads may require additional leveling; tent spots are mostly for smaller tents; fire rings; limited firewood is available for gathering in the vicinity; water at a single hand pump; vault facilities; gravel driveways; limited supplies are available in McKenzie Bridge, 9 miles southwest.

SEASON & FEES: $3.00 for a standard site, $4.00 for a riverside site; mid-May to September; upper loop is open for winter camping with no services; 16 day limit.

NATURAL FEATURES: Located on the west slope of the Cascades on a tree-dotted hillside overlooking the confluence of Ollalie Creek with the McKenzie River; Three Sisters Wilderness lies just to the south and the Mount Washington Wilderness Area is to the east.

ATTRACTIONS: Fishing in the McKenzie River; rafting; boating; a boat launch is located 0.3 mile south of this camping area; the 26-mile-long McKenzie River Trail passes-by on the opposite bank of the river.

NOTES: The views from the upper sites, near the highway, are vast and captivating. The lower sites, right on the grassy riverbank, have a more restricted view, but enjoy a somewhat quieter atmosphere.

PARADISE
Willamette National Forest

LOCATION: Western Oregon northeast of Springfield.

ACCESS: From Oregon State Highway 126 at milepost 54 +.1 (4 miles east of McKenzie Bridge, 37 miles west of Sisters), turn north onto a paved access road, and immediately west (left); proceed west for 0.1 mile to the campground.

FACILITIES: 64 level sites; sites are medium-sized with good separation provided by dense vegetation; 'premium' sites, along the river, are a bit smaller than sites along the highway; parking pads are paved, with some pull-throughs spacious enough to accommodate large vehicles; some nice, grassy tent sites, including some located along the river; fire rings; limited firewood is available for gathering in the vicinity; water at faucet-fountains throughout; restrooms with supplementary vault facilties; paved driveways; campground host; limited supplies are available in the small community of McKenzie Bridge.

SEASON & FEES: $6.00 for a standard site, $8.00 for a 'premium'site, $12.00 and $16.00 for multiple sites; May to September; 16 day limit.

NATURAL FEATURES: Located on the west slope of the Cascades along the south bank of the McKenzie River; units are all situated amid tall trees, hardy ferns, and a green forest floor; Blue River Reservoir is a few miles west; Three Sisters Wilderness is to the south, and the Mount Washington Wilderness Area is to the east.

ATTRACTIONS: Fishing in the McKenzie River; rafting; boat launch located east of the camping area; a trail through the campground connects with the 26-mile-long McKenzie River Trail.

NOTES: The dense forest here at Paradise creates a 'coastal rainforest' atmosphere. The campground trail passes through a virtual tunnel of thick vegetation.

MCKENZIE BRIDGE
Willamette National Forest

LOCATION: Western Oregon between Springfield and Bend.

ACCESS: From Oregon State Highway 126 at milepost 49 +.8 (1 mile west of McKenzie Bridge, 9 miles east of Blue River), turn south onto a gravel access road; continue for 100 yards to the campground entrance.

FACILITIES: 20 level sites in 2 loops; most sites are fairly large with good separation; A Loop sites are a bit larger than B Loop sites; parking pads are gravel; many sites are straight-ins but some are pull-throughs spacious enough to accomodate very large vehicles; some nice grassy tent sites; fire rings; firewood is available for gathering in the vicinity; water at a hand pump in each loop; vault facilities; gravel driveways; campground host; limited supplies in the community of McKenzie Bridge; complete supplies and services are available in Springfield, 47 miles west.

SEASON & FEES: $4.00 for a single unit, $8.00 for a multiple unit; mid-May to September; 16 day limit.

NATURAL FEATURES: Located on the west slope of the Cascades along the north bank of the McKenzie River; sites are situated amid tall conifers and moderate underbrush; Blue River Reservoir is a few miles west; Three Sisters Wilderness is southeast of here.

ATTRACTIONS: Boating (boat launch adjacent); fishing in the McKenzie River; 2 picnic areas have river access, picnic tables and barbecue grills; a number of nearby forest roads lead up into the surrounding mountains; variety of water recreation activities at Blue River Reservoir.

NOTES: This campground is easily accessible yet far enough from the highway to eliminate any disturbing traffic noise. Some sites have river access within a few yards. McKenzie Bridge has a nice, sheltered/shady, forested atmosphere with lots of elbow room.

166

DELTA
Willamette National Forest

LOCATION: Western Oregon between Springfield and Bend.

ACCESS: From Oregon State Highway 126 at milepost 45 +.4 (4.5 miles east of Blue River, 5.5 miles west of Bridge), turn south onto Forest Road 19; drive 0.2 mile, across a wooden trestle bridge; turn west (right) and continue (parallel to Highway 126) for 1 mile to the campground.

FACILITIES: 39 level sites; most sites are spacious and well separated; parking pads are gravel, average to large, straight-ins or pull-throughs; some large, level, grassy tent spots; fire rings at all sites; barbecue grills and fire rings at multiple sites; water at a single hand pump; vault facilities (H); gravel driveways; campground host; limited supplies in Blue Pool; complete supplies and services are available in Springfield, 43 miles west.

SEASON & FEES: $5.00, $7.00 for a premium site, $10.00 for a multiple site; May to September; 16 day limit.

NATURAL FEATURES: Located on the west slopes of the Cascades at 1200'; the McKenzie River flows past the north edge of the campground; the South Fork of the McKenzie flows along the south side; an open grassy flat stretches along the riverbank; most sites are in moderately dense forest; the Three Sisters Wilderness lies to the east.

ATTRACTIONS: Stream fishing; an "Old Growth Timber Grove" nature trail starts from across a footbridge at the west end of the campground; Blue River Lake, a few miles north, offers most types of water recreation. Cougar Reservoir, to the south, is right on the western edge of the Three Sisters Wilderness.

NOTES: The fact that Delta is across the river from the highway makes it secluded enough to be quiet and peaceful. Though there are many, recreational opportunities in the nearby area, Delta is seldom filled to capacity.

BLACK CANYON
Willamette National Forest

LOCATION: Western Oregon southeast of Eugene.

ACCESS: From Oregon State Highway 58 at milepost 27 +.3 (8 miles west of Oakridge, 33 miles east of Eugene), turn north into the campground.

FACILITIES: 75 sites in 6 loops; parking pads are paved; some spacious pull-through units are located rather close to the highway; riverside spots are smaller; there are some very nice tent spots, some with gravel tent pads; fire rings; some gatherable firewood is available in the vicinity; water at several faucets; vault facilities; campground host; paved driveways; adequate supplies and services in Oakridge; complete supplies and services are available in Eugene.

SEASON & FEES: $4.00 for a standard single site, $7.00 for a 'premium' (riverside) site, $8.00 for a multiple site, $14.00 for a multiple riverside site; May to October; 16 day limit.

NATURAL FEATURES: Located on the west slopes of the Cascades at less than 1000' of altitude; many sites are right on the south bank of the Willamette River; a deep channel is just offshore here, at a bend in the Willamette River; campground vegetation--ferns, moss and trees--is dense enough to be mistaken for a rain forest.

ATTRACTIONS: Boating; paved boat ramp; rafting; stream fishing; an adjacent picnic area has barbecue grills; ranger-naturalist programs on summer evenings; a trail leads through the campground to a gravel river beach.

NOTES: This campground, in the Black Canyon of the Willamette, is the last on the free-flowing Willamette River, because a few miles downstream the Lookout Point Dam restricts its flow. The rainforest atmosphere at this campground suggests settings on the Oregon Coast. 'Premium' sites along the river offer some really great views. Another nearby campground is Shady Dell, located at milepost 29. It has 10 sites rather near the highway.

BLUE POOL
Willamette National Forest

LOCATION: Southwest Oregon southeast of Eugene.

ACCESS: From Oregon State Highway 58 at milepost 44 +.7 (10 miles east of Oakridge, 41 miles west of the intersection of Oregon State Highway 58 with U.S. 97), turn south into the campground.

FACILITIES: 24 sites in 3 loops; most units are small, with average to good separation; parking pads are paved, small to medium straight-ins; pads are fairly level, though the campground is built on a slight slope; several rather small, private but very nice tent spots, including some walk-in sites, are located toward the west end of the campground; steel fire rings; limited firewood is available for gathering in the area, so b-y-o is recommended; water at several faucets; vault facilities; campground host; paved driveways; adequate supplies and services are available in Oakridge.

SEASON & FEES: $5.00 for a single unit, $10.00 for a double unit; May to September; 16 day limit.

NATURAL FEATURES: The "Blue Pool" is a deep, natural pool of water in Salt Creek flows right along next to many of the campsites; forested peaks of the Cascades surround this narrow valley; tall cedars, maples and pines and a considerable amount of underbrush provide separation between the sites.

ATTRACTIONS: An open, grassy, 'poolside' picnic area is a beautiful spot; it has barbecue grills and a large upright fireplace; stream fishing; Salt Creek Falls, a 266' cascade, is located 10 miles to the east.

NOTES: Blue Pool Campground is located in a secluded wooded glen quite near the highway. The adjacent day use area is one of the nicer picnic spots in this part of the country. This really neat place is perfect for a daytrip or an overnight stay.

SHADOW BAY
Willamette National Forest

LOCATION: Southwest Oregon southeast of Eugene.

ACCESS: From Oregon State Highway 58 at milepost 58 +.9 (26 miles east of Oakridge, 25 miles west of the intersection of Oregon State Highway 58 with U.S. 97), turn north onto Forest Road 5897; proceed north for 6.5 miles on a winding paved road; turn left onto Forest Road 5896; continue 1.8 miles on a fairly steep access road down to the campground.

FACILITIES: 103 sites in 6 loops; sites vary in size from medium to large, with average to good separation; parking pads are gravel; most pads are straight-ins, several long enough for large rv's; some beautiful tent spots; a few walk-in sites; fireplaces; some firewood is available for gathering in the area; water at several faucets; restrooms; holding tank disposal station near the entrance; paved driveways; adequate supplies and services in Oakridge.

SEASON & FEES: $6.00 for a single unit, $12.00 for a double unit; May to September.

NATURAL FEATURES: Located in the heart of the Cascade Range on the east shore of Waldo Lake; sites farthest from the lakeshore are on a grassy hilltop, with some trees for shelter and separation; sites closer to the lake are more on a forested slope; Diamond Peak rises to almost 9000' in the Diamond Peak Wilderness to the south.

ATTRACTIONS: Boating; fishing; swimming; foot trails in the area include the Shoreline Trail and the Waldo Lake Trail; the Pacific Crest Trail passes nearby; winter sports are popular in the Waldo Lake area.

NOTES: Shadow Bay is one of several campgrounds along the lake shore. This campground has easy access, is sufficiently removed from the mainstream of traffic, and is seldom filled to capacity. If the proper weather conditions exist, Waldo Lake appears to be a mirror reflecting the images of surrounding mountain peaks.

PRINCESS CREEK
Deschutes National Forest

LOCATION: Southwest Oregon southeast of Eugene.

ACCESS: From Oregon State Highway 58 at milepost 63 +.8 (28 miles east of Oakridge, 23 miles west of the intersection of Oregon State Highway 58 with U.S. 97), turn south into the campground.

FACILITIES: 46 sites in 2 loops; sites are good-sized and fairly well separated; parking pads are gravel; pads are mostly level pull-throughs, many ample enough for large rv's; some very nice tent sites, especially in the eastern loop; fireplaces; some firewood is available for gathering in the area; water at several faucets; vault facilities; campground host; paved driveways; adequate supplies and services are available in Oakridge.

SEASON & FEES: $6.00 for a single unit, $12.00 for a double unit; May to October; 14 day limit.

NATURAL FEATURES: Located in the heart of the Cascade Range on the north shore of Odell Lake; striking Diamond Peak pierces the skyline across the lake to the south; the lakeside sites are adequately sheltered/shaded, while units away from the shore are heavily forested; all sites have a view of the lake; Willamette Pass, at 5126', is just a short distance up the highway to the west.

ATTRACTIONS: Boating; boat ramp and dock are located between the 2 loops; fishing; the Pacific Crest Trail passes-by the lake's west shore; a winter sports area is nearby at Willamette Pass; about 8 miles to the west (just off Highway 58), is 266' Salt Creek Falls.

NOTES: Though many of the sites are close to the highway, there is an abundance of forest cover to muffle the traffic noise. Odell Lake is beautiful, and Princess Creek Campground is convenient, spacious and generally well maintained.

SUNSET COVE
Deschutes National Forest

LOCATION: Southwest Oregon north of Crater Lake.

ACCESS: From Oregon State Highway 58 at milepost 66 +.8 (19 miles west of the intersection of Oregon State Highway 58 with U.S. 97, 32 miles east of Oakridge), turn south into the campground.

FACILITIES: 21 sites; sites are mostly medium-sized with fair to good separation; a few pull-throughs are long enough for large vehicles; parking pads are gravel; because of the slope, many parking pads may require additional leveling; some good spots for smaller tents; fireplaces; firewood is available for gathering in the area; water at several faucets; waste water receptacles at several locations; vault facilities; driveway is broken pavement; adequate supplies and services are available in Oakridge.

SEASON & FEES: $5.00 for a single unit, $10.00 for a double unit; May to October; 14 day limit.

NATURAL FEATURES: Nestled in the heart of the Cascade Range on a forested hillside along the north shore of Odell Lake; very prominent Diamond Peak rises to almost 9000' across the lake to the south; campsites are located in a dense pine forest with very little underbrush.

ATTRACTIONS: Boating; boat ramp and floating dock; fishing; views through the trees of Odell Lake and Diamond Peak from most sites; the drive along Highway 58 and over Willamette Pass offers travelers some fine mountain scenery.

NOTES: Some of these sites are rather near the highway, so you may want to check out another forest campground, Odell Creek, which is located 2 miles further south on a gravel road. It has similar facilities, but no boat launch. Odell Lake is a beautiful, sapphire-blue mountain lake surrounded by emerald-green forested slopes.

CRESCENT LAKE
Deschutes National Forest

LOCATION: Southwest Oregon north of Crater Lake.

ACCESS: From Oregon State Highway 58 at milepost 69 +.5 (17 miles west of the intersection of Oregon State Highway 58 with U.S. 97, 35 miles east of Oakridge), turn south onto Forest Road 60; drive 2.0 miles on this paved, curvy road; turn west (right) at an information sign and continue 0.7 mile; turn south (left) into the campground.

FACILITIES: 46 sites; most sites are average-sized, with medium-length, gravel, straight-in parking pads; several units have long pull-throughs; many sites will require some additional leveling; fireplaces; some firewood is available for gathering in the vicinity; water at faucets throughout; vault facilities; paved driveways; campground host; limited supplies on Highway 58; adequate supplies and services are available in Oakridge.

SEASON & FEES: $6.00 for a single unit, $12.00 for a double unit; May to October; 14 day limit.

NATURAL FEATURES: Located on a bay on the sloping, forested east shore of Crescent Lake, where Cresent Creek flows into the lake; Crescent Lake is a glacially formed lake nestled amid the forested slopes of the Cascades; tall timber and grass are the predominant forms of campground vegetation; some of the sites are right along the bay and some are creekside.

ATTRACTIONS: Boating; paved boat ramp; fishing; swimming; water skiing; lake views through the trees from most sites; foot trails in the area; nearby Whitefish Horse Camp is located at a trailhead to Summit Lake.

NOTES: Because of its proximity to the highway and a marina, this campground tends to be very popular with weekend boaters. For a more secluded camp spot, you might want to check out Spring Campground, another large forest camp, located at the south end of Crescent Lake, 5 miles from here.

DIAMOND LAKE
Umpqua National Forest

LOCATION: Southwest Oregon north of Crater Lake National Park.

ACCESS: From the intersection of Oregon State Highways 138 and 230 (80 miles northeast of Medford, 3 miles south of Diamond Lake), drive west on Highway 230 for 0.3 mile; turn north (right) onto Forest Road 4795 (paved); continue 2.3 miles along the East Shore Road; turn west (left) into the campground.

FACILITIES: More than 200 sites in 3 tiers; sites are rather small and close together; most parking pads are paved straight-ins; additional leveling may be necessary; a few good-sized tent sites, but many are small; fire rings; firewood is often for sale, some firewood is available for gathering on nearby forest lands; water at several faucets; central restrooms; campground host; paved driveways; limited supplies at a small store near the south end of the campground and at a resort near the north end.

SEASON & FEES: $6.00 for a single unit, $9.00 for a double unit, $1.00 extra for a lakeside unit; May to October; 14 day limit.

NATURAL FEATURES: Located in the Southern Cascades on the sloping, forested east shore of Diamond Lake; the 3000-acre lake is completely surrounded by heavily forested mountains; campground vegetation consists primarily of tall conifers, moderate underbrush, and a pine needle-and-grass forest floor.

ATTRACTIONS: Boating (2 ramps); fishing; swimming; foot and equestrian trails in the area, including access to the Pacific Crest Scenic Trail; information center located near the entrance; ranger-directed evening programs.

NOTES: As remote as it is, Diamond Lake is still a very popular recreation area. An important attraction here is the fantastic scenery. All sites have views, across the lake, of Mount Bailey. Sunsets on the lake can be phenomenal!

BROKEN ARROW
Umpqua National Forest

LOCATION: Southwest Oregon north of Crater Lake National Park.

ACCESS: From the intersection of Oregon State Highways 138 and 230 (3 miles south of Diamond Lake, 80 miles northeast of Medford), drive west on Highway 230 for 0.3 mile; turn north (right) onto Forest Road 4795 (paved); proceed 0.7 mile; turn west (left) onto South Shore Road; continue 0.5 mile and turn south (left) into the campground.

FACILITIES: 148 sites in 11 loops; sites are average to large, with minimal to good separation; parking pads are paved, and some are long enough for large vehicles; many units have large, level tent spots; gravel table areas; barbecue grills and/or fire rings; firewood is often for sale, some firewood is available for gathering in the area; water at several faucets; restrooms; holding tank disposal station; paved driveways; campground host; limited supplies at a small store about 1 mile north.

SEASON & FEES: $5.00 for a single unit, $7.00 for a double unit; May to September; 14 day limit.

NATURAL FEATURES: Located in the Southern Cascades on an open forest hillside near the south shore of Diamond Lake; the lake is visible through the trees from some sites; campground vegetation consists mostly of grass, conifers, and very little underbrush.

ATTRACTIONS: Boat ramp; fishing; picnic area; nearby foot and equestrian trails, including access to the Pacific Crest Scenic Trail; information center in Diamond Lake, 3 miles north.

NOTES: A striking attraction in the Diamond Lake area is the fantastic scenery! Mt. Thielsen, just to the east, reaches to over 9000'. It's visible from the lake, from many points around the lake, and from the approaching highways.

FAREWELL BEND
Rogue River National Forest

LOCATION: Southwest Oregon between Medford and Crater Lake National Park.

ACCESS: From Oregon State Highway 62 at milepost 56 +.9 (14 miles west of the Annie Springs entrance to Crater Lake National Park, 57 miles east of Medford), turn west into the campground.

FACILITIES: 61 sites in 3 loops; sites are large and well separated; parking pads are paved straight-ins, some long enough to accommodate large vehicles; most sites are quite level; fire rings and barbecue grills at each site; firewood is available for gathering in the area; water at several faucet/fountains; restrooms (H); several waste water receptacles; paved driveways; minimal supplies at a resort 0.5 mile south on Highway 62; complete supplies and services are available in Medford.

SEASON & FEES: $6.00; May to September; 14 day limit.

NATURAL FEATURES: Located in the Southern Cascades on the southeast bank of the Rogue River; most of the sites are well separated by tall hardwoods, conifers and considerable underbrush; about half the sites are streamside.

ATTRACTIONS: A large, grassy, central area contains a children's playground (most of the play equipment was constructed from natural materials); Rogue River Gorge viewpoint, 0.5 miles south, overlooks the historic river where it rushes through a narrow gorge; Crater Lake National Park is 15 miles northeast; trailhead for the Upper Rogue River Trail is located a few miles south.

NOTES: Though a few sites may be rather close to the highway, the forest serves as an effective partition between most campsites and the traffic. The closeness of the legendary Rogue River creates a distinctive spirit at Farewell Bend.

UNION CREEK
Rogue River National Forest

LOCATION: Southwest Oregon between Medford and Crater Lake National Park.

ACCESS: From Oregon State Highway 62 at milepost 56 +.1 (15 miles west of the Annie Springs entrance to Crater Lake National Park, 56 miles northeast of Medford), turn west into the campground.

FACILITIES: 99 sites in 5 loops; sites are large and very well distanced, with trees and shrubs for good separation; parking pads are fairly level, gravel straight-ins; many pads are spacious enough to accommodate large vehicle combinations; some nice, secluded tent spots; fireplaces; firewood is available for gathering in the area; water at several faucets; vault facilities; waste water receptacles; paved driveways; camper supplies at a resort 1 mile north on Highway 62; complete supplies and services are available in Medford.

SEASON & FEES: $4.00; May to September; 14 day limit.

NATURAL FEATURES: Located on a heavily timbered flat along both sides of Union Creek, where Union Creek flows into the Rogue River; campground vegetation consists mainly of tall conifers, fairly dense underbrush and a pine needle forest floor; Crater Lake is located 20 miles east.

ATTRACTIONS: Rogue River Gorge viewpoint, 0.5 mile north, overlooks the river where it rushes through a narrow gorge; trailhead for the Upper Rogue River Trail is located a few miles south; foot trails follow Union Creek along both banks; picnic area with shelters; Crater Lake National Park is 15 miles northeast; ranger-naturalist programs on summer evenings.

NOTES: The campsites at Union Creek are spacious and private--and some are creekside. The campground is neatly divided into two sections by this clear, mountain stream spanned by a picturesque wooden bridge.

177

MAZAMA
Crater Lake National Park

LOCATION: Southwest Oregon south of Crater Lake.

ACCESS: From Oregon State Highway 62 at the Annie Springs entrance station (57 miles northwest of Klamath Falls, 71 miles northeast of Medford), drive north 100 yards and turn east (right) into the campground.

FACILITIES: 198 level sites in 7 loops; sites are fairly large and well separated (for a national park campground); parking pads are paved, many are fairly long pull-throughs; some very nice, spacious tent areas; fireplaces; b-y-o firewood; water at several faucets; restrooms; showers are available at a private lodge nearby; holding tank disposal station; paved driveways; limited supplies at Rim Village, 4 miles north; complete supplies and services are available in Klamath Falls and Medford.

SEASON & FEES: $6.00 for camping, plus $5.00 for the park entrance fee; May to September.

NATURAL FEATURES: Located on a light to moderately forested flat; sites are in among tall trees, or on open grassy areas; Crater Lake itself is located 4 miles north; peaks of the Cascades encircle this lake which has formed in a volcanic caldera; Annie Creek flows through a chasm several hundred feet below the campground level.

ATTRACTIONS: Annie Creek Nature Trail descends 1.7 miles to the creek; Pacific Crest Trail passes near the campground and extends the length of the park; Visitor Center at Rim Village; Rim Drive completely circles the lake; cruises on the lake from Cleetwood Cove; fishing permitted in the lake and streams of the park; ranger-naturalist programs on summer evenings.

NOTES: Many of these nice campsites are very near the edge of the Annie Creek chasm. Crater Lake, the second deepest lake in the western hemisphere, is a magnificent sight--from the rim or from the lake itself.

SPRING CREEK
Winema National Forest

LOCATION: Southwest Oregon north of Klamath Falls.

ACCESS: From U.S. Highway 97 just 100 yards south of milepost 241 (33 miles north of Klamath Falls, 104 miles south of Bend), turn west onto Forest Road 9732 (gravel); drive west and south on a steep and winding road for 3.0 miles to the campground entrance; continue 0.6 mile to the campsites.

FACILITIES: 26 fairly level sites; sites are very large and well spaced; parking pads are gravel, mostly level, and spacious enough for large trailers; large, level spots, surrounded by tall thin timber, for tents; fireplaces; an abundance of firewood is available for gathering; water at several faucets; 2 restrooms with auxiliary vaults; waste water and trash receptacles at each site; gravel driveways; limited supplies in Chiloquin, 5 miles south; complete supplies and services are available in Klamath Falls.

SEASON & FEES: $2.00.

NATURAL FEATURES: Located on a forested flat along Spring Creek, where the stream is wide, deep and slow-moving; vegetation is quite dense, with very tall conifers, underbrush and tall grass; timbered hills and mountains surround the campground.

ATTRACTIONS: Stream fishing in Spring Creek; foot trail from the campsites down to the creek and a picnic area; nearby Qux-Kanee Overlook provides a fantastic vista of the entire Klamath Basin.

NOTES: Spring Creek Campground is not usually busy-- probably due, in part, its rough access. Maneuvering the access road might be a little difficult for some towing vehicles. This secluded retreat has lots of elbow room at a good price. Mosquitoes seem to be less of a problem here than at nearby Collier Memorial State Park.

COLLIER
State Park

LOCATION: Southwest Oregon north of Klamath Falls.

ACCESS: From U.S. Highway 97 at milepost 244 +.1 (30 miles north of Klamath Falls, 107 miles south of Bend) turn east onto a paved access road; proceed east and south for 0.4 mile to the campground.

FACILITIES: 68 level sites, including 50 with full hookups; sites are mostly medium-sized, with only a little vegetation for separation; most parking pads are paved, some are pull-throughs spacious enough to accomodate large vehicles; some roomy, level tent sites; fireplaces; firewood is usually for sale, or b-y-o; water at several faucets; restrooms with showers (H); holding tank disposal station; paved driveways; limited supplies in Chiloquin, 5 miles south; complete supplies and services are available in Klamath Falls.

SEASON & FEES: $8.00 for a standard site, $10.00 for a full-hookup site; April to October; 10 day limit.

NATURAL FEATURES: Located in an open forest in a large valley between the southern Cascades and the Fremont Mountains; Spring Creek flows into the Williamson River near here; campground vegetation consists of tall trees, very little underbrush, sparse grass, and a forest floor of pine needles.

ATTRACTIONS: Collier Memorial Logging Museum--an outdoor display of logging machinery from bygone eras--is adjacent; a paved trail leads from the campground to the museum; stream fishing in Spring Creek and the Williamson River; creekside day use area; picnicking; playground; ranger-naturalist evening programs.

NOTES: Collier Campground is in a lovely setting along a clear, rushing stream. It's popular with campers, fishermen, and mosquitoes. (A mosquito control program is in effect.) Beyond the State Park, a gravel road leads several miles north to Williamson River Forest Service Campground.

WILLOW LAKE
Jackson County Park

LOCATION: Southwest Oregon northeast of Medford.

ACCESS: From Oregon State Route 140 at milepost 28 +.6 (40 miles east of Medford, 40 miles west of Klamath Falls), turn north onto County Road 30/37 at a "Willow Lake" sign ; drive 10.7 miles north on a curvy paved road; at milepost 23 +.5, turn sharply left onto Willow Lake Road (Forest Road 3020); proceed southwest for 1.5 (paved) miles to the campground.

FACILITIES: 71 sites, including some with hookups; sites are average-sized, generally well separated; parking pads are gravel, and many pull-throughs are long enough for large vehicles; some pads may require additional leveling; about 30 sites have nice, large tent areas in an open forest setting; fireplaces; some firewood is available for gathering in the vicinity; water at several faucets; central restroom with showers, supplemented by vault facilities; holding tank disposal station; gravel driveways; camper supplies and laundry facilities are located at the adjacent marina/general store/restaurant.

SEASON & FEES: $6.00 for a standard site, $7.00 for a partial-hookup site, $8.00 for a full-hookup site; $1.00 extra for each adult beyond 2 per site.

NATURAL FEATURES: Located at 3000' on the forested west shore of man-made Willow Lake; timbered peaks of the southern Cascades, including 9500' Mount McLaughlin, surround this mountain lake; vegetation in the camping area consists of tall, thin conifers with hanging moss, and moderate underbrush.

ATTRACTIONS: Boat launch and dock; rental boats; fishing; sailing; water-skiing; swimming beach; day use area.

NOTES: The drive to this fairly secluded lake is enjoyable in its own right. Mount McLaughlin's stately presence adds a touch of near-surrealism to the local landscape.

WHISKEY SPRINGS
Rogue River National Forest

LOCATION: Southwest Oregon northeast of Medford.

ACCESS: From Oregon State Highway 140 at milepost 28 +.6 (40 miles east of Medford, 40 miles west of Klamath Falls), turn north onto County Road 30/37 at a sign for "Willow Lake"; drive 9 miles north on a curvy paved road; turn east (right) at milepost 25 +.3 onto an access road with broken pavement, and proceed for 0.4 mile to the campground entrance.

FACILITIES: 36 level sites; campsites are large and well spaced; parking pads are gravel; some sites have double-wide straight-in pads, and some have pull-throughs spacious enough to accomodate very large rv's; some large, level tent areas are located in among the trees; fireplaces; firewood is available for gathering in the area; water at faucets throughout; vault facilities; gravel driveways; limited supplies at a small store on Willow Lake, 4 miles west; complete supplies and services are available in Medford and Klamath Falls.

SEASON & FEES: $4.00; May to September; 14 day limit.

NATURAL FEATURES: Located on a heavily forested flat in the southern Cascades, just west of the Sky Lakes Wilderness Area; fairly clear of underbrush; the soil and gravel are an unusual reddish color; a small stream flows through the campground.

ATTRACTIONS: Nature trail; footbridge across the small creek; day use area has picnic sites, barbecue grills, and horseshoe pits; forest roads lead up into the Cascades toward the Sky Lakes Wilderness Area; Willow Lake, 4 miles west, is popular for boating, fishing, swimming and other water sports.

NOTES: The sites at Whiskey Springs are easily accessible, secluded, and roomy. It's unlikely this camping facility is often filled to capacity because the major local water feature, Willow Lake, is several miles from here.

DOE POINT
Rogue River National Forest

LOCATION: Southwest Oregon between Klamath Falls and Medford.

ACCESS: From Oregon State Highway 140 at milepost 30 +.4 (38 miles west of Klamath Falls, 42 miles east of Medford), turn south, then immediately west onto a paved access road which parallels the highway; drive west 0.2 mile to the campground.

FACILITIES: 25 sites in 2 loops; sites are medium to large and fairly well-separated; some pads are very long, and many are double-wide in order to accomodate a vehicle and trailer side-by-side; a few pads may require additional leveling; most sites have adequately level tent spots; fireplaces; some firewood is available for gathering in the vicinity; water at several faucets; central restrooms; paved driveways; campground host; limited supplies about 1 mile east on Highway 140; complete supplies and services are available in Medford and Klamath Falls.

SEASON & FEES: $6.00; May to September; 14 day limit.

NATURAL FEATURES: Located on the forested north shore of Fish Lake in the southern Cascades; a number of sites are right along the lake, which is encircled by timbered slopes; vegetation in the campground consists primarily of tall conifers and a considerable amount of underbrush, providing good separation between sites.

ATTRACTIONS: Nature trail leads around the lake; a picnic area, with kitchen shelters, is located between the 2 loops; boat ramp and dock at Fish Lake Campground, 0.7 mile east; great views across the lake.

NOTES: This campground is located in a mountain setting with hard-to-top scenery and generally excellent fishing near at hand. The lake is stocked annually and fish grow quickly because of an abundance of food.

FISH LAKE
Rogue River National Forest

LOCATION: Southwest Oregon between Klamath Falls and Medford.

ACCESS: From Oregon State Highway 140 at milepost 30 +.4 (38 miles east of Klamath Falls, 42 miles west of Medford), turn south and immediately east onto a paved access road which parallels the highway; drive east 0.5 mile to the campground.

FACILITIES: 17 sites; sites are mostly average-sized with some separation; parking pads are gravel, typically long, and some are double-wide; most sites are level enough for tents; fireplaces; some firewood is available for gathering in the vicinity; water at several faucets; central restrooms; waste water receptacles; paved driveways; campground host; limited supplies are available less than 1 mile east, on Highway 140; complete supplies and services are available in Medford and Klamath Falls.

SEASON & FEES: $6.00; May to September; 14 day limit.

NATURAL FEATURES: Located on a timbered hillside on the north shore of Fish Lake in the southern Cascades; the campground area has an open forest atmosphere with tall pines and very little underbrush; views of the lake through the trees from many sites; elevation is 4900'.

ATTRACTIONS: Fishing; boating; paved and lighted boat ramp and dock; visitor center nearby at Lake of the Woods; a foot trail leads around the east end of the lake and connects with the Pacific Crest Trail.

NOTES: The fishing here is reportedly in the very good-to-excellent category. An annual stocking program and the nearly ideal environmental conditions are cited as reasons for the good fish production. The campground is situated far enough from the highway to be reasonably protected from the disturbance of traffic.

ASPEN POINT
Winema National Forest

LOCATION: Southwest Oregon between Klamath Falls and Medford.

ACCESS: From Oregon State Highway 140 at milepost 36 +.3 (32 miles west of Klamath Falls, 48 miles northeast of Medford), turn south onto Forest Road 3704; drive 0.6 mile on this paved access road; turn west (right) and immediately south (left) into the campground.

FACILITIES: 60 sites in 2 loops; sites are fairly large with good separation for the most part; parking pads are gravel and mostly level; most pads are pull-ins, with several pull-throughs spacious enough to accomodate very large vehicles; a few walk-in tent sites; fireplaces; some firewood is available for gathering in the area; water at faucets throughout; centrally located restrooms; holding tank disposal station is located across the access road; paved driveways; campground host; limited supplies and phone at a resort 0.5 mile south; complete supplies and services are available in Medford and Klamath Falls.

SEASON & FEES: $6.00; May to September; 16 day limit.

NATURAL FEATURES: Located in an open forest setting along the northeast shore of Lake of the Woods in the southern Cascades; campground vegetation is composed of tall conifers, very little underbrush and a carpet of forest material; Mountain Lakes Wilderness lies to the east, and Sky Lakes Wilderness is to the north; elevation is 5100'.

ATTRACTIONS: Fishing; boating; boat launch and dock; swimming beach, no lifeguard; day use picnic area; Billie Creek Nature Trail is one of several foot trails in the area; Lake of the Woods Visitor Center is on Highway 140.

NOTES: Aspen Point has been a popular campground since the 1920's. There are huge stone fireplaces and picnic tables here which were built in the 1930's.

SUNSET
Winema National Forest

LOCATION: Southwest Oregon between Klamath Falls and Medford.

ACCESS: From Oregon State Highway 140 at milepost 36 +.3 (32 miles west of Klamath Falls, 48 miles northeast of Medford), turn south onto Forest Road 3704 (paved); drive 1.3 miles south and east to a "T" intersection; turn south (right) onto Dead Indian Road; continue for 0.9 mile; turn west (right) into the campground.

FACILITIES: 66 sites in 3 loops; sites are good-sized and fairly well-separated; parking pads are mostly level, paved straight-ins, some spacious enough to accomodate very large vehicles; a number of sites have large, level, gravel tent pads; fireplaces; firewood is available for gathering in the vicinity; water at faucet-fountains throughout; centrally located restrooms; holding tank disposal station is located 2 miles north near Aspen Point Campground; paved driveways; campground host; limited supplies and phone at a resort 2 miles north; complete supplies and services are available in Klamath Falls.

SEASON & FEES: $6.00; May to September; 16 day limit.

NATURAL FEATURES: Located on the forested east shore of Lake of the Woods in the southern Cascades; campground vegetation consists of fairly dense conifers with considerable underbrush; Mountain Lakes Wilderness lies to the east and Sky Lakes Wilderness is to the north.

ATTRACTIONS: Boat launch and dock; fishing; swimming; Sunset Trail leads 1 mile along the shore to Rainbow Bay Picnic Area; Lake of the Woods Visitor Center is located on Highway 140.

NOTES: 9500' Mount McLoughlin is visible across the lake to the north. Nice, off-the-highway campground.

GOOSE LAKE
State Park

LOCATION: South-central Oregon on the Oregon-California border.

ACCESS: From U.S. 395 in the hamlet of New Pine (15 miles south of Lakeview, 43 miles north of Alturas, California), turn west onto State Line Road; proceed 1.2 miles and turn north (right) into the campground.

FACILITIES: 48 level sites, all with partial hookups; sites are narrow and long, with minimal separation; parking pads are paved, medium-length straight-ins; excellent, large, grassy tent spots; fireplaces; firewood is usually for sale, or b-y-o; water at faucets in each site; restrooms with showers; paved driveway; campground host; gas and groceries in New Pine; adequate supplies and services are available in Lakeview and Alturas.

SEASON & FEES: $9.00 for a site, $3.00 for an extra vehicle; mid-April to the end of October; 10 day limit.

NATURAL FEATURES: Located in a large, high desert basin surrounded by low, rounded, mountains covered by grass, sage, and some medium-height trees; the east shore of large, shallow Goose Lake is within walking distance; campground vegetation consists of watered and mown grass and short-to-medium height hardwoods; most campsites have some sort of shelter/shade; elevation 4700'.

ATTRACTIONS: Day use area near the lake shore; fishing for warm-water species (bullhead, perch, etc.); fishing from a boat is suggested; small, simple, boat launch area; also good to excellent fishing in the local mountains.

NOTES: This is a nice campground that's near a primary highway, and yet in many respects it's really somewhat off the beaten path, too. The campground reportedly never fills up. Goose Lake could almost be described as an enormous, blue puddle that straddles the Oregon-California border--although it has been sounded to 24 feet, its average depth is only 8 feet.

Interesting scenery. Reminds me of Vantage around lake. Campground is not near lake & does not have a view of lake.

Oregon 83

✕ CROOKED RIVER
The Cove Palisades State Park

LOCATION: Central Oregon west of Madras.

ACCESS: From U.S. 97/Oregon State Highway 26 at Avenue D in mid-town Madras, proceed west and south on Avenue D (which becomes Culver Highway) to the town of Metolius; turn west onto Jefferson Avenue; continue west then south to Gem Lane; turn west onto Gem Lane, cross a railroad track, and follow this road west then south to a sign "The Cove Palisades"; turn west onto a paved park road; continue west 1 mile and turn south (left) into Crooked River Campground ("Loop E").(Total distance from Madras to Crooked River is 10 miles.) Whew!

FACILITIES: 91 partial-hookup sites; units are level, small to average, with minimal separation; parking pads are paved, level and medium-sized; some grassy spots for tents; fire rings; firewood is usually for sale, or b-y-o; water at faucets throughout; central restrooms with showers; holding tank disposal station at the entrance; paved driveways; minimal supplies at a general store, 1 mile east; adequate supplies and services are available in Madras.

SEASON & FEES: $7.00 without hookups, $9.00 with hookups, $3.00 for an extra vehicle; some sites open all year, with reduced fees October to April; 10 day limit.

NATURAL FEATURES: Located on the east rim above a deep basaltic canyon containing Lake Billy Chinook, a reservoir located at the confluence of 3 rivers--Crooked, Metolius, and Deschutes; campground vegetation consists of mown lawns and a few planted shade trees.

ATTRACTIONS: Boating; fishing; water skiing; swimming; hiking; river access from several points; the drive along the canyon rim provides spectacular views of the area.

NOTES: The Cove Palisades State Park is a 'hidden' secret. Access is rather complicated, but the facilities are a welcome surprise! The park road beyond Crooked River (3 miles to the nearest river access) is steep and winding.

I didn't go all the way to this campground because the road turned into gravel so I turned around. I later learned it was just a short stretch of gravel.

Oregon 84

X DESCHUTES RIVER
The Cove Palisades State Park

LOCATION: Central Oregon west of Madras.

ACCESS: From U.S. 97/Oregon State Highway 26 at Avenue D in mid-town Madras, proceed west and south on Avenue D (which becomes Culver Highway) to the town of Metolius; turn west onto Jefferson Avenue; continue west then south to Gem Lane; turn west onto Gem Lane, cross a railroad track, follow this road west then south to a sign "The Cove Palisades"; turn west onto a paved park road; continue west 6 miles down a steep, winding road to Deschutes River Campground (Loops A, B & C).(Total distance from Madras--15 miles.)

FACILITIES: 181 sites, including 87 with partial hookups; sites are mostly small to medium, with minimal to adequate separation; parking pads are paved, and mostly straight-ins; some may require leveling; tent spots are grass or bare earth; fire rings or fireplaces at each site; firewood usually for sale, or b-y-o; water at faucets throughout; central restrooms with showers; holding tank disposal station on the rim; paved driveways; minimal supplies at the marina; adequate supplies and services in Madras.

SEASON & FEES: $7.00 for a standard site, $9.00 for a partial-hookup site, $3.00 for an extra vehicle; some park sites open all year with reduced fees October to April; 10 day limit.

NATURAL FEATURES: Located deep in a dry, rocky canyon near the confluence of Crooked, Metolius and Deschutes Rivers; campsites are located in a grove of pine and juniper surrounded by towering basaltic escarpments.

ATTRACTIONS: Boating; fishing; waterskiing; swimming areas; hiking; several nearby river access points; marina; amphitheater near Loop A for ranger-naturalist programs.

NOTES: A number of these sites are distinctively different--built into rocky walls with huge boulders for separation. Other sites have grass and trees for cool comfort.

OCHOCO LAKE
State Park

LOCATION: Central Oregon between Prineville and Mitchell.

ACCESS: From U.S. 26 at milepost 26 +.2 (7.2 miles east of Prineville, 43 miles west of Mitchell), turn south into the campground.

FACILITIES: 22 sites; sites are average-sized with minimal to adequate separation; parking pads are mostly small to medium, paved straight-ins; some pads may require additional leveling; fireplaces or fire rings at each site; b-y-o firewood is recommended; water at several faucets; centrally located restrooms; waste water receptacles; showers and minimal supplies are available at a private resort nearby; adequate supplies and services are available in Prineville.

SEASON & FEES: $7.00 for a site, $3.00 for an extra vehicle; April to October; 10 day limit.

NATURAL FEATURES: Located on a lightly forested bluff above the north shore of Ochoco Lake, which is surrounded by tree-dotted ridges; the Ochoco Mountains rise to almost 7000' across the lake to the east; short and medium junipers are the predominant types of trees in the campground; some of the sites have bare earth floors, while others have a carpet of mown grass.

ATTRACTIONS: Boating; windsurfing; gravel boat launch; fishing; day use area adjacent to the campground; John Day Fossil Beds National Monument is located northwest of Mitchell.

NOTES: Ochoco Lake Campground has simple but congenial facilities in a conveniently situated roadside location. The country around here is a slightly less arid version of the Central Oregon high desert. For those who prefer camping at an even more removed area, Prineville Reservoir is located 17 miles south of Prineville. It has 70 campsites, a boat ramp and a swimming beach.

OCHOCO DIVIDE
Ochoco National Forest

LOCATION: Central Oregon between Prineville and John Day.

ACCESS: From U.S. Highway 26 just west of milepost 50 (34 miles east of Prineville, 16 miles west of Mitchell), turn south into the campground.

FACILITIES: 28 sites on a slight slope; sites are average to large and have minimal separation; parking pads are gravel; some pads are small straight-ins and others are pull-throughs large enough to accommodate medium-sized rv's; some pads may require additional leveling; many nice, grassy tent spots; steps are cut into the slope at many sites to provide easier access to tables and fireplaces; limited firewood is available for gathering in the vicinity; water at 2 faucets; vault facilities; waste water receptacles; paved driveways; limited supplies and services are available in Mitchell.

SEASON & FEES: $3.00; May to September; 14 day limit.

NATURAL FEATURES: Located in the Ochoco Mountains in a high, dry open forest, just west of Ochoco Divide; a rivulet near the divide flows westward down to Ochoco Lake and ultimately to the Deschutes River; campsites are situated on a grassy, tree-dotted slope.

ATTRACTIONS: There are some commanding vistas from atop Ochoco Divide--especially to the east; a jeep trail leads off from the eastern end of the campground; the drive along Highway 26, east of here, passes by some interesting geological formations; 2 sections of the John Day Fossil Beds National Monument are located near Mitchell and, further east, near Dayville.

NOTES: Ochoco Divide Campground has sort of an 'airy' quality as a result its mountainside position. The campsites are not very far from the highway, but the traffic on U.S. 26 is generally quite light anyway. Good price, too.

CLYDE HOLLIDAY
State Park

LOCATION: Central Oregon between Mt. Vernon and John Day.

ACCESS: From U.S. 26 at milepost 155 +.2 (1.3 miles east of Mt. Vernon, 7 miles west of John Day), turn south into the campground.

FACILITIES: 24 level sites, all with partial hookups; sites are fairly large with some separation; parking pads are paved, and most are spacious enough for very large rv's; a few hiker/biker sites are available; some very nice, large tent spots on level lawns; fireplaces; firewood is usually for sale, or b-y-o; centrally located restrooms with showers (H); water at each site; holding tank disposal station near the entrance; paved driveways; campground host; limited supplies and services are available in Mt. Vernon and John Day.

SEASON & FEES: $9.00 for a site, $3.00 for an extra vehicle; April to October; 10 day limit.

NATURAL FEATURES: Located along the John Day River; the park has manicured lawns and a variety of trees which provide limited shelter/shade; semi-arid terrain, with lightly timbered ridges along either side of the river, beyond the immediate vicinity; the Strawberry Mountain Range, with peaks rising to 9000', lies to the southeast.

ATTRACTIONS: Large, grassy day use area adjacent to the campground; a visitor center is located at the John Day Fossil Beds National Monument, a few miles west on Highway 19.

NOTES: The city-park-like setting for these campsites is unexpected here in dry Central Oregon. The Clyde Holliday 'oasis' is close enough to a sizable community to be convenient, but far enough from it to be detached. Some striking geological features can be seen in the John Day Valley.

DEPOT PARK
Grant County Park

LOCATION: Central Oregon in Prairie City.

ACCESS: From U.S. 26 (Front Street) at milepost 175 in mid-town Prairie City, turn south onto Main Street; continue south for 0.4 mile; turn east (left) into the park.

FACILITIES: 17 fairly level sites, some with hookups; sites are average in size with minimal separation; parking pads are paved, level, would accommodate medium-sized vehicles; a nice level lawn area is designated for tents; fireplaces; b-y-o firewood; water at many sites and the restroom; restroom with coin showers; holding tank disposal station at the entrance; telephone at the washroom; paved driveways; limited supplies and services are available in Prairie City.

SEASON & FEES: $3.00 for a tent site, $6.00 for a partial-hookup site, $1.00 for a hiker/biker site; $1.00 for use of the holding tank disposal station.

NATURAL FEATURES: Located in the John Day River Valley, north of the John Day River; campsites are quite open, on lawns with a few tall hardwoods for limited shelter/shade; views of the Strawberry Mountains to the south.

ATTRACTIONS: The park has an open, grassy area for recreation; access to the Strawberry Mountain Wilderness, south of Prairie City; the Depot Museum, with limited hours of operation, is located in a renovated railroad depot building which was moved to this location.

NOTES: Depot Park is located far enough from the highway to be quiet, yet conveniently close to Prairie City's business district. The pleasant, green surroundings in the park stand in stark contrast to the region's semi-arid terrain. A good stop for central Oregon travelers.

DIXIE
Malheur National Forest

LOCATION: Eastern Oregon between John Day and Baker.

ACCESS: From U.S. 26 at milepost 184 +.9 (9.5 miles east of Prairie City, 23 miles west of Unity) turn northwest onto a gravel forest road; continue 0.3 mile to the campground.

FACILITIES: 11 sites; sites are medium to good-sized, with good to excellent separation; parking pads are gravel, some large enough to accommodate medium-sized vehicles; additional leveling may be necessary at many sites; some nice secluded tent sites are located among the tall trees; fireplaces or barbecue grills; firewood is usually abundant; water at a single hand pump; vault facilities; waste water receptacle; pack-it-in/pack-it-out trash removal system; gravel driveways; limited supplies and services in Prairie City; adequate supplies and services are available in Baker, 50 miles northeast.

SEASON & FEES: No fee.

NATURAL FEATURES: Located on a forested hillside at 5000' at the southern tip of the Blue Mountains; nearby Dixie Summit, west on Highway 26, is at 5280'; a small creek flows through the campground and adjacent picnic area; vegetation in the camp area consists of tall timber and a little underbrush.

ATTRACTIONS: Hiking; berry picking; day use area adjacent to the campground has picnic facilities and a picturesque wooden foot bridge over the small stream.

NOTES: This campground will seldom be full to capacity because it's a bit off the beaten path, and has no major water feature to attract crowds. It's just a pleasant, simple, secluded forest camp, and would be a cool stop in the warmth of the Eastern Oregon summer. Hopefully, the price will stay the same.

UNITY LAKE
State Park

LOCATION: Eastern Oregon south of Baker.

ACCESS: From U.S. 26 at milepost 210 + .3 (2 miles west of Unity, 19 miles east of the intersection of U.S. 26 with Oregon State Highway 7), turn northeast onto Oregon Secondary Highway 245; proceed east and north for 2.2 miles; turn left onto a paved access road and continue 0.5 mile to the park and campground.

FACILITIES: 15 level sites, including 10 sites with electric hookups; sites are average-sized with very little separation; parking pads for 10 sites in the main loop are paved; a second loop has gravel pads; some parking pads are adequate for large vehicles; fireplaces; b-y-o firewood is recommended; centrally located restrooms (H) with solar showers; water at several faucets in the main loop, but sites in the second loop have no nearby water; holding tank disposal station and a telephone at the entrance; paved driveways; limited supplies and services are available in Unity, 5 miles south.

SEASON & FEES: $8.00 for a standard site, $9.00 for a partial-hookup site; April to October; 10 day limit.

NATURAL FEATURES: Located on a dry sage flat on a breezy bluff slightly above man-made Unity lake; some lawns with planted hardwoods in the campground, plus a few small trees and some natural grass and sage around the lake; the Blue Mountains rise to the north and west.

ATTRACTIONS: Boating; boat ramp; fishing; day use area with mown lawns and barbecue grills; nearby mountains, lakes and streams are accessible by forest roads.

NOTES: This is a pleasant place to enjoy eastern Oregon if you prefer a prairie environment over a mountain setting. There's enough local geological relief, plus some distant mountain views, to add a touch of embellishment to the semi-arid scene.

EMMIGRANT SPRINGS
State Park

LOCATION: Northeast Oregon east of Pendleton.

ACCESS: From Interstate 84 exit 234 eastbound (24 miles east of Pendleton), travel east along the frontage road on the south side of I-84 for 0.6 mile to the park; from I-84 exit 234 westbound (28 miles west of LeGrande) cross the Interstate to the south frontage road, then proceed west 0.5 mile to the park entrance; turn left into the campground.

FACILITIES: 51 sites, including 18 with full hookups; size and spacing of most units is typical of Oregon parks, but sites in one of the loops are a little larger than the others; paved parking pads; excellent spots for tents; fire rings; firewood for sale or b-y-o ; water at faucets throughout; restrooms with showers; paved driveways; gas and groceries at Meecham, 1 mile east; adequate supplies and services are available in Pendleton.

SEASON & FEES: $8.00 for a standard site, $10.00 for a full-hookup site, $3.00 for an extra vehicle; April to October; 10 day limit.

NATURAL FEATURES: Located on a flat in a forest of tall conifers; very little low-level vegetation within the campground, but some recent plantings of trees may eventually provide a little extra separation between sites; located 7 miles east of Blue Mountain Summit; elevation 4000 feet; generally quite mild during the summer.

ATTRACTIONS: Nature trails; outdoor exhibit located near the park entrance; the historic spring for which the park is named is located just west of the park; large community building available by reservation; day use area.

NOTES: Here is an excellent stop for Interstate travelers, (particularly those who've spent a day or two crossing the barrens of southern Idaho and eastern Oregon). And it's not as heavily used as you might think. Freeway noise may be a bother in some sites, but otherwise it's fine.

HILGARD JUNCTION
State Park

LOCATION: Northeast Oregon west of LeGrande.

ACCESS: From Interstate 84 exit 253 (9 miles west of LeGrande, 43 miles east of Pendleton), turn south onto Oregon State Highway 244, and proceed 0.1 mile to the campground entrance on the east (left) side of the highway.

FACILITIES: 18 sites; most units are level, small to medium in size, with minimal separation; short to medium-length parking pads; excellent spots for tents; fire rings; limited amount of firewood available for gathering in the vicinity; water at faucets in several locations; restrooms; holding tank disposal station near the campground; paved driveways; fairly complete supplies and services are available in LeGrande.

SEASON & FEES: $8.00 for a site, $3.00 for an extra vehicle; reduced fees October to April; open all year; 10 day limit.

NATURAL FEATURES: Located in a small canyon on a grassy flat on the north bank of the Grande Ronde River; nearly all campsites are right along the river; light to moderate shelter/shade in the campground; dry climate.

ATTRACTIONS: Outdoor historical exhibit with displays of historical documents; fishing; day use area directly to the west of the campground.

NOTES: Although this park, like most Oregon parks, is very well maintained, the relative openness of the campground and the noise from the freeway may be objectionable to some. It's the closest public campground to LeGrande, the hub of recreational activity in this part of Oregon. Emmigrant Springs State Park, 18 miles west, is a recommended alternative.

MINAM
State Recreation Area

LOCATION: Northeast corner of Oregon north of La Grande.

ACCESS: From Oregon State Highway 82 at milepost 33 +.6 (0.1 mile west of the hamlet of Minam, 34 miles north of La Grande), turn north at the west end of the bridge which crosses the river; follow a narrow gravel road which parallels the river for 1.7 miles to the campground.

FACILITIES: 12 sites; camp units are level, of average size and within view of one another; gravel parking pads; good tent-pitching possibilities; fireplaces; firewood is available for collecting in the area; water at a single hydrant; vault facilities; paved loop drive; nearest minimal supplies at a small store and motel in Minam; fairly complete supplies and services are available in La Grande.

SEASON & FEES: $7.00 for a site, add $2.00 for four or more adults per camp unit, $3.00 for an extra vehicle; April to October; 10 day limit.

NATURAL FEATURES: Located on a small grassy flat in a narrow canyon on the Wallowa River; some shelter/shade provided by trees along the perimeter of the campground; additional trees have been planted.

ATTRACTIONS: Plenty of river access points between the highway and the campground and beyond; many deep pools in the river which reportedly provide good fishing.

NOTES: This is a nice little campground which is surprisingly quite popular. It's been included because of its good sportsman's access, and because it's one of the few public camping areas in these parts.

WALLOWA LAKE
State Park

LOCATION: Northeast corner of Oregon south of Enterprise.

ACCESS: From mid-town Enterprise, travel south on Oregon State Highway 82, through the small community of Joseph, then along the east shore of Wallowa Lake to the park (a total of 12 miles from Enterprise).

FACILITIES: 210 sites, including 120 with full hookups, in a half-dozen loops; sites are of average size for an Oregon state park and are reasonably well spaced, but not very private; parking spaces are paved, many are long pull-throughs; excellent spots for tents; fireplaces; some firewood for sale, but very little is available for gathering, so b-y-o is suggested; water at faucets throughout; restrooms with showers; holding tank disposal station; paved driveways; marina and lodge nearby; gas, groceries and laundromat in Joseph; adequate supplies and services are available in Enterprise.

SEASON & FEES: $8.00 for a standard site, $10.00 for a full-hookup site, $3.00 for an extra vehicle, $2.00 for boat space; April to October; 10 day limit.

NATURAL FEATURES: Located at the south end of 283-foot-deep Wallowa Lake; glacial moraines tower 1200 feet above the lake surface; very tall conifers in the campground; grass and pine needle ground cover; very little low-level vegetation; deer are frequent visitors to the campground.

ATTRACTIONS: Boating; fishing; foot trails; amphitheater for scheduled ranger-naturalist programs in the summer; children's play area.

NOTES: Although it's in a relatively isolated region, Wallowa Lake's campground is *very* popular. (Get there early on holiday weekends.) The burial place of the famed Nez Perce Indian leader, Chief Joseph, is at the north of the lake.

FAREWELL BEND
State Park

LOCATION: Eastern Oregon north of Ontario.

ACCESS: From Interstate 84 at Exit 353 (22 miles northwest of Ontario, 50 miles southeast of Baker), drive northwest on Huntington Road, parallel to I-84, for 1.0 mile to the park entrance; turn northeast (right) and then northwest (left) into the campground; Loop B is 0.1 mile on the left; Loop A is 0.2 mile straight ahead and on the right.

FACILITIES: 96 level sites, including 53 with partial hookups (in Loop A); parking pads are average-sized straight-ins; pads are paved in Loop A, and gravel in Loop B; all sites have good tent-pitching areas; fireplaces or fire rings; b-y-o firewood is recommended; water faucets throughout; centrally located restroom with showers in Loop A, and vault facilities in Loop B; holding tank disposal station; paved driveways in Loop A, gravel driveways in Loop B; limited supplies are available at a store near the I-84 interchange; complete supplies and services are available in Ontario.

SEASON & FEES: $7.00 for a primitive site, $9.00 for a partial-hookup site; reduced fees October-to-April; open all year; 10 day limit.

NATURAL FEATURES: Located on a bliff at a bend on the Snake River, where the river is very wide and generally slow-moving;the grounds are watered and mowed, planted with young-to-mature trees for shade and separation; rolling treeless hills to the south and tall treeless peaks to the north across the river.

ATTRACTIONS: Boating; fishing; large cement boat ramp; huge day use area.

NOTES: This is an historically significant site--where the Oregon Trail pioneers camped before heading cross-country toward the Columbia River. A number of sites in Loop A have a good view across the river.

Washington

Washington is a fine state.

It can be argued, quite successfully, we believe, that few, if any, other states can top Washington in the area of scenic variety. From the rain forests of the Olympic Peninsula, to the emerald isles of Puget Sound, to the misty Cascades, to the arid Columbia Basin, to the golden Palouse Hills-- Washington packs a lot more into a lot less territory than other western states. (You could spend a month, a year, or more just getting to know the Sound alone.)

And in spite of all the stories told of the state's incessant rain (many of which, we suspect, are fabricated by Southern Californians), it doesn't rain *all* the time, *all* over Washington. (Ask any tenured Washingtonian what he does when he plans a camping trip, and it *does* rain, he'll reply, "We go anyway".)

Even with a population density that's greater than average for the western states, Washington has a surprisingly large number of excellent camping areas.

And while many cite Oregon as being the western leader in state park development, Washington certainly doesn't take second place to its sister to the south in that area. It *may* be our misconception, but Washington's state parks, unlike those of some other states, don't have an overused look; somehow, most of the parks maintain a fresh appearance.

A lot of the credit for the excellent recreational environment in Washington has to go to the untold number of outdoor-oriented individuals who have made a concerted, and effective, effort to maintain Washington's highly desireable natural environment.

Washington *is* a fine place.

KLAHOWYA
Olympic National Forest

LOCATION: Northwest Washington on the north side of the Olympic Peninsula northeast of Forks.

ACCESS: From U.S. 101 at milepost 211 +.9 (20 miles northeast of Forks, 41 miles west of Port Angeles), turn north onto a gravel access road and continue 0.3 mile to the campground entrance.

FACILITIES: 48 sites in two loops; most units are level, spacious and moderately spaced; parking spaces are paved and consist of a few pull-alongs, but mostly straight-ins; many sites, including a couple of walk-ins, are right on the river's edge; fireplaces; firewood is available for collecting, but may be wet; water at faucets every half dozen sites; vault facilities (H); gravel loop driveways; nearest supplies (limited) in Sappho, 10 miles west, or Fairholm, 8 miles east; adequate supplies in Forks; complete supplies and services are available in Port Angeles.

SEASON & FEES: $4.00; open all year, but no water or fee in winter; 14 day limit.

NATURAL FEATURES: Located on the north bank of the Soleduck River in a narrow, steep-sided 'corridor'; moderately dense rain forest with lots of hanging moss on the trees; cool and moist most of the year.

ATTRACTIONS: "Pioneers' Path" nature trail meanders through the forest within the campground, with signs along the trail that tell of man's past influence on this area; fishing.

NOTES: This strikingly beautiful campground exhibits the somber, moody atmosphere typical of rain forest camps. Even on cloudless days not much sun filters through the giant trees. You may hear a little highway noise, but most of it is dampened (no pun intended) by the lush vegetation.

FAIRHOLM
Olympic National Park

LOCATION: Northwest Washington on the north side of the Olympic Peninsula west of Port Angeles.

ACCESS: From U.S 101 at milepost 220 +.9 at Fairholm (26 miles west of Port Angeles, 33 miles east of Forks), turn north onto the paved campground access road; proceed 0.3 mile to the campground.

FACILITIES: 87 sites in three loops, including 16 walk-in sites just above the lake shore; most sites are pretty slopey and of average size for a national park campground; small to medium, gravel parking pads and table areas; fireplaces; b-y-o firewood; water from faucets at restrooms; central restroom in each loop; holding tank disposal station; paved driveways; small store and gas station on the highway near the campground entrance; adequate supplies in Forks, complete supplies and services are available in Port Angeles.

SEASON & FEES: $5.00; open all year; 14 day limit.

NATURAL FEATURES: Located on a moderately steep hillside at the west end of Crescent Lake; dense conifer and hardwood forest, plus enough low-level brush in the campground for some campsite separation; the entire area is surrounded by densely forested mountains.

ATTRACTIONS: Self-guiding 0.75 mile nature trail; other trails lead through the campground loops and down to the lake; designated swimming area (quite near the highway); boat launch and docks; fishing.

NOTES: Crescent Lake is perhaps the most picturesque of the easily accessible lakes on the Peninsula. There are some truly spectacular mountain vistas in this area. Many campers consider the walk-ins to be the best campsites.

SALT CREEK
Clallam County Recreation Area

LOCATION: Northwest Washington on the north edge of the Olympic Peninsula west of Port Angeles.

ACCESS: From Washington State Highway 112 at milepost 53 +.9 (11 miles west of Port Angeles), turn north onto Camp Hayden Road; continue 3.5 miles to the recreation area entrance.

FACILITIES: 80 sites in two sections: the first consists of 48 closely spaced rv sites in three parallel rows; the second group of sites would be preferable for tenters, since the location affords substantially more protection from the elements than the first (see below); additional leveling is needed at many sites; fire rings; firewood is usually for sale, or b-y-o; central restroom with showers, plus auxiliary vault facilities; resident manager; nearest supplies (limited) at a small store at the intersection of Highway 112 and Camp Hayden Road.

SEASON & FEES: $4.00 for Clallam County residents, $6.00 for non-county residents; 1 vehicle and 6 people per site; open all year.

NATURAL FEATURES: Located on a high bluff above the Strait of Juan de Fuca; one area is located on an open grassy, slightly sloping flat surrounded by a conifer and hardwood forest; a second area is situated on a forested point just to the west of the first section; typically very windy.

ATTRACTIONS: Large children's play area; foot trails to viewpoints and to the beach; abandoned harbor defense bunkers.

NOTES: Although the facilities are adequate and reasonably priced, the big attraction here is the view-- wow! On a clear day you can see Puget Sound far to the east, and the southern tip of Vancouver Island to the north.

ELWHA
Olympic National Park

LOCATION: Northwest Washington on the north side of the Olympic Peninsula west of Port Angeles.

ACCESS: From U.S. 101 at milepost 239 +.5 (at the east end of the Elwha River bridge, 9 miles west of Port Angeles), turn south onto Elwha Valley Road (paved); continue 3.1 miles to the campground entrance on the east side of the road.

FACILITIES: 41 sites, including 7 walk-ins; most sites are very level and of average size for a park service campground, with minimal separation; paved, mostly short to medium, straight-in parking spaces, plus a few pull-throughs; excellent tent-pitching opportunities for small to medium sized tents; fireplaces; b-y-o firewood; water at several faucets; central restroom; shelter with a large stone fireplace; paved driveways; ranger station 1 mile south; limited supplies (and showers) at a resort on the main highway; complete supplies and services are available in Port Angeles.

SEASON & FEES: $5.00; open all year; 14 day limit.

NATURAL FEATURES: Located on a wooded flat in the Elwha River Valley; Elwha River is 200 yards west of the campground; moderately dense conifer and hardwood forest; in somewhat more open forest than many other campgrounds in the Olympics.

ATTRACTIONS: Elwha Campground Trail, a 0.7 mile loop; nearby amphitheater for scheduled ranger-naturalist programs in the summer; fishing.

NOTES: Although this campground is very popular in the summer, it's nearly deserted in winter. That's unfortunate, since this valley can be enjoyed year 'round. Bring your rain gear, though.

X ALTAIRE
Olympic National Park

LOCATION: Northwest Washington on the north side of the Olympic Peninsula west of Port Angeles.

ACCESS: From U.S 101 at milepost 239 +.5 (at the east end of the Elwha River bridge, 9 miles west of Port Angeles), turn south onto the Elwha Valley Road (paved); proceed south 4.5 miles (0.5 mile past the Elwha Ranger Station) to the campground access road; turn west, go down a steep paved road 0.1 mile to the campground.

FACILITIES: 32 sites; sites are level and reasonably good-sized with nominal separation; all parking spaces are paved; most units have straight-in parking pads, some have pull-throughs; good tent-pitching possibilities; fireplaces; b-y-o firewood; water at faucets in several locations; restrooms; spacious shelter with a large stone fireplace; paved driveways; nearest supplies (and showers) at a resort on the main highway; complete supplies and services are available in Port Angeles.

SEASON & FEES: $5.00; May to October; 14 day limit.

NATURAL FEATURES: Located on a small flat on the bank of the swiftly flowing Elwha River; fairly dense conifer and hardwood forest, but little in the way of ground-level vegetation; tall, heavily timbered ridges on either side of the river; typically quite damp/wet.

ATTRACTIONS: Whiskey Bend Trail leads off from the ranger station; scenic drive to the south on the Elwha Valley Road; fishing.

NOTES: This is really a pretty nice little campground: very level, somewhat off the beaten path, the sound of the rushing river for background music. Note that, although Altaire is closed during the winter, Elwha campground, 1.5 miles north, is open all year.

Beautiful river. Very pretty campground.

HEART O' THE HILLS
Olympic National Park

LOCATION: Northwest Washington on the north side of the Olympic Peninsula south of Port Angeles.

ACCESS: From U.S. 101 in mid-town Port Angeles, turn south onto South Race Street (street signs will indicate that this is the way to Hurricane Ridge); proceed south for 6.3 miles to the entrance station and the campground just beyond, on the east side of the road. (Note that the last several miles of the access road are steep and winding.)

FACILITIES: 105 sites in 5 loops; overall, the camp units are slightly larger than average for a national park campground, with average privacy; paved parking pads; additional leveling will be needed in most sites; adequate space for medium-sized tents; handicapped access units available; fireplaces; b-y-o firewood; water at central faucets; restrooms with camper service sinks; paved driveways; complete supplies and services are available in Port Angeles.

SEASON & FEES: $5.00; open all year; 14 day limit.

NATURAL FEATURES: As the name implies, this is hilly country; dense forest in and around the campground, with some head-high vegetation for campsite separation; wide, deep valleys and sharply-defined mountains in the vicinity.

ATTRACTIONS: Visitor centers at park headquarters in Port Angeles and at Hurricane Ridge; several trailheads nearby; amphitheater for scheduled ranger-naturalist programs.

NOTES: While Heart O' The Hills may be crowded during the summer months, staying here provides you with access to some of the finest scenery in the park, the most notable of which is found at Hurricane Ridge, 13 miles south. If you manage to get here during clear weather, you won't soon forget the astounding vistas which can be enjoyed throughout this region.

DUNGENESS
Clallam County Recreation Area

LOCATION: Northwest Washington on the north edge of the Olympic Peninsula east of Port Angeles.

ACCESS: From U.S. 101 at milepost 260 (11 miles east of Port Angeles, 4 miles west of Sequim), turn north onto Kitchen-Dick Lane; continue 3.3 miles to a point where the road curves east (right) and becomes Lotzgessel Road; proceed 0.2 mile east on Lotzgessel Road to Voice of America Road; turn north (left) onto V O A Road (watch for the large "Dungeness Recreation Area" sign) and continue 0.6 mile to the recreation area.

FACILITIES: 90 sites; most sites are level and fairly good-sized with quite a bit of privacy; gravel parking spaces are primarily long straight-ins, but there are some large pull-throughs as well; nice grassy tent spots; fire rings; firewood is usually for sale, or b-y-o; central faucets; restrooms; paved driveways; fairly complete supplies and services are available in Sequim; complete shopping in Port Angeles.

SEASON & FEES: $4.00 for Clallam County residents, $6.00 for non-residents; February 1 to September 30.

NATURAL FEATURES: Located in a large pine grove on a bluff above 7-mile-long Dungeness Spit, the country's largest natural sand hook; the area abounds in marine wildlife; windy, but not as wet as most of the peninsula.

ATTRACTIONS: Trails from near the campground to Dungeness Spit; beachcombing; clamming; children's play area; hunting October to January.

NOTES: Some of the most sweeping panoramas of the Olympic Peninsula region are available here: the Olympic Mountains, in full view to the south; Vancouver Island to the north; the Strait of Juan de Fuca to the west; Puget Sound to the east.

SEQUIM BAY
State Park

LOCATION: Northeast corner of the Olympic Peninsula east of Port Angeles.

ACCESS: From U.S. Highway 101 at a point 4 miles east of Sequim and 14 miles west of Discovery Bay, turn north into the park; the campground is a short distance north of the entrance.

FACILITIES: 86 sites, including 26 full-hookup units, in 2 loops; sites in the upper loop are primarily for large vehicles--they have paved, level, pull-through parking pads; the lower loop has smaller sites with better separation-- parking pads are smaller straight-ins which may need additional leveling; small, but nice, tent spots in the lower loop; fireplaces; b-y-o firewood is recommended; water at several faucets; restrooms with showers; paved driveways; complete supplies are available in Sequim.

SEASON & FEES: $6.00 for a standard site, $8.50 for a full-hookup site; open all year, with limited facilities in winter; 10 day limit.

NATURAL FEATURES: Located on the forested shore of Sequim Bay in the 'rain shadow' of the Olympic Mountains--considerably less rain falls here than in the rest of the Olympic Peninsula; some sites are right on the edge of the bay, which is quite well-protected from the elements; Dungeness Spit, a miles-long natural sand jetty, juts out from the Peninsula into the Strait of Juan de Fuca nearby.

ATTRACTIONS: Boat ramp; fishing; swimming; nature trails; playground; large, open, grass recreation areas; Dungeness National Wildlife Refuge and Dungeness Recreation Area nearby.

NOTES: Because of its mild, dry climate, the Sequim Bay area is occasionally termed the 'Banana Belt of the Pacific Northwest'.

MORA
Olympic National Park

LOCATION: Northwest Washington on the west side of the Olympic Peninsula west of Forks.

ACCESS: From U.S 101 at milepost 193 +.15 (2 miles north of Forks, 9 miles south of Sappho), turn west-southwest onto LaPush Road and drive 8.4 miles to the Quilliute Prairie Fire Department building; turn west (right) onto Mora Road, and continue 3.3 miles to the campground entrance.

FACILITIES: 90 sites in five loops; all sites are level, medium-sized and fairly well separated (for a national park campground); paved parking pads; adequate space for medium to large tents in most sites; fireplaces; b-y-o firewood; water at central faucets; central restrooms; holding tank disposal station; paved driveways; groceries, gas, laundromat and showers at the intersection of LaPush/Mora Roads, 3.3 miles east; adequate supplies and services are available in Forks.

SEASON AND FEES: $5.00; open all year.

NATURAL FEATURES: Located on the north bank of the swift, deep Quilliute River; very dense rain forest with lots of ferns and twiggy hardwoods; cloudy/rainy throughout the year, but somewhat less in summer than during other seasons.

ATTRACTIONS: Ocean beaches 1.5 miles west, with trails that lead north and south along the coast; riverside campfire circle for ranger-naturalist talks; fishing.

NOTES: Mora Campground is located in the narrow coastal section of Olympic National Park. There is a very quiet, (some might say somber) atmosphere associated with this area. Several of the most scenic beaches in the Park are near here. There are some particularly nice sites on the bank of the Quilliute River.

BOGACHIEL
State Park

LOCATION: Northwest Washington on the west side of the Olympic Peninsula south of Forks.

ACCESS: From U.S. 101 at milepost 186 (5.5 miles south of mid-town Forks, 0.4 mile north of the Bogachiel River bridge), turn west onto a short paved access road which leads to the park entrance.

FACILITIES: 42 sites; sites are of average size and are level; the units at the south end of the campground are a little larger and are right along the river's edge (but closer to the bridge and associated highway noise); small to medium, gravel parking pads; 2 kitchen shelters; fireplaces; firewood is available for gathering in the vicinity, but is likely to be wet, so b-y-o is recommended; water at faucets throughout the campground; restrooms with showers; holding tank disposal station; paved driveways; resident ranger-manager; adequate supplies are available in Forks.

SEASON & FEES: $6.00 for a site, $2.00 for an extra vehicle; open all year; 10 day limit.

NATURAL FEATURES: Located on the north/east bank of the wide, swift and deep Bogachiel River; a small creek crossed by a footbridge flows through the campground; dense rain forest in the region, but the campground is in a slightly more open forest setting.

ATTRACTIONS: The Bogachiel is a renowned steelhead and salmon fishery; boat launch; big game hunting on nearby national forest lands.

NOTES: This campground, although nice, doesn't appear to be quite up to the standards set by other Washington state parks. The deteriorating effect of the elements (it rains *a lot* here) no doubt has taken its toll. A good hunter's and fisherman's camp, though.

HOH
Olympic National Park

LOCATION: Northwest Washington on the west side of the Olympic Peninsula east/southeast of Forks.

ACCESS: From U.S. 101 at milepost 178 +.5 (13 miles south of Forks, 21 miles north of Kalaloch), turn east onto the Hoh Valley Road (paved, but winding and bumpy); continue east 19 miles to the campground; (allow a minimum of 45 minutes for the trip).

FACILITIES: 95 sites in 3 loops; most sites are level, generously sized and well spaced (for a national park campground); most parking spaces are paved, short to medium-length straight-ins, with some medium to long pull-throughs; most units offer good tent-pitching opportunities; a number of campsites are right along the river; fireplaces; b-y-o firewood from outside the park; water at central faucet-fountains; restrooms; holding tank disposal station; paved driveways; ranger station; nearest supplies (very limited) at a small store 12 miles west on the Hoh Road; adequate supplies and services are available in Forks.

SEASON & FEES: $5.00; open all year, with limited facilities in winter; 14 day limit.

NATURAL FEATURES: Located on a moderately forested flat along the bank of the Hoh River; Hoh Rain Forest, with its incomparable variety of flora and fauna; elevation 583'.

ATTRACTIONS: Visitor center; self-guided nature trails; amphitheater for evening campfire programs during the summer.

NOTES: Yes, we've disregarded distance off the main highway to bring you this campground. It is so truly unique that it's more than worth the extra time getting here. Spend a day or two listening to the river and silently walking the rain forest trails, and you'll remember the experience for a lifetime.

KALALOCH
Olympic National Park

LOCATION: Northwest Washington on the west coast of the Olympic Peninsula south of Forks.

ACCESS: From U.S. 101 at milepost 157 +.7, at the small settlement of Kalaloch (34 miles south of Forks, 70 miles north of Hoquiam), turn west into the campground entrance.

FACILITIES: 179 sites in 6 loops; majority of the units are about average in size for a national park campground and fairly well separated; small, paved, reasonably level straight-in parking pads (a few are pull-alongs); most sites have large, level tent spaces; fireplaces; b-y-o firewood; water at faucets in each loop; central restrooms; paved loop driveways; ranger station nearby; very limited supplies at a nearby resort; adequate supplies are available in Forks.

SEASON & FEES: $5.00; open all year; 14 day limit.

NATURAL FEATURES: Located on a windswept bluff above the ocean beach; campground vegetation consists of short to medium height trees and leafy bushes which provide a fairly good windbreak; several inviting beaches are accessible from here.

ATTRACTIONS: Beachcombing; amphitheater for scheduled ranger-naturalist programs during the summer.

NOTES: The beaches in this area are varied in their nomenclature and points of interest. Some have proper nouns for names, like Ruby Beach; most are merely numbered: Beach 2, Beach 3, Beach 6, and so on. Each beach has its own special appeal: Ruby beach is adorned with spires of stone called "seastacks"; steep, colorful cliffs rise above Beach 6; the shoreline north of Beach 4 is noted for its tidepools.

WILLABY
Olympic National Forest

LOCATION: Northwest Washington on the west side of the Olympic Peninsula north of Hoquiam.

ACCESS: From U.S. 101 at milepost 125 +.5 (38 miles north of Hoquiam, 66 miles south of Forks), turn east onto the South Shore Lake Quinault Road (paved); the campground entrance is 1.6 miles east, on the north side of the road.

FACILITIES: 19 sites; most sites are medium-sized with fairly good spacing and visual separation between most sites; parking pads are paved, mostly short, straight-ins which may require some additional leveling; some units have large, framed-and-gravelled tent pads; paved pathways; fireplaces; firewood is available for gathering in the vicinity, but may be wet much of the year, so b-y-o is suggested; water at faucet-fountains throughout the campground; restroom; paved loop driveway; nearest supplies (limited) at the small general store in Quinault, 0.6 mile east; complete supplies and services are available in the Aberdeen-Hoquiam area.

SEASON & FEES: $6.00; May to September; 14 day limit.

NATURAL FEATURES: Located on a relatively steep hillside a few yards from deep blue (when the sun shines) Lake Quinault; very tall conifer forest with an abundance of ferns and other low-level vegetation; mild temperatures year-round; annual rainfall averages 145 inches.

ATTRACTIONS: Fishing; boat launch; paved/gravel self-guiding nature trail 0.2 mile west.

NOTES: About half of the campsites provide you with somewhat of a view of Lake Quinault through the trees. Only smaller trailers are recommended due to the narrow driveway and small parking spaces. Willaby is the first campground off U.S. 101 on this road. There are several other nice camping areas at the east end of the lake, 13 to 19 miles from here.

FALLS VIEW
Olympic National Forest

LOCATION: Northwest Washington on the east side of the Olympic Peninsula.

ACCESS: From U.S. 101 at a point 3.8 miles south of Quilcene and 8 miles north of Brinnon, turn west into the campground.

FACILITIES: 30 sites in 2 loops; sites are average to large, with fair to excellent separation; small to medium, paved parking pads are mostly straight-ins which may require some additional leveling; some campsites have ample room for large tents; terraced arrangement for tables; fireplaces; firewood is available for gathering near the campground; water at faucets; vault facilities; paved driveways; limited to adequate supplies and services are available in Quilcene.

kind of rough

SEASON & FEES: $5.00, only one vehicle permitted per site; May to September; 14 day limit.

NATURAL FEATURES: Located on the densely forested west slope of the Quilcene Range of the Olympic Mountains; the Big Quilcene River flows through a deep ravine here; waterfall nearby on the river; Mt. Walker is 1 mile to the east, and 2 miles farther east is Dabob Bay on Puget Sound; Buckhorn Wilderness Area is to the west.

ATTRACTIONS: Hiking trail to the falls on the Big Quilcene River; 4-wheel drive trails lead east to Mt. Walker and west to the Buckhorn Wilderness Area boundary.

NOTES: An alternative campground, just 3 miles south, is Rainbow. It has a narrow, steep, gravel driveway and 9 forested sites. The drive along Highway 101 to Falls View and Rainbow is first class! In this section, the highway leaves the coast and meanders between a sheer forested bluff and a pleasant valley. These campgrounds are unlike others in the area because they're situated several miles from the shore.

SEAL ROCK
Olympic National Forest

LOCATION: Northwest Washington on the east side of the Olympic Peninsula.

ACCESS: From U.S. 101 at a point 10 miles south of Quilcene and 2 miles north of Brinnon, turn east into the campground.

FACILITIES: 41 sites in 3 tiers; sites are small to average, with fairly reasonable separation; most parking pads are small to medium gravel straight-ins, some are pull-throughs; additional leveling may be necessary; tent spots are fairly clear of underbrush and adequate for medium-sized tents; some sites have framed-and-gravelled tent pads; fireplaces; very little firewood is available in the immediate area, so b-y-o is recommended; water at several faucets; restrooms; paved driveways are narrow with limited space for large vehicles to maneuver; minimal supplies and services in Brinnon; adequate supplies and services are available in Shelton, 38 miles south.

SEASON & FEES: $6.00; April to October; 14 day limit.

NATURAL FEATURES: Located on a forested hillside overlooking Dabob Bay and Hood Canal; Olympic Mountains to the west; fairly dense vegetation in the camping area consists of conifers, hardwoods, bushes and ferns; rocky beach.

ATTRACTIONS: Boat ramp; fishing; swimming; day use area with picnic facilities; hiking and clamming on the beach; a scenic drive follows along the Dosewallips River westward from U.S. 101 toward the Brothers Wilderness Area and Olympic National Park.

NOTES: Seal Rock is a typically peaceful campground on a sheltered bay with great views through the trees from virtually all sites. The drive along U.S.101 in this region is superscenic--between the Bay to the east and the Olympics to the west.

DOSEWALLIPS
State Park

LOCATION: Northwest Washington on the east side of the Olympic Peninsula.

ACCESS: From U.S. Highway 101 at a point 1 mile south of Brinnon and 24 miles north of Hoodsport, turn west into the campground.

FACILITIES: 128 sites, including 40 with full hookups; site size varies from medium to very large; separation is minimal to good; some parking pads are gravel, some are paved; most pads are level, and a few are spacious enough to accomodate the largest rv's; most units offer excellent tent-pitching opportunities; fireplaces; b-y-o firewood is recommended; water at several faucets; restrooms with showers; paved driveways; minimal supplies in nearby Brinnon; adequate supplies and services are available in Shelton, 35 miles south.

SEASON & FEES: $6.00 for a standard site, $8.50 for a full-hookup site; open all year, with limited facilities in winter; 10 day limit.

NATURAL FEATURES: Located where the Dosewallips River flows into Hood Canal; sites are situated on both sides of the highway; vegetation ranges from very open to quite dense; there are large mown lawns between sites in the western section and long, sandy beaches near sites in the eastern section; the Olympic Mountains rise to the west.

ATTRACTIONS: Boating; fishing; swimming; hiking; clamming; oyster gathering; a drive along the Dosewallips River leads west toward the Brothers Wilderness and Olympic National Park.

NOTES: Having access to both Hood Canal and the Dosewallips River here opens-up opportunities for a diversity of recreational activities. The fairly mild climate draws campers, boaters, beachcombers and fishermen year-round.

POTLATCH
State Park

LOCATION: Western Washington on the east side of the Olympic Peninsula northwest of Olympia.

ACCESS: From U.S. 101 at a point 0.5 mile south of the community of Potlatch and 4.5 miles north of the intersection of U.S. 101 and Washington State Highway 106, turn west into the campground.

FACILITIES: 37 small sites, including 18 with full hookups; a few trees provide minimal separation between sites; parking pads are level, gravel, and some are long enough to accomodate large rv's; fireplaces; b-y-o firewood; water at several faucets; restrooms with showers; holding tank disposal station at the entrance; paved driveways; minimal supplies in Potlatch; adequate supplies and services are available in Shelton, 12 miles south.

SEASON & FEES: $6.00 for a standard site, $8.50 for a full-hookup site; $3.00 for a primitive walk-in site; open all year, with limited facilities in winter; 10 day limit.

NATURAL FEATURES: Located on a forested flat just across the highway from the shore of Hood Canal, a major arm of Puget Sound; The Great Bend of Hood Canal is immediately off the day use facility's beach; Olympic Mountains rise to the west.

ATTRACTIONS: Extensive day use area is located east across the highway from the campground: sandy beach with bath house, playground and mown lawns; boating; fishing; clamming; crabbing; hiking and jeep trails lead westward toward Olympic National Park.

NOTES: The scenery in this part of the country is first-rate--east across Hood Canal and west toward the Olympic Mountains. This campground is *not* a well-kept secret. It's quite popular, so the 'early arrival' recommendation is appropriate in this case.

SCHAFER
State Park

LOCATION: Olympic Peninsula west of Olympia.

ACCESS: From U.S 12/Washington State Highway 8 at milepost 14 +.8 (5 miles west of Elma, 5 miles east of Montesano), turn north onto a paved road at the "Schafer State Park" sign; continue north and east for 9.1 miles along the East Fork of the Satsop River; turn south (right) into the campground.

FACILITIES: 47 sites, including 6 with partial hookups; sites are average to slightly above average in size; some separation between sites; parking pads are gravel/dirt and level; some pads are long enough to accomodate very large rv's; large, level tent spaces; fireplaces; b-y-o firewood is recommended; water at several faucets; restrooms; holding tank disposal station; community kitchen/shelter; paved driveways; adequate supplies and services are available in Montesano and Elma.

SEASON & FEES: $6.00 for a standard site, $8.00 for a partial-hookup site; open all year, but only on weekends and holidays during the winter; 10 day limit.

NATURAL FEATURES: Located on a forested flat along the East Fork of the Satsop River; a rain forest atmosphere is created by tall moss-covered hardwoods and a carpet of ferns and tiny plants.

ATTRACTIONS: Good river beach access; fishing; hiking trails; day use area across the road from the campground has picnic shelters, a children's play area, and horseshoe pits.

NOTES: This lush green campground's atmosphere is one of quiet detachment from the mainstream of traffic just a few miles to the south.

LAKE SYLVIA
State Park

LOCATION: Northwest Washington in the southern section of the Olympic Peninsula near Montesano.

ACCESS: From mid-town Montesano (near milepost 10 +.5 on Washington State Highway 8 and U.S. Highway 12), travel west on Pioneer Avenue to Third Street; turn north onto Third Street and proceed 1.5 miles on a rather steep, winding, paved road to the park entrance.

FACILITIES: 35 sites; most sites are small to medium in size and somewhat closely spaced; level, medium-length, gravel parking spaces; medium-sized, grassy tent areas; hiker/biker units on the east end of the camping area; fireplaces; firewood for sale by park concessionaire in the summer, or b-y-o; water at faucets throughout the campground; central restroom with showers; holding tank disposal station; paved driveways; some groceries are available from the park concessionaire; adequate supplies are available in Montesano.

SEASON & FEES: $6.00 for a site, $2.00 for an extra vehicle; open all year, with limited facilities October to April; 10 day limit.

NATURAL FEATURES: Located on a point of land on the east shore of small Lake Sylvia; tall hardwoods mixed with some conifers; some underbrush in the campground provides nominal campsite separation; sand/grass swimming beach.

ATTRACTIONS: Self-guided nature trail; swimming; boating (no motors); children's playground in the day use area; trout fishing.

NOTES: This is a pleasant, albeit popular, campground which offers activities which are in keeping with the sylvan setting. The lake is a favorite with canoeists and inflatable floaters because of the motorless boating requirement. There's a nice view of the lake from most campsites.

OCEAN CITY
State Park

LOCATION: Western Washington in the southwest corner of the Olympic Peninsula west of Aberdeen-Hoquiam.

ACCESS: From the intersection of Washington State Highways 109 and 115 (16 miles west of Hoquiam), travel south 1 mile on Route 115 to the park entrance on the west side of the highway.

FACILITIES: 178 sites, including 48 with full-hookups, in three loops: 130 standard sites with small gravel parking pads are located in two loops which flank the entrance station; large, grassy areas ideal for tent-pitching; the 48 hookup units are situated in a third loop west of the entrance station, close to the beach; large, level, paved, straight-in or pull-through parking spaces; fireplaces; firewood is usually for sale, or b-y-o; water at faucets; central washroom with showers in each loop; holding tank disposal station; paved driveways; resident ranger-manager; very limited supplies are available in Ocean City, 2 miles north, or Ocean Shores, 2 miles south.

SEASON & FEES: $6.00 for a standard site, $8.50 for a full-hookup site, $2.00 for an extra vehicle; open all year; 10 day limit.

NATURAL FEATURES: Located on a fairly level stretch of shoreline on the Pacific Ocean; the loops with the standard sites have large evergreens and hardwoods for privacy and shelter/shade; the hookup loop is more open, with a beach view from some sites; expansive ocean beach; usually breezy.

ATTRACTIONS: Beachcombing; fishing; clamming; hiking.

NOTES: Although there are few sites with an ocean view here, the beach is just a few minutes' walk from any of the campsites. Irrespective of its summer/weekend popularity, it's still an excellent campground.

TWIN HARBORS
State Park

LOCATION: Southwest Washington south of Westport.

ACCESS: From the intersection of Washington State Highway 105 and the Highway 105 north spur (4 miles south of Westport): there are several park entrances to the south and to the east of the intersection.

FACILITIES: 321 sites in several sections on both sides of the highway: the largest area, on the east side of the highway in a grove of tall trees, has level sites of moderate size, with medium-length pads; a second major area is on the west side of the highway along the beach (usually available by assignment only); 50 full-hookup units are located on the southeast corner of the intersection in an open, paved/gravel "parking lot" arrangement; fireplaces; firewood is usually for sale, or b-y-o; water at faucets; central restroom with showers in each section; holding tank disposal station; resident ranger-manager; nearest supplies (limited) are available in Westport.

SEASON & FEES: $6.00 for a standard site; $8.50 for a full-hookup site; $2.00 for an extra vehicle; open all year; 10 day limit.

NATURAL FEATURES: Long windswept ocean beaches; the sites in the large section on the east side of the highway afford substantially more protection from the wind (and sun, when it shines) than those on the west.

ATTRACTIONS: Beach trail; beachcombing (best in winter); limited clamming; access to the well-known charter fishing fleet of Westport.

NOTES: This is the largest campground on the Washington coast. Quite a few of the camp units are very close to the highway. Still, it's a nice place with a variety of camping opportunities--more enjoyable at times other than summer weekends.

GRAYLAND BEACH
State Park

LOCATION: Southwest Washington south of Westport.

ACCESS: From Washington State Highway 105 at the south edge of the town of Grayland, turn west onto County Line Road; the park entrance is 0.1 mile west of the highway.

FACILITIES: 60 full-hookup sites in two sections north and south of the entrance road; camp units are relatively narrow, with minimal to average separation between sites; long, level, paved straight-in parking spaces; small to medium-sized, level, grassy tent areas; fireplaces; firewood is occasionally for sale, or b-y-o; central restroom with showers; wide, paved roadways; resident ranger-manager; limited to adequate supplies are available in Grayland.

SEASON & FEES: $8.50 for a site, $2.00 for an extra vehicle; sites are pre-assigned during seasonal peaks; open all year; 10 day limit.

NATURAL FEATURES: Located a few hundred yards from the sea, but without an ocean view; mown grass, short pine and hardwoods between most campsites; medium to tall vegetation around the perimeter of the campground; expansive beach within easy walking distance; often rainy, usually windy.

ATTRACTIONS: Trail to the beach; beachcombing (best in winter); limited clamming.

NOTES: This campground was apparently designed primarily with the recreational vehicle camper in mind. The grounds are very nicely landscaped and maintained. Most of the campsites are quite "open", although some privacy and protection from the elements is provided by the evergreens which have been planted throughout the campground. Recreation and tourism are major sources of income for the community of Grayland.

225

FORT CANBY
State Park

LOCATION: Extreme southwest Washington at the mouth of the Columbia River.

ACCESS: From U.S. 101 at mid-town Illwaco, turn west/southwest onto the Fort Canby road (paved, winding), and proceed 3.3 miles to the park entrance; the campground is 1 mile northwest of the entrance station.

FACILITIES: 250 sites, including 60 full hookup units, in a maze of small loops; sites are level, with medium to long, paved parking pads; excellent tent-pitching possibilities; fireplace/barbecue grill combination fire appliances; b-y-o firewood; water at faucets in each loop; restrooms (H) with showers; holding tank disposal station; paved driveways; resident ranger-manager; camping supplies are available from a park concessionaire; adequate supplies are available in Illwaco.

SEASON & FEES: $6.00 for a standard site, $8.50 for a full hookup unit, $2.00 for an extra vehicle; open all year; 10 day limit.

NATURAL FEATURES: Located on an open flat a short distance from the ocean, at the mouth of the Columbia River; a substantial amount of low-level vegetation provides some separation between campsites; often windy.

ATTRACTIONS: Lewis and Clark Interpretive Center, open daily during the summer; Cape Disappointment Lighhouse, constructed in the 1850's, is the oldest West Coast lighthouse still in operation; four nature trails; nice beach; boat launch; fishing; good beachcombing, particularly in winter.

NOTES: Fort Canby has a greater variety of attractions and activities than the other state parks in this part of Washington State. This area's recorded history dates back 200 years or more. Fort Canby itself was operated as a Columbia River defense post from the 1870's to the end of World War II. Very nice, interesting park. Worth the stop.

LARABEE
State Park

LOCATION: Northwest Washington south of Bellingham.

ACCESS: From Interstate 5 exit 250 (4 miles south of Bellingham, 20 miles north of Burlington), turn west onto Washington State Highway 11; follow Highway 11 west then south for 7 miles to the park entrance; turn west (right) into the campground.

FACILITIES: 87 sites, including 26 with full hookups, on a hillside; sites are small to average-sized, with nominal separation; some parking pads are gravel, some are paved (including larger ones designated for trailers); the slope has been terraced for the tables and pads, but many pads may require additional leveling; several sites have shelters over the tables; a few walk-in sites; fireplaces; b-y-o firewood is recommended; water at several faucets; restrooms with showers; holding tank disposal station; paved driveway; complete supplies and services in Bellingham.

SEASON & FEES: $6.00 for a standard site, $8.50 for a full-hookup site, $2.00 for an extra vehicle; open all year with limited facilities in winter; 10 day limit.

NATURAL FEATURES: Located on a forested hillside along the forested shore of Samish Bay; there is a view of Puget Sound from some sites; the camping area has a mown grassy lawn with huge trees, ferns and boulders.

ATTRACTIONS: Fishing; boat launch; swimming; playground; foot trails in the area--some leading to the shore where marine life can be observed in tidal pools; nearby Bellingham has a museum and interesting architectural exhibits.

NOTES: The scenic drive along Highway 11 to this park is truly alluring. It follows along the shore and through a tunnel of lush, green vegetation. Some sites are rather close to the highway, but an encircling rail fence provides an effective boundary.

BAYVIEW
State Park

LOCATION: Northwest Washington northeast of Anacortes.

ACCESS: From Washington State Highway 20, at a point 5 miles east of Anacortes and 7 miles west of Interstate 5, turn north onto a paved road signed for "Bayview State Park"; drive 7 miles north to the small community of Bay View; at the north edge of Bay View, turn east into the campground.

FACILITIES: 68 sites, including 9 with full hookups, in 3 loops; sites vary in size from small to large; separation varies from minimal to excellent; most parking pads are gravel straight-ins or paved pull-alongs; many sites have large, level tent spots; fireplaces; b-y-o firewood is recommended; water at several faucets; 1 main restroom, with showers, supplemented by vault facilities; paved main driveway; resident ranger-manager; fairly complete supplies and services are available in Anacortes.

SEASON & FEES: $6.00 for a standard site, $8.50 for a full-hookup site; open all year, with limited facilities in winter; 10 day limit.

NATURAL FEATURES: Located on a hillside above Padilla Bay of Puget Sound; 1 loop encircles a large flat grassy meadow; a second loop is set on a heavily forested hillside east of the meadow; a third section, with hookups, sits on a grassy bluff overlooking the bay; some sites have a view of the bay but most are tucked away in a densely forested area; a long, sandy beach is located across the highway from the campground.

ATTRACTIONS: Boating; fishing; swimming; a short trail leads from the campground, through the forest, and down to the beach; Padilla Bay Interpretive Center nearby; Washington State Ferry terminal in Anacortes.

NOTES: The view from the bluff overlooking Padilla Bay is quite impressive, particularly westerly toward Anacortes.

DECEPTION PASS
State Park

LOCATION: Northwest Washington on Whidbey Island.

ACCESS: From Washington State Highway 20 (at a point 6.6 miles south of Anacortes and just south of the Deception Pass Bridge), turn west into the park; proceed less than a mile down a fairly steep access road; turn north (right) into the campground.

FACILITIES: 230 sites in 2 main areas on a hillside; sites are small to medium in size, with average to very good separation; most parking pads are small, gravel straight-ins which may require additional leveling; some nice, secluded, small to medium tent spots; fireplaces; b-y-o firewood is recommended; water at numerous faucets; restrooms with showers; holding tank disposal station; paved driveways; limited supplies are available at a small store 1 mile south on Highway 20; adequate supplies and services are available in Oak Harbor, 10 miles south.

SEASON & FEES: $6.00 for a site, $2.00 for an extra vehicle; open all year with limited facilities in winter; 10 day limit.

NATURAL FEATURES: Located on a heavily forested hillside on the northwest corner of Whidbey Island in Puget Sound; the park encompasses 2474 acres on 8 islands in the Sound; Pass Lake and Cranberry Lake are located near the campground within the main section of the park; tall cedars and pines tower over lush ferns and underbrush in this densely forested campground setting.

ATTRACTIONS: Fishing; hiking; swimming; beachcombing along salt and fresh water beaches; boat ramp; playground; boat rentals and camper supplies are available from a concessionaire in the park.

NOTES: Most sites have no direct view of Puget Sound, but are within an easy walk of long, sandy West and North Beaches. The alluring surroundings and a variety of activities in the park make this a pleasant and popular retreat.

FORT EBEY
State Park

LOCATION: Northwest Washington on Whidbey Island.

ACCESS: From Washington State Highway 20 (at a point 8 miles south of Oak Harbor), turn west onto Libby Road; continue west 0.9 mile; turn south onto Valley Drive; drive 0.6 mile south, then turn west (right) into the campground; (sections of the access roads are steep and twisty).

FACILITIES: 50 sites in 2 main loops; sites are mostly average-sized with good separation; gravel parking pads; some pull-through pads are spacious enough to accommodate very large rv's; some parking pads may require additional leveling; a few walk-in sites; fireplaces; b-y-o firewood is recommended; water at several faucets; restrooms with showers; paved driveways; adequate supplies and services are available in Oak Harbor, 9 miles northeast.

SEASON & FEES: $6.00 for a site, $2.00 for an extra vehicle; open all year, with limited facilities in winter; 10 day limit.

NATURAL FEATURES: Located on Whidbey Island on a bluff overlooking Puget Sound; small Lake Pondilla is within the park; the surrounding vegetation is quite distinctive: a ceiling of extremely tall straight pines towers over a very dense vine-covered forest floor; rocky beach nearby.

ATTRACTIONS: Boating; fishing; swimming on the Sound and at Lake Pondilla; nature trails; historic World War II harbor defense bunker; Keystone Ferry terminal nearby.

NOTES: Fort Ebey State Park overlooks Puget Sound from the west shore of Whidbey Island. In clear weather you may see Port Townsend, the San Juan Islands and the Strait of Juan de Fuca in the distance.

FORT CASEY
State Park

LOCATION: Northwest Washington on Whidbey Island.

ACCESS: From the intersection of Washington Highways 20 and 525 (5 miles southeast of Coupeville, 22 miles north of the Mukilteo-Clinton ferry terminal), drive west on Highway 20 for 3.4 miles to the Keystone ferry terminal; drive past the terminal 0.6 mile; turn south (left) into the campground.

FACILITIES: 25 sites; most units are small and level; very little separation between sites; parking pads are level, gravel, medium to long pull-throughs; small, level tent spaces with a grass surface; fireplaces; b-y-o firewood; water at faucets; restroom with showers; paved driveway; adequate supplies and services are available in Coupeville.

SEASON & FEES: $6.00 for a site, $2.00 for an extra vehicle; open all year, with limited facilities in winter; 10 day limit.

NATURAL FEATURES: Located along an open shoreline on the west coast of Whidbey Island; campground vegetation consists primarily of sparse grass, bushes and a few small conifers; a short, tree-dotted ridge rises behind the sites; a rocky beach skirts the sites on the shore side; views of the Olympic Mountains and Puget Sound.

ATTRACTIONS: Fishing; hiking; boat launch nearby; a bluff above the campground has a picnic area and an excellent view of Puget Sound; well-preserved coast artillery available for public observation and inspection; Fort Casey Interpretive Center located in Admiralty Point Lighthouse.

NOTES: Fort Casey's 1890 defense post offers several historically significant displays. Although the campground's sites may not be spacious, its location next to the Keystone ferry terminal provides an element of convenience for many Puget Sound travelers.

SOUTH WHIDBEY
State Park

LOCATION: Northwest Washington on Whidbey Island.

ACCESS: From the intersection of Washington State Highways 20 and 525 (4 miles east of Keystone, 5 miles southeast of Coupeville), drive south 5 miles on Highway 525 to Smuggler's Cove Road; turn west (right) and drive 4 miles west then south on Smuggler's Cove Road; turn west (right) into the campground.

FACILITIES: 54 sites in 2 loops; most sites are level and of average size; good separation provided by the forest; parking pads are gravel, and mostly straight-ins; some pads are spacious enough to accomodate large rv's; fireplaces; b-y-o firewood is recommended; water at numerous faucets; restrooms with showers; holding tank disposal station near the entrance; driveway in the lower loop is paved, the upper loop drive is gravel; limited supplies and services are available in Freeland, 8 miles southeast.

SEASON & FEES: $6.00 for a site, $2.00 for an extra vehicle; open all year, weekends and holidays only during the winter; 10 day limit.

NATURAL FEATURES: Located on a forested hillside on the western coast of Whidbey Island in Puget Sound; sites are surrounded by dense vegetation of ferns, bushes, and tall cedars; some views of Puget Sound and the Olympic Mountains; sandy beach.

ATTRACTIONS: Boating (boat ramp nearby at Bush Point); swimming; clamming and crabbing; nature trails in the campground area; foot trail to the sandy beach; amphitheater for scheduled ranger-naturalist programs.

NOTES: Access to this park is through a corridor of dense vegetation. From the beach and a number of sites, there is a captivating view of the Olympic Mountains to the west across Puget Sound.

WENBERG
State Park

LOCATION: Northwest Washington north of Everett.

ACCESS: From Interstate 5 exit 206 (10 miles north of Everett, 21 miles south of Mount Vernon), turn west onto Lake Goodwin Road; drive west 0.4 mile to a fork in the road; take the right fork; drive 4.5 miles north to "East Lake Goodwin Road"; turn left; drive 1.5 miles west, and turn north (right) into the park.

FACILITIES: 75 sites in 3 loops, including 16 with partial hookups; hookup sites have large, gravel pull-through pads which are very close together; sites 17 to 75 are primarily for tents or small rv's, and are mostly medium-sized with average separation; many pads will require some additional leveling; fireplaces; b-y-o firewood is recommended; water at several faucets; restrooms with showers; kitchen shelter; holding tank disposal station; paved driveways; minimal supplies are available in the park; adequate supplies and services are available in Lakewood, 5 miles east.

SEASON & FEES: $6.00 for a standard site, $8.00 for a partial-hookup site, $2.00 for an extra vehicle; May to September with limited facilities in winter; 10 day limit.

NATURAL FEATURES: Located on the shore of Lake Goodwin between the Cascade Mountains and the Pacific Coast; most campsites are in a fairly open grassy area surrounded by dense stands of majestic pines and cedars.

ATTRACTIONS: Boating; fishing; swimming; paved trail from the campground to the beach; nature trail; playground; Tulalip Indian Reservation is located just south of the park.

NOTES: Water recreation is a big drawing card for this fresh water preserve surrounded by forested slopes. Wenberg State Park's proximity to 'Pugetopolis' makes it very popular, so you may prefer an off-season, mid-week visit.

FORT WORDEN
State Park

LOCATION: Northwest Washington on the Olympic Peninsula north of Port Townsend.

ACCESS: From Washington State Highway 20 at the Whidbey Island ferry terminal, drive northeast through Port Townsend on Water Street; turn left onto Monroe Street and follow a well-marked route through a residential area 1.5 miles to the park entrance (at the intersection of "W" Street and Cherry Street); continue north on Cherry Street through the park 0.2 mile, then east 0.4 mile on Admiralty Avenue to the campground.

FACILITIES: 50 level sites, all with full hookups; sites are small to medium with minimal separation; paved, level parking pads; large, grassy tent spots; fireplaces; b-y-o firewood; water at numerous faucets; restrooms with showers; paved driveways; minimal supplies near the campground; adequate supplies and services are available in Port Townsend.

SEASON & FEES: $8.50 for a site; open all year with limited facilities in winter; 10 day limit.

NATURAL FEATURES: Located on an open, grassy flat between a sandy beach and a forested hillside, near Point Wilson on Admiralty Bay; sweeping view of Puget Sound to the east.

ATTRACTIONS: Fishing; boat launch; beach access; 6 miles of hiking trails; playground; National Historic Landmark District with renovated 1900 military buildings available as short-term rental housing; Marine Science Center; Coast Artillery Museum.

NOTES: Fort Worden is a naturally beautiful place that's also very popular for its historic interest. It serves as a center for many regional conferences and festivals throughout the year.

FORT FLAGLER
State Park

LOCATION: Northwest Washington on Marrowstone Island, east of Port Townsend.

ACCESS: From Washington State Highway 20 at a point 5 miles south of Port Townsend and 8 miles north of the intersection of Highway 20 and U.S. 101, turn east onto Four Corners Road; drive through the small community of Hadlock, then east across Indian Island and onto Marrowstone Island; at a fork in the road just east of the Marrowstone Island bridge, turn north (left); continue 4 miles (paved) to the park.

FACILITIES: 116 sites in 3 loops; some sites are small, slopey, and well separated by forest vegetation; other sites are large and level, with no separation; parking pads are gravel, most are straight-ins; pads vary from small and sloped to large and level; many excellent tent spots; fireplaces; b-y-o firewood is recommended; water at several faucets; restrooms with showers; holding tank disposal station; paved driveways; camper supplies in the park; adequate supplies and services are available in Port Townsend.

SEASON & FEES: $6.00 for a site; $2.00 for an extra vehicle; open all year with limited facilities in winter; 10 day limit.

NATURAL FEATURES: Located at the northern tip of Morrowstone Island in Puget Sound; sites 1-47 are on a forested hillside with some scenic views through the trees; sites 48-96 are along the treeline near the beach; sites 97-116 are on an open, grass flat along the beach; great views of Admiralty Inlet and Whidbey Island.

ATTRACTIONS: Boat launch; fishing; clamming; beach access; hiking; playground; tours of 1898 Fort Flagler.

NOTES: Fort Flagler's limited accessibility (it is reachable only by bridge or by boat), adds an element of seclusion to its attributes.

OLD FORT TOWNSEND
State Park

LOCATION: Northwest Washington south of Port Townsend.

ACCESS: From Washington State Highway 20 at a point 4.2 miles south Port Townsend (at the Whidbey Island ferry terminal) and 9 miles north of the intersection of Highway 20 and U.S. 101, turn east onto Old Fort Townsend Road; continue 2.3 miles to the campground.

FACILITIES: 40 sites in 2 distinctly different sections: the upper loop is on a slope--sites are average-sized, well separated, with short, paved straight-in parking pads; the lower section is on a flat--sites are small, with paved, parallel, pull-through parking pads and very little separation; small to medium tent spots throughout; fireplaces in the upper loop, barbecue grills in the lower section; kitchen shelter; restroom with showers in the upper loop, vault facilities in the lower section; holding tank disposal station; paved driveways; adequate supplies and services are available in Port Townsend.

SEASON & FEES: $6.00; May to September; 10 day limit.

NATURAL FEATURES: Old Fort Townsend State Park is located on a 150-foot cliff above Port Townsend Bay; sites 1-27 are in a dense conifer forest, sites 28-40 are on an exposed, grassy flat; views of Admiralty Inlet, Puget Sound and the Cascade Mountains.

ATTRACTIONS: Fishing; clamming; beach access; day use area has a playground and group picnicing facility; hiking trails and nature walk.

NOTES: Historically significant Fort Townsend was established as a U.S Army post in 1856. This somewhat secluded 377-acre park offers a fine view of Port Townsend Bay and the Cascade Range to the east. This is a neat little place that's usually not as bustling as some of the other parks in the Sound area.

KITSAP MEMORIAL
State Park

LOCATION: Northwest Washington on the west side of the Kitsap Peninsula north of Bremerton.

ACCESS: From Washington State Highway 3 at milepost 57 (3 miles south of Port Gamble, 21 miles north of Bremerton), turn west onto the paved park access road; continue 0.3 mile to the park entrance; the campground is to the north, just inside the entrance.

FACILITIES: 43 sites in two sections; sites 1 through 18 are parallel to each other in a single line on the east side of the camping area; the remainder of the camp units are in a loop on the north side; gravel parking spots; most sites can accommodate a medium-sized tent or rv; all campsites are level; fireplaces; presto logs for sale, or b-y-o; water at several faucets; restrooms with showers; holding tank disposal station just outside the park entrance; paved driveways; limited supplies in Port Gamble; fairly complete supplies and services are available in the Poulsbo area, 6 miles south.

SEASON & FEES: $6.00 for a site, $2.00 for an extra vehicle; open all year; 10 day limit.

NATURAL FEATURES: Located on a bluff above Hood Canal (a major inlet on Puget Sound); some shelter is provided by tall pine trees and a substantial amount of shrubbery between the sites in the loop; pasture adjacent to the park; great variety of clams, oysters, geoduck and octopus in the nearby waters.

ATTRACTIONS: Beach trail; beachcombing; clamming; fishing; ball field; children's play area; shelters; community building; museums in Port Gamble.

NOTES: As seen from here, the Olympic Mountains, a few miles to the west, seem to rise right out of Hood Canal. Beachcombing here can be highly rewarding, particularly during the winter months.

FAY BAINBRIDGE
State Park

LOCATION: Northwest Washington on Bainbridge Island west of Seattle.

ACCESS: From Washington State Highway 305 at milepost 4 +.3 (4 miles north of Winslow, 8 miles south of Poulsbo), turn east onto NE East Day Road; proceed 1.4 miles to a "T" intersection; turn north (left) onto Sunrise Road, and continue 1.6 miles to the park entrance, on the east side of Sunrise Road.

FACILITIES: 35 sites in two sections: the first area, with 10 "primitive" sites and a small shelter, is on a rather steep hillside near the entrance; the second camp area consists of 25 level units, each with water hookup, in a single line along the open beach; the beach sites have medium-length, gravel parking pads and good tent spots; fireplaces; b-y-o firewood; water at faucets; restrooms with showers; sanitary disposal station; resident ranger-manager; nearest supplies (limited) in Winslow; fairly complete supplies and services are available in the Poulsbo area.

SEASON & FEES: $6.50 for a hookup site, $2.00 for an extra vehicle; $3.00 for a primitive site, $4.50 for a primitive site with a vehicle; open all year; 10 day limit.

NATURAL FEATURES: Primitive sites are located on a forested hillside; beach sites are in the open, with evergreens planted between many sites; views across Puget sound to the east and north; long, driftwood-strewn, sand/pebble beach.

ATTRACTIONS: Beachcombing; clamming; playground; boat launch; Old Port Madison bell is on display near the entrance; Suquamish Museum and Tribal Center nearby.

NOTES: The primitive camping area might serve as a convenient stop for cyclists touring the West Sound, although some tenters might find the sites to be a little too sloped. (Well, they *are* well-drained!) The park has a very popular day use area as well.

SCENIC BEACH
State Park

LOCATION: Northwest Washington on the west side of the Kitsap Peninsula northwest of Bremerton.

ACCESS: From Washington State Route 3 at milepost 43 +.5 (the Newberry Hill exit, 8 miles north of Bremerton), travel west on Newberry Hill Road 3 miles to a "T" intersection; turn north (right) and follow the road 5 miles in a long sweeping 180 degree curve to Seabeck (you'll now be headed south); 0.1 mile south of the Seabeck elementary school, turn west onto Scenic Beach road, and drive 1.5 miles to the park entrance.

FACILITIES: 52 sites in two loops; virtually all sites are spacious and private; parking spaces are very long, level, oiled gravel, pull-throughs or straight-ins; adequate level space for large tents; many tables are installed on the hillside above the parking spots, with steps for easy accessibility; fireplaces; b-y-o firewood; water at faucets every few sites; restroom with showers in each loop; holding tank disposal station; paved driveways; resident ranger-manager; nearest supplies (quite limited) in Seabeck; fairly complete supplies and services are available in Bremerton.

SEASON & FEES: $6.00 for a site, $2.00 for an extra vehicle; April 1 to September 30, weekends only in winter; 7 day limit.

NATURAL FEATURES: Located on a heavily forested hillside; 0.3-mile-long beach on Hood Canal (a major inlet in Puget Sound); spectacular views of the Olympic Mountains.

ATTRACTIONS: Trails to the beach; beachcombing; fishing; boat ramp 1 mile; children's playgrounds in the campground and in the day use area.

NOTES: Scenic Beach is an extraordinarily well designed and well managed park. The environment here is superb. It gets a little busy on summer weekends, so you may enjoy it more in spring or fall. Terrific place!

ILLAHEE
State Park

LOCATION: Northwest Washington on the Kitsap Peninsula northeast of Bremerton.

ACCESS: From mid-town Bremerton at the intersection of Washington State Highways 303 and 304 (near the ferry terminal), travel north on Route 303 for 2.1 miles to its intersection with State Highway 306 (Sylvan Way); turn east onto Route 306 and proceed 1.5 miles to the park entrance (just north of the end of Highway 306).

FACILITIES: 25 sites in one large loop; spacious, fairly private campsites; paved parking pads; about half of the units have medium-length pull-through pads, the remainder have straight-ins; fairly good spots for medium-sized tents, but the campground was probably designed more with rv's in mind; most spaces will probably require some additional leveling; fireplaces; b-y-o firewood; water at faucets throughout the campground; central restroom with showers; holding tank disposal station; paved driveways; resident ranger-manager; fairly complete shopping opportunities in Bremerton.

SEASON & FEES: $6.00 for a site, $2.00 for an extra vehicle; open all year; 10 day limit.

NATURAL FEATURES: Located on a gently rolling hillside at the junction of 3 major arteries of Puget Sound: Port Orchard Bay, Sinclair Inlet and Rich Passage; vegetation consists primarily of tall conifers and ferns; rail fences throughout the grounds enhance the natural landscaping; 1800' of saltwater frontage in the park.

ATTRACTIONS: Beachcombing; fishing; boat launch with excellent moorage; playground; a pair of naval guns 'guards' the park entrance; Puget Sound Naval Shipyard and Shipyard Museum in Bremerton.

NOTES: Although this park and campground may sustain a high level of activity during the busy months, it's worth the visit just to see the nicely landscaped grounds.

240

MANCHESTER
State Park

LOCATION: Western Washington on the Kitsap Peninsula east of Bremerton.

ACCESS: From Washington State Highway 160 near milepopst 3 (4.5 miles east of Port Orchard, 3 miles west of Southworth), turn north onto Colchester Road; travel north 1.7 miles to East Main Street in Manchester; turn west (left) onto East Main, go 1 block, then jog north (right) onto Beach Drive East; proceed 1.9 miles to East Hilldale Road; turn right onto East Hilldale, and continue 0.3 mile to the park entrance. (Did you find it OK?)

FACILITIES: 50 sites in 2 loops; most sites are medium-sized, fairly well spaced, and separated by shrubbery; about half of the units have long pull-through parking pads, the remainder have long straight-ins; paved or gravel parking surfaces; level, medium to large tent areas; fireplaces; b-y-o firewood; water at faucets throughout the campground; restroom with showers in each loop; holding tank disposal station at the entrance; paved roadways; resident ranger-manager; limited supplies in Manchester; adequate supplies are available in Port Orchard.

SEASON & FEES: $6.00 for a site, $2.00 for an extra vehicle; open all year, but weekends and holidays only October to April; 10 day limit.

NATURAL FEATURES: Located on a forested bluff above Clam Bay and Rich Passage in Puget Sound; several varieties of conifers, hardwoods, and ferns; a small creek flows through the center of the campground.

ATTRACTIONS: Interpretive trail constructed by local scout troops starts near the park entrance; wide, paved pathways along the beach; early twentieth century naval buildings; fishing; scuba diving/snorkeling.

NOTES: One of the drawing points of this park is its easy accessibility from the Seattle-Tacoma area: less than an hour from Seattle by ferry, or via highway from Tacoma.

BELFAIR
State Park

LOCATION: Western Washington southwest of Bremerton.

ACCESS: From the intersection of Washington State Highways 3 and 300 in Belfair (10 miles southwest of Bremerton), drive southwest on Highway 300 for 3 miles; turn south (left) into the park, then immediately right, to the campground.

FACILITIES: 194 sites, including 47 with full hookups, in 3 loops; small to medium campsites with minimal to excellent separation; level, paved or gravel parking pads vary from small to large; excellent tenting opportunities; fireplaces; b-y-o firewood is recommended; water at several faucets; restrooms with showers; holding tank disposal station; paved driveways; adequate supplies and services are available in Belfair.

SEASON & FEES: $6.00 for a standard site, $8.50 for a full-hookup site; open all year, with limited facilities from October to March; 10 day limit.

NATURAL FEATURES: Located along the shore of Hood Canal, a major arm/inlet of Puget Sound; most sites are in a dense forest of very tall conifers, ferns and considerable underbrush; the loop closest to Hood Canal is more open and includes some lawn areas; Olympic Mountains to the west; Cascade Mountains are visible across the Canal to the east; Big Mission Creek and Little Mission Creek flow through the park and into the Canal.

ATTRACTIONS: Fishing; swimming in a lagoon; beachcombing; clamming; oyster gathering; playground; hiking.

NOTES: Because Highway 300 virtually ends at this campground, there is very little traffic noise to disturb even those campers closest to the highway. Sites vary from open/sunny camp units within view of the Canal, to wooded sites alongside a rippling brook.

TWANOH
State Park

LOCATION: Northwest Washington north of Olympia.

ACCESS: From Washington State Highway 106 at a point 7 miles south of Belfair and 13 miles north of the intersection U.S. 101 and State Route 106, turn east into the campground.

FACILITIES: 46 sites, including 9 with full hookups; sites are close together with minimal separation; level, gravel parking pads--some long enough to accomodate large rv's; interior lawn area for tents; some walk-in sites; fireplaces; b-y-o firewood is recommended; water at several faucets; kitchen shelter; restrooms with showers; paved driveway; campground host; limited supplies at a small store adjacent to the park; adequate supplies and services are available in Belfair.

SEASON & FEES: $6.00 for a standard site, $8.50 for a full-hookup site, $2.00 for an extra vehicle; April to October; 10 day limit.

NATURAL FEATURES: Located in a small, densely forested area across the highway from the south shore of Hood Canal; vegetation in the camping area includes some tall bushy trees, ferns and a mown lawn; temperate climate; Olympic Mountains just to the west, Cascade Mountains some distance to the east.

ATTRACTIONS: Boat launch; extensive sandy beach; fishing; swimming; nature trails; playground; tennis court nearby.

NOTES: Twanoh State Park is located in one of the more scenic areas along Hood Canal. An extensively developed resort area stretches for miles in either direction along Highway 106. This park is *very* popular. Another state park campground, Jarrell Cove, is located about 15 miles east off Highway 3. Some of its 20 sites may be available if Twanoh is filled.

SALTWATER
State Park

LOCATION: Western Washington on the east side of Puget Sound between Seattle and Tacoma.

ACCESS: From Interstate 5 at Des Moines (exit 149 if southbound, 149B if northbound, midway between Seattle and Tacoma), turn west onto Washington State Highway 516; continue 1.5 miles to the intersection of State Highways 516 and 509; turn south onto Highway 509 and proceed 1.4 miles to the park entrance; turn west, then south, and go down a hill to a large parking lot; turn east and proceed through the lot and under the highway bridge into the campground. (Got that?)

FACILITIES: 52 sites in two sections: the first area, as you enter the campground, is comprised mostly of large pull-through sites out in the open, and seems to have been designed with rv's in mind; the second section, to the east of the first, has small to average sites in a more wooded setting; gravel parking pads, most requiring a little extra leveling; fireplaces; b-y-o firewood; water at several faucets; restrooms with showers; holding tank disposal station; paved driveways; resident ranger; fairly complete shopping in Des Moines.

SEASON & FEES: $6.00 for a site, $2.00 for an extra vehicle; open all year; 10 day limit.

NATURAL FEATURES: Located in wooded Kent Smith Canyon, a few yards east of Puget Sound's Poverty Bay; a creek flows along the south edge of the campground.

ATTRACTIONS: Foot trails; limited clamming; playground in the day use area; scuba diving.

NOTES: This campground has been included with some misgivings: it can be a very busy place, and there are "Lock Your Valuables..." signs posted in the park. However, it's the closest public campground to Seattle and may be useful to many campers. Use at your discretion.

DASH POINT
State Park

LOCATION: Western Washington on the east side of Puget Sound north of Tacoma.

ACCESS: From Washington State Highway 509 at milepost 8 +.3 (8 miles north of Interstate 5 exit 133 at Tacoma, 6 miles west of the intersection of Highway 509 and State Route 99 near Federal Way), turn south (i.e., right, if approaching from Tacoma) into the campground entrance. (Note that the highway lies basically in an east-west direction at this point.)

FACILITIES: 138 sites in two sections; 110 standard units in an area south (directly ahead) of the entrance; good-sized, semi-private sites; hard-packed gravel straight-in or pull-through pads of varying lengths; space for medium to large tents; water at several points; also 28 partial hookup sites in an area west (to the right) of the entrance, closer to the highway; several pull-throughs here, but mostly straight-ins; fireplaces; b-y-o firewood; central restroom with showers in each section; holding tank disposal station; paved driveways; closest complete shopping is in Federal Way.

SEASON & FEES: $6.00 for a standard site, $8.00 for a partial-hookup site, $2.00 for an extra vehicle; open all year; 10 day limit.

NATURAL FEATURES: Located in a heavily wooded area, with a mixture of hardwoods and conifers; very thick carpet of forest material; beach area on Puget Sound within walking distance.

ATTRACTIONS: Many foot trails, including a beach access trail; close to major urban shopping centers.

NOTES: This campground is on the outskirts of one of the Northwest's major cities, so the park is predictably crowded in the summer. It is surprisingly *un*populated during much of the rest of the year. Improvements to the hookup area have recently been accomplished.

MILLERSYLVANIA
State Park

LOCATION: Western Washington south of Olympia.

ACCESS: From Interstate 5 exit 95 (12 miles south of Olympia, 11 miles north of Centralia), drive east on Washington State Highway 121 for 2.8 miles; at a "T" intersection, turn north (left) onto a paved access road; continue 0.7 mile and turn west (left) into the campground.

FACILITIES: 164 sites, including 52 with partial hookups; sites are standard to large, with average to excellent separation; parking pads are all level, gravel, and some are spacious enough for large rv's; excellent tent spots; fireplaces; b-y-o firewood is recommended; water at several faucets; restrooms with showers; kitchen shelter; holding tank disposal station; paved driveways; camper supplies at a small local store; adequate to complete supplies and services are available in Olympia and Centralia.

SEASON & FEES: $6.00 for a standard site, $8.50 for a partial-hookup site; open all year, with limited facilities in winter; 10 day limit.

NATURAL FEATURES: Located on a densely forested flat; vegetation in the camp area consists of very tall conifers, large ferns, and some low-level bushes; Deep Lake and Spruce Creek are located nearby, within the park boundary; the Cascade Mountains and Mt. Rainier rise 50 miles to the east.

ATTRACTIONS: Boat launch; fishing; swimming beaches; playground; mown lawns in the picnic area; several foot paths, including Timber Island Ecology Trail which passes through a game sanctuary; jogging and fitness trails.

NOTES: Millersylvania's campground offers many comfortable camp units in a serene forest atmosphere. Its inviting freshwater beaches attract scores of water sports enthusiasts.

ALDER LAKE
City of Tacoma Park

LOCATION: Southwest Washington west of Mount Rainier National Park.

ACCESS: From Washington State Highway 7 at a point 31 miles south of Tacoma and 19 miles west of the Nisqually Entrance to Mount Rainier National Park, turn south into the park.

FACILITIES: 32 sites, including 18 with partial hookups, in 2 areas; hookup sites are in a large, gravel parking area overlooking the lake; 16 additional sites are located along a gravel drive leading down toward the lake (many of these sites have pull-along parking pads in need of additional leveling); there are a few exemplary tent spots near the lake; fireplaces; b-y-o firewood is recommended; water at central faucets; vault facilities; limited supplies are available in Alder and La Grande.

SEASON & FEES: $4.00 for a standard site, $6.00 for a partial hook-up site; April to October, with limited facilities in winter; 14 day limit.

NATURAL FEATURES: Located on Alder Lake, a 287-square-mile reservoir, created by Alder Dam on the Nisqually River as a source of water for the city of Tacoma; forested slopes surround the lake; some campsites have shade trees and grassy areas for tent-pitching; other sites are very open and have a gravel surface.

ATTRACTIONS: Boating; fishing; swimming; Mount Rainier National Park, 20 miles east, has fabulous scenery, visitor center at Paradise Point, and museum at Longmire.

NOTES: Alder Lake Campground is in a prime location: within 30 miles of the Tacoma urban area, and 20 miles from a world-renowned national park. The lake environment and the recreational facility here are excellent. This campground might serve well as a very attractive alternative to the campgrounds in Mount Rainier National Park.

RAINBOW FALLS
State Park

LOCATION: Western Washington southwest of Olympia.

ACCESS: From Washington State Highway 6 at a point 15.8 miles east of Interstate 5 exit 77 (Chehalis) and 35 miles east of U.S. 101 (Raymond), turn north and drive across a bridge into the park.

FACILITIES: 47 level sites; sites are mostly average-sized with average separation; some parking pads are paved, remainder are gravel; some pads are large enough for medium-sized rv's; most units will easily accomodate large tents; a few walk-in sites; fireplaces; b-y-o firewood is recommended; water at several faucets; centrally located restroom with showers supplemented by vault facilities; kitchen shelter; holding tank disposal station at the entrance; paved driveways; limited supplies in Doty, 1 mile west, complete supplies and services are available in Chehalis.

SEASON & FEES: $6.00 for a site, $2.00 for an extra vehicle; open all year, with limited facilities in winter; 10 day limit.

NATURAL FEATURES: Located in the Chehalis River Valley north of the Willapa Hills; sites are engulfed in a rainforest atmosphere with tall trees, hanging moss, and luxuriant ferns.

ATTRACTIONS: Fishing in the Chehalis River; playground and large lawn for recreational activities in the interior of the park; nature trails; suspension bridge over the river; day use area on the north bank of the river.

NOTES: Portions of Rainbow Falls State Park were constructed years ago by the CCC. There are a number of structures here which are characteristic of that era. The sylvan setting is established by tall moss-covered conifers towering over a thick, pine needle forest floor.

LEWIS AND CLARK
State Park

LOCATION: Western Washington south of Olympia.

ACCESS: From U.S. 12 at a point 2.6 miles east of Interstate 5 exit 68 (the exit is signed for "Mt. St. Helens Viewpoint & Visitor Center") and 30 miles west of Morton, turn south onto a paved access road; proceed 1.7 miles, then turn west (right) into the campground.

FACILITIES: 25 campsites in 2 loops; gravel parking pads are typically smaller straight-ins, although a few are pull-throughs long enough to accommodate larger rv's; additional leveling may be required; adequate, but somewhat sloped, areas for medium-sized tents; fireplaces; b-y-o firewood is recommended; kitchen shelter; water at several faucets; restrooms; paved/gravel driveways; minimal supplies at a small store on U.S. 12; complete supplies and services are available in Chehalis, 12 miles north.

SEASON & FEES: $6.00; open all year, with limited facilities in winter; 10 day limit.

NATURAL FEATURES: Located on a forested hillside in the Cowlitz River Valley; a creek flows through the day use area; views of Mt. St. Helens from an observation platform at the information center, 1 mile south of the campground.

ATTRACTIONS: Playground; open recreation space in the day use area; hiking trails through an old-growth forest exhibit; amphitheater for ranger-naturalist programs; Jackson House Historic Site just north of the park; Mount St. Helens Viewpoint and Visitor Center, 1 mile south, has information about the 1980 volcanic eruption.

NOTES: This secluded little camping area is located just a few yards from a picturesque creek and a tiny waterfall. A major attraction here is its closeness to the Mount St. Helens Volcanic Site.

MAYFIELD LAKE
Lewis County Park

LOCATION: Western Washington west of Mount Rainier.

ACCESS: From U.S. 12, at a point 15 miles west of Morton and 17 miles east of the intersection of U.S. 12 and Interstate 5 at exit 68, turn northwest onto Beach Road; travel 1 mile to the park, then turn right into the campground.

FACILITIES: 54 sites in 2 loops; sites are average or better in size, with average separation; parking pads are gravel; a few units are roomy enough to accommodate large rv's; some additional leveling may be necessary; tent spots vary in size and levelness; fireplaces; b-y-o firewood is recommended; water at several faucets; restrooms with showers; holding tank disposal station at the far north end of the park; paved driveways; minimal supplies at a small store on Highway 12; complete supplies and services are available in Chehalis, 30 miles northwest.

SEASON & FEES: $6.00 for a site; $2.00 for an extra vehicle; additional $4.00 reservation fee; May to September; 10 day limit.

NATURAL FEATURES: Mayfield Lake is a reservoir formed by Mayfield Dam on the Cowlitz River; sites are situated in an open, grass area or near tall trees; some sites are on a bluff overlooking the lake while others are right on the lakeshore; Mount St. Helens National Volcanic Monument is to the south; Mount Rainier is located to the east.

ATTRACTIONS: Boating; fishing; water skiing; sandy beach for swimming; playground; hiking trails; dam tours; nearby White Pass skilift operates during summers for sightseeing.

NOTES: Mayfield Lake is 13 miles long and has 33 miles of shoreline. It provides various recreational activities and the park offers some of the best camping facilities in this part of Washington.

SEAQUEST
State Park

LOCATION: Southwest Washington south of Olympia.

ACCESS: From Interstate 5 exit 49 (30 miles south of Chehalis, 10 miles north of Kelso), turn east onto Washington State Highway 504 (Spirit Lake Road); drive east 5 miles, then turn north (left) into the park entrance.

FACILITIES: 70 sites, including 16 with full hookups, in 3 loops; sites are average to large and fairly well separated; parking pads are gravel and adequate for medium to large vehicles; additional leveling may be necessary; some sites have secluded tent spots; fireplaces; b-y-o firewood; water at several faucets; restrooms, with showers, are supplemented by vault facilities; holding tank disposal station; paved driveways; resident ranger-manager; complete supplies and services are available in Castle Rock, 5 miles east.

SEASON & FEES: $6.00 for a standard site, $8.50 for a full-hookup site; open all year, with limited facilities from October to April; 10 day limit.

NATURAL FEATURES: Located among a fairly dense mixture of tall firs and hardwoods; Mount Saint Helens National Volcanic Monument is located 30 miles east; Silver Lake is accessible across the highway to the south; the Cowlitz River lies a few miles west.

ATTRACTIONS: Hiking trails; extensive day use area has mown lawns, picnic shelters, playground, horseshoe pits and a ball field; boating, fishing and swimming at Silver Lake; adjacent Mount Saint Helens Visitor Center features displays explaining the 1980 volcanic eruption.

NOTES: One of the best reasons for staying here (or just spending a few hours in the area) is the Mount Saint Helens Visitor Center, just west of the Seaquest Park entrance. The exhibits and slide/film presentations are really fascinating (particularly to children).

PARADISE POINT
State Park

LOCATION: Southwest Washington north of Portland, Oregon.

ACCESS: From Interstate 5 exit 16 (5 miles south of Woodland, 16 miles north of the Oregon border), on the *east* side of I-5, turn north onto a frontage road (Paradise Point Park Road) and continue 1 mile to the campground.

FACILITIES: 70 sites in 2 loops; sites in one loop are close to the Interstate, have minimal separation, with parking spaces level and long enough for large rv's; units in the second loop are smaller and adequately separated; additional leveling may be necessary in the second loop; most parking pads are paved; tent spots tend to be either large, level and in the open, or small and private; fireplaces; b-y-o firewood; water at several faucets; restrooms with showers; holding tank disposal station; driveways are paved; resident ranger-manager; adequate supplies and services are available in Woodland.

SEASON & FEES: $6.00 for a standard site, $3.00 for a primitive site; open all year, but weekends and holidays only in winter; 10 day limit.

NATURAL FEATURES: Located along the East Fork of the Lewis River between the Pacific Ocean and the Coast Range; the loop that's close to the highway is quite open and has manicured lawns and a rail fence bordering the driveway; the second loop is more forested and is situated on a hillside amid a mixture of hardwoods and conifers.

ATTRACTIONS: Hiking trails; day use area includes a boat ramp and river access; fishing.

NOTES: Before the highway became a major thoroughfare, Paradise Point may have been a "paradise", but now many of the sites are within 100 yards of I-5's traffic. (The day use area is actually beneath an I-5 bridge.) The grounds are well-maintained, and a row of trees tries to camouflage the freeway.

BATTLEGROUND LAKE
State Park

LOCATION: Southwest Washington north of Portland, Oregon.

ACCESS: From the intersection of Washington Highways 502 and 503 (west of the community of Battleground), drive east on Highway 502 (Main Street) for 0.8 mile to mid-town Battleground; turn north onto 142nd (Grace Street); drive 0.6 mile north and turn east (right) onto 229th (Heissen Road); drive east then north on Heissen Road for 2.3 miles to 249th; at that intersection, turn left onto a paved park access road leading west a few hundred yards to the campground.

FACILITIES: 70 sites in 2 areas; sites are average or better in size and separation; parking spaces are paved and typically level; several long pull-throughs for large rv's; fireplaces; b-y-o firewood is recommended; water at several faucets; restrooms with showers; resident ranger-manager; paved driveways; adequate supplies and services are available in Battleground.

SEASON & FEES: $6.00 for a standard site, $3.00 for a walk-in site; open all year, with limited facilities in winter; 10 day limit.

NATURAL FEATURES: Located on the forested shore of Battleground Lake (the lake's waters have collected in an extinct volcano); forested slopes have tall pines, hardwoods and ferns with some open grassy areas; sites 1-35 are densely forested, while sites 36-70 are in a more open area which tent campers may find more suitable.

ATTRACTIONS: Fishing; boating; sandy swimming beach; nature trails; equestrian trails and a horse camp; large day use area has shelters, mown lawns and picnic facilities.

NOTES: Battleground Lake is a neat place! But because it's only a few miles from the Portland-Vancouver metropolitan area, it's normally filled to capacity early in the day during the warmer months.

DOUGLAS FIR
Mt. Baker-Snoqualmie National Forest

LOCATION: Northwest Washington northeast of Bellingham.

ACCESS: From Washington State Highway 542 at a point 2.5 miles east of the community of Glacier, turn north (left) into the campground.

FACILITIES: 30 level sites in 2 loops; sites are average or better in size, and well separated by dense vegetation; some excellent tent spots on a soft forest floor; some ground-level fireplaces and some stone fire rings; firewood is usually available for gathering; water at 2 hand pumps; vault facilities; the loop nearer to the river has a gravel driveway and the loop up on a knoll has a paved driveway; resident concessionaire; limited supplies in Maple Falls, 10 miles west of Glacier on Highway 542.

SEASON & FEES: $6.00 for a site, $3.00 for an extra vehicle; May to October; 14 day limit; operated by a concessionaire.

NATURAL FEATURES: The Nooksack River flows alongside the lower loop of the campground; the upper loop is on a forested knoll; all sites are surrounded by dense rain forest-like vegetation--lush ferns cover the soft pine-needle forest floor, moss grows on rocks and trees and hangs from the tree limbs; the extinct volcano, Mount Baker, rises to almost 11,000' not quite 10 miles south.

ATTRACTIONS: Stream fishing; Horseshoe Bend hiking trail begins south across the highway; an extensive network of hiking trails is located in the Mount Baker area; nearby Kulshan Ridge provides an excellent view of Mount Baker.

NOTES: The surrounding rainforest vegetation here, between the Nooksack River to the south and a rock-faced bluff to the north, creates a serene atmosphere in this campground. The river can be seen or heard from virtually all sites.

COLONIAL CREEK
Ross Lake National Recreation Area

LOCATION: North-central Washington between Winthrop and Newhalem.

ACCESS: From Washington State Highway 20 at milepost 130 (20 miles east of Newhalem, 63 miles west of Winthrop), turn south or north into the 2 respective sections of the campground.

FACILITIES: 164 sites in 2 sections; most sites are average or larger in size, with fairly good separation; parking pads are gravel, short to medium straight-ins or pull-throughs; some sites may require additional leveling; many small, private tent spots; a few walk-in tent sites; fireplaces; b-y-o firewood is recommended; water at several faucets or hydrants; restrooms (H); holding tank disposal station located in the southern unit; paved driveways; campground hosts; nearest reliable source of supplies and services is Marblemount, 40 miles west.

SEASON & FEES: $5.00; May to November.

NATURAL FEATURES: Located on a forested hillside near the south end of Diablo Lake; very tall conifers, hardwoods, and varying amounts of underbrush provide good separation; tall peaks of the Cascades tower over the lake and the campground.

ATTRACTIONS: Boating and related water sports on Diablo Lake and Thunder Creek; self-guiding nature trail; Thunder Creek Hiking Trail; evening interpretive programs; Diablo Lake is at the southern tip of expansive Ross Lake National Recreation Area.

NOTES: This campground tends to fill early due to its location right beside the lake and on the highway. A few lakefront sites provide for tentside mooring of boats. Some sites may be a bit close to the highway or to a neighboring camper, but the dense vegetation helps to subdue extraneous noise.

LONE FIR
Okanogan National Forest

LOCATION: North-central Washington between Winthrop and Newhalem.

ACCESS: From Washington State Highway 20 at milepost 168 +.4 (24 miles west of Winthrop, 49 miles east of Newhalem), turn southeast into the campground.

FACILITIES: 27 sites; units are a bit small but very well separated; small to medium-sized parking pads are gravel straight-ins or pull-throughs; many may require additional leveling; some secluded tent spots have been carved out of the dense vegetation; fireplaces; firewood is available for gathering in the vicinity; water at several faucets; vault facilities (H); gravel driveway; limited supplies and services are available in Winthrop.

SEASON & FEES: $5.00; June to September; 14 day limit.

NATURAL FEATURES: Located on the east slopes of the tallest peaks of the Cascade Range; tiny Pine Creek joins Early Winters Creek at this point; sites are surrounded by dense forest with tall conifers and considerable underbrush.

ATTRACTIONS: A principal activity is hiking in the Cascades: Cutthroat Lake Trailhead is 1 mile west and the Pacific Crest Trail is accessible from near milepost 157 +.7 on Highway 20; stream fishing; the superscenic North Cascades Highway continues west from here over 5477' Washington Pass.

NOTES: This is a high-altitude campground with a relatively short season. Near here are great views of several landmarks, including "The Needles" to the north, Silver Star Mountain to the east, and Liberty Bell Mountain to the west. Lone Fir is a good base camp for exploring the Cascades.

KLIPCHUCK
Okanogan National Forest

LOCATION: North-central Washington between Winthrop and Newhalem.

ACCESS: From Washington State Highway 20 at milepost 175 +.1 (18 miles west of Winthrop, 55 miles east of Newhalem), turn northwest onto a paved access road; continue 1.3 miles to the campground entrance.

FACILITIES: 46 sites; most units are average-sized and have excellent separation; parking pads are gravel, short to medium straight-ins; vehicles will probably require some additional leveling; small to medium-sized tents can be tucked into small nooks among the trees; stairs lead from parking pads to some table and tent areas; fireplaces; some is firewood available for gathering in the vicinity; water at several faucets; 3 restrooms (H); paved driveway; limited supplies and services are available in Winthrop.

SEASON & FEES: $5.00; May to September; 14 day limit.

NATURAL FEATURES: Located on a forested hillside in a narrow valley along Early Winters Creek; campground vegetation consists of dense stands of conifers and hardwoods, with considerable grass and underbrush; high timbered ridges on both sides of the valley; peaks of the Cascades rise just west of the campground area.

ATTRACTIONS: Stream fishing; hiking on several mountain trails, including those to Cedar Falls and Rattlesnake Creek, which ultimately join the Pacific Crest Trail; the drive across the North Cascades Highway from here toward Newhalem offers magnificent mountain scenery.

NOTES: A conscientious attempt was made in this campground to provide the most level sites possible, considering the steep terrain. The dense vegetation provides excellent privacy and a peaceful environment.

EARLY WINTERS
Okanogan National Forest

LOCATION: North-central Washington between Winthrop and Newhalem.

ACCESS: From Washington State Highway 20 at milepost 177 +.7 (16 miles west of Winthrop, 58 miles east of Newhalem), turn left or right at the east end of the Early Winters Creek Bridge. (Sites are located on both sides of the highway.)

FACILITIES: 7 sites on the north and 7 sites on the south side of the highway; sites are small to average in size, with average separation; parking pads are gravel, short to medium, straight-ins; additional leveling may be necessary in some instances; medium-sized tent areas; fireplaces; firewood is available for gathering in the vicinity; water at several faucets; vault facilities; gravel driveways; limited supplies and services are available in Winthrop, 16 miles east.

SEASON & FEES: $5.00; May to September; 14 day limit.

NATURAL FEATURES: Located on the east slope of the Cascade Mountains in a valley bordered by high rocky ridges; Early Winters Creek, a swiftly flowing mountain stream, joins the waters of the Methow River a short distance to the east; terrain along the river is level but a bit rocky; medium-sized pines and moderate underbrush provide some shelter and separation for the campsites, many of which are creekside.

ATTRACTIONS: Stream fishing; Cedar Creek Trailhead is 3 miles west; a very scenic drive along the North Cascades Highway, over Washington Pass, starts here and continues westward through North Cascades National Park.

NOTES: This is a good base-of-operations camp for exploration of the inviting mountain areas to the west. Many sites are so close to the creek that most highway noise would be moderated by the sound of the rushing water.

PEARRYGIN LAKE
State Park

LOCATION: North-central Washington north of Winthrop.

ACCESS: From Washington State Highway 20 (Riverside Avenue) at milepost 192 +.9 in mid-town Winthrop, turn north onto Bluff Street; continue 1.5 miles, and turn east (right) onto the state park access road; continue 1.7 miles and turn right again into the park; the entrance station is 0.7 mile, and the campground is 0.6 mile farther.

FACILITIES: 83 sites, including 57 with full hookups; site size is typical for a state park; minimal separation, except for a few lakeside sites which are well separated; most parking pads are gravel; one loop is designed for trailers; parking pads are medium to large straight-ins and pull-throughs; fairly level, grassy tent spots; fireplaces; b-y-o firewood; several faucets; restrooms with showers; holding tank disposal station at the entrance; paved driveways; adequate supplies and services are available in Winthrop.

SEASON & FEES: $6.00 for a standard site, $8.50 for a full-hookup site, $3.00 for an extra vehicle; May to November; 10 day limit.

NATURAL FEATURES: Located on the grassy north shore of beautiful Pearrygin Lake; watered and mown lawns are dotted with some small trees; expanses of gently rolling, partially forested hillsides surround the park.

ATTRACTIONS: Boating; swimming; waterskiing; windsurfing; gravel boat launch and floating docks; large day use area with sandy beach and picnic facilities; outstanding view up the valley toward the rugged peaks of the Cascade Mountains.

NOTES: At Pearrygin Lake, some lucky lakeside campers can tie up their boats within a few feet of their tents. This is a *very* crowded park on summer weekends, so reservations are recommended. Try to plan a visit during non-peak times.

LOUP LOUP
Okanogan National Forest

LOCATION: North-central Washington between Twisp and Okanogan.

ACCESS: From Washington State Highway 20 at milepost 214 +.7 (12 miles east of Twisp, 18 miles west of Okanogan), turn north onto Forest Road 42 (paved); continue 0.5 mile north and west; turn north (right, still on Road 42); continue 0.6 mile, and turn west (left) into the campground.

FACILITIES: 27 level sites in 2 tiered loops; the larger loop is close to the road, the lower loop is further away, down along a creek; very large sites with good separation; parking pads are gravel straight-ins or pull-throughs, some spacious enough for large rv's; most tent areas are large and level; fireplaces; ample firewood is available for gathering; water at several faucets; vault facilities; gravel driveway; limited supplies and services are available in Twisp.

SEASON & FEES: $4.00; May to September; 14 day limit.

NATURAL FEATURES: Located in the foothills of the Cascades, between steep, forested slopes east and west; a small creek runs through a meadow near the day use area; moderately dense vegetation in the campground's main loop consists of tall conifers with hanging moss; the lower 5 units, along the creek, have tall grass and typical creekside brush.

ATTRACTIONS: Secluded camp with lots of elbow room; nearby opportunities for backcountry exploration; Loup Loup Winter Sports Area is close by; Road 42 leads north to Conconully State Park and Reservoir.

NOTES: This is a super stop, near a main highway, for a traveler seeking forest tranquility. Another nearby forest campground, JR, is located near milepost 214. It has 7 small sites, right along Highway 20.

LEADER LAKE
Department of Natural Resources

LOCATION: North-central Washington between Twisp and Okanogan.

ACCESS: From Washington State Highway 20 at milepost 224 + .3 (9 miles west of Okanogan, 22 miles east of Twisp), turn northeast onto a paved single-lane road; continue on this twisty road 0.4 mile to the campground.

FACILITIES: 25 sites in 3 main sections; gravel/dirt parking pads vary from small to very large; some parking spots are straight-ins, some are pull-throughs, and some are however-you-can-manage; most will require additional leveling; a few sites have framed-and-leveled tent pads; fireplaces; b-y-o firewood is recommended; NO DRINKING WATER; vault facilities; pack-it-in/pack-it-out trash removal system; gravel driveways; adequate supplies and services are available in Okanogan.

SEASON & FEES: No fee; 5 day limit.

NATURAL FEATURES: Located on the east slope of the Cascades, in a basin surrounding a picturesque mountain lake; all sites are on a rocky hillside along the lakeshore; vegetation varies from fairly dense timber to just a few sparse bushes; moderately forested hills surround the area; a small stream flows into the lake near its southwest corner.

ATTRACTIONS: Boating; fishing; paved boat ramp; Conconully State Park and Reservoir are accessible from here by traveling north on some back roads.

NOTES: This campground is quite popular, even with its limited facilities. The scenery is exceptionally pleasant, and virtually all sites have a lake view. A companion Department of Natural Resources campground, Rock Creek, is located off Highway 20 at milepost 223, and 4 miles north on a gravel road.

ALTA LAKE
State Park

LOCATION: North central Washington north of Wenatchee.

ACCESS: From Washington State Highway 153 at milepost 1 +.7 (33 miles south of Twisp, 1.7 miles west of the intersection of U.S. 97 and Highway 153), turn south onto a steep, winding, but paved access road; continue 2 miles to the campground.

FACILITIES: 147 sites in 3 loops; sites along the lakeshore tend to be small and close together; sites across the roadway above the lake are larger and better separated; most parking pads are small straight-ins, and many will require some additional leveling; small to medium, somewhat sloped tent spots; fireplaces; limited firewood is available for gathering in the vicinity, b-y-o is suggested; water at several faucet-fountains; restrooms with showers; holding tank disposal station; driveways in the upper loops are paved, lower loop drive is gravel; limited to adequate supplies in Pateros, 5 miles northeast.

SEASON & FEES: $6.00 for a standard site, $2.00 for an extra vehicle; open all year, with limited facilities in winter; 10 day limit.

NATURAL FEATURES: Located in the forested foothills of the Cascade Mountains on the shore of Alta Lake; 97 sites are on a forested hillside above the lake; 50 sites are in a less sheltered section closer to the shore; spacious day use area has a sandy beach, mown lawns and picnic spots.

ATTRACTIONS: Boating; fishing; exceptionally nice sandy swimming beach; nature trail leads to a scenic overlook; golf course nearby; winter sports area.

NOTES: Alta Lake is a strikingly beautiful mountain lake surrounded by dense stands of tall conifers. The relatively mild climate makes this a popular spot year-round. Early arrival, especially on summer weekends, is encouraged.

MONEY CREEK

Mt. Baker-Snoqualmie National Forest

LOCATION: West-Central Washington west of Skykomish.

ACCESS: From U.S. 2 at a point 4 miles west of Sky-komish and 9 miles east of the national forest boundary, turn south onto a paved access road; cross a bridge over the South Fork of the Skykomish River; turn left or right into the campground. (Sites are east and west of the entrance.)

FACILITIES: 24 level sites in two loops; most sites are average or better in size, and very well separated by dense vegetation; considerable diversity in parking pads: gravel or paved, straight-ins or pull-throughs, small to large, single or double; some excellent tent sites located among the trees; fire rings; firewood is available for gathering in the vicinity; water at faucets; vault facilities; most driveways are paved; limited supplies are available in Skykomish.

SEASON & FEES: $6.00 for site, $4.00 for an extra vehicle; May to October; 14 day limit.

NATURAL FEATURES: Located on the western slope of the Cascade Mountains; distant peaks are visible across the river; Money Creek flows into the South Fork of the Skykomish River here amid rain forest-like vegetation; several sites are situated right along the south riverbank.

ATTRACTIONS: Foot-trails in the campground; stream fishing; sandy river beach; picnicing near the campground; nearby 4-wheel-drive roads lead south toward the Alpine Lakes Wilderness.

NOTES: The drive along U.S. 2 through the deep-green Skykomish River Canyon is in itself worth the trip. Because Money Creek Campground is close to the metropolitan area and easy to find, it's very popular. As an alternative, Beckler River Campground, 2 miles north of Skykomish, has similar facilities. Sites at Beckler River are more likely to be available during peak camping times.

I didn't like this campground. The South unit is up away from the lake & you can't see the lake from the north unit.

LAKE WENATCHEE
State Park

LOCATION: Central Washington northwest of Wenatchee.

ACCESS: South Unit: From the intersection of U.S. 2 and Washington State Highway 207 (20 miles east of Stevens Pass, 16 miles north of Leavenworth), drive north on Highway 207 for 3.5 miles to the sign "Southshore - Lake Wenatchee"; turn west (left); drive past the 3 entrances to Nason Creek Forest Service Campground to the park entrance. North Unit: continue north on Highway 207 for 1.0 mile past the south unit access; turn left into the campground.

FACILITIES: South Unit, 100 sites; North Unit, 97 sites; parking pads are paved and most will accomodate large rv's; some will need additional leveling; framed-and-gravelled tent pads; fireplaces; some firewood is available for gathering in the vicinity; water at several faucets; restrooms with showers; holding tank disposal station; paved driveways; limited supplies at a store 0.5 mile on Highway 207; adequate supplies and services are available in Leavenworth.

SEASON & FEES: $6.00; April to October, some sites are kept open for winter parking; 10 day limit.

NATURAL FEATURES: Located on the north and south shores of glacier-fed Lake Wenatchee; the densely forested Cascade Mountains encircle the lake; campground vegetation consists of very tall conifers and moderate underbrush.

ATTRACTIONS: Boating; fishing; most day use facilities, boat ramp and sandy swimming beach are located along the south shore; boat and horse rentals; miles of hiking trails; playground; amphitheater; winter sports area.

NOTES: Lake Wenatchee is a gem of a lake. Early arrival at this very popular recreation area is recommended, particularly on summer weekends.

Not a pretty campground although there are some sites on the creek. The trees arent pretty. Dry & dusty looking.

Washington 62

NASON CREEK
Wenatchee National Forest

LOCATION: Central Washington north of Leavenworth.

ACCESS: From the intersection of U.S. Highway 2 and Washington State Highway 207 (20 miles east of Stevens Pass, 16 miles north of Leavenworth), drive 3.5 miles north on Highway 207 to a "Southshore Lake Wenatchee" sign; turn west (left) and continue 0.1 mile on a paved road to the campground.

FACILITIES: 68 sites in 3 loops; most sites are level and well separated by timber; parking pads are mostly gravel straight-ins, with a few pull-throughs spacious enough for larger rv's; many sites will accomodate large tents; fireplaces at some sites, barbecue grills at others; firewood is available for gathering in the vicinity; water at several faucet-fountains; restrooms; holding tank disposal station; paved driveways; campground host; limited supplies at a small store 1 mile north; adequate supplies and services are available in Leavenworth.

SEASON & FEES: $6.00; May to November; 14 day limit.

NATURAL FEATURES: Located in a fairly open conifer forest along the bank of Nason Creek, on the eastern slope of the Cascade Mountains; many of the campsites are creekside; forested mountains completely encircle this area, including nearby Lake Wenatchee.

ATTRACTIONS: Fishing in the creek; boating, fishing, swimming and waterskiing on Lake Wenatchee, 1 mile northwest; hiking and horseback riding in Lake Wenatchee State Park.

NOTES: Nason Creek is a very likable campground in itself, but having Lake Wenatchee and all its attractions close at hand is a bonus. This campground is also a good alternative to the one at the state park; although the park's facilities, for about the same cost, may make the park a better buy.

TUMWATER
Wenatchee National Forest

LOCATION: Central Washington northwest of Wenatchee.

ACCESS: From U.S. Highway 2 at a point 9 miles northwest of Leavenworth and 7 miles south of Coles Corner (and just north of a highway-crossing over the Wenatchee River), turn east into the campground.

FACILITIES: 80 sites, 60 in one main loop, plus 20 more sites in a spur to the west along Chiwaukum Creek; excellent separation; parking pads are average-sized, dirt straight-ins; small to medium-sized tent spots; fireplaces; firewood available for gathering; water at several hydrants; restrooms; holding tank disposal station; paved driveways; adequate supplies and services are available in Leavenworth.

SEASON & FEES: $6.00; May to November; 14 day limit.

NATURAL FEATURES: Located in very densely forested Tumwater Canyon on the eastern slope of the Cascade Mountains; Chiwaukum Creek flows into the Wenatchee River here; all sites are very secluded and separated by stands of tall conifers; some campsites are right along the creek; Alpine Lakes Wilderness lies to the west; Tumwater Botanical area is located to the south.

ATTRACTIONS: Fishing in the creek and river; a hiking trail winds from the campground, along the river and creek, then back to the campground; group picnic area; trailhead to Alpine Lakes Wilderness nearby; Leavenworth Recreation Area is 10 miles south.

NOTES: Though the campground is close to the highway, traffic noise is muffled by the sound of the creek and river tumbling over the rocks. Highway 2 passes through a narrow canyon in this section, and there's just enough room for the road and the river.

TRONSEN
Wenatchee National Forest

LOCATION: Central Washington north of Ellensburg.

ACCESS: From U.S. 97 at milepost 165 (18 miles south of Leavenworth, 1 mile northeast of Swauk Pass), turn west into the campground.

FACILITIES: 31 sites; sites are larger than average and fairly well separated; parking pads are gravel, mostly level, and medium to large in size; some large tent spots; fireplaces; firewood is available for gathering in the area; water at several faucets; vault facilities; gravel driveways; minimal supplies at a small store and cafe 12 miles south on Highway 97; adequate supplies in Leavenworth or Cle Elum; complete supplies and services are available in Ellensburg and Wenatchee.

SEASON & FEES: $5.00; May to October; 14 day limit.

NATURAL FEATURES: Located on a forested flat in the Wenatchee Mountains near the summit of Swauk Pass at 4105'; somewhat open forest of very tall conifers, some low-level underbrush, and patches of grass; Tronsen Meadow extends south from here; Tronsen Creek flows past the campground and northward where it eventually joins the Wenatchee River.

ATTRACTIONS: Hiking; stream fishing; U.S. 97 follows along the east slope of the Cascades through some magnificent scenic areas.

NOTES: Interestingly, at this spot near the top of a mountain pass, the sites are more level than at campgrounds along the highway to the south and west. A dense stand of tall trees and underbrush separates most of the campsites from the highway, so traffic noise shouldn't be much more disturbing than the sound of mountain waters tumbling over the rocks in Tronsen Creek.

SWAUK
Wenatchee National Forest

LOCATION: Central Washington northeast of Cle Elum.

ACCESS: From U.S. 97 at milepost 159 +.8 (4 miles southwest of Swauk Pass, 20 miles northeast of Cle Elum), turn south and immediately east onto an access road which parallels the highway; continue 0.2 mile (past the day use area) to the campground.

FACILITIES: 23 sites; most sites are average-sized with reasonable separation; parking pads are gravel, average-sized straight-ins and well leveled (considering the terrain); good tent sites in grassy areas among the trees; fireplaces; some firewood is available for gathering; water at several faucets; centrally located restroom with auxillary vaults; gravel driveways; limited supplies at a store/cafe, 6 miles south on Highway 97; adequate supplies in Cle Elum; complete supplies and services are available in Wenatchee and Ellensburg.

SEASON & FEES: $5.00; mid-April to November; 14 day limit.

NATURAL FEATURES: Located 4 miles west of Swauk Pass in the Wenatchee Mountains; Swauk Creek tumbles right past many of the sites on its way toward the Yakima River; the campground itself is situated in a moderately dense conifer forest in a narrow valley.

ATTRACTIONS: Stream fishing; Sculpture Rock Trail leads from south of the creek (across a small wooden footbridge); day use area includes a ball field, children's play area, kitchen shelters and a large upright stone fireplace for group use.

NOTES: Some of these campsites are rather close to the highway (within 50 yards), but forest vegetation muffles the sound of traffic, and the campground is below the actual level of the highway. From most sites, the sound of the rushing creek might be louder than the sound of traffic.

MINERAL SPRINGS
Wenatchee National Forest

LOCATION: Central Washington north of Ellensburg.

ACCESS: From U.S. 97 at milepost 156 +.1 (8 miles southwest of Swauk Pass, 16 miles northeast of Cle Elum), turn west and cross a small bridge to the campground.

FACILITIES: 12 sites in 2 loops; sites are average or better in size, and fairly well separated; parking pads are mostly level, gravel, pull-alongs or straight-ins of varying lengths; some very nice tent spots; fireplaces; firewood is available for gathering in the vicinity; water at faucets at both ends of the campground; vault facilities; gravel driveways; minimal supplies at a resort and cafe across the highway; adequate supplies in Cle Elum; complete supplies and services are available in Ellensburg.

SEASON & FEES: $4.00; May to December; generally available for camper parking, without water or fee, in winter; 14 day limit.

NATURAL FEATURES: Located on a bluff 100 feet above the creek and highway, in a narrow valley where Medicine Creek flows from the west into Swauk Creek; sites are in an open conifer forest with tall trees and some underbrush; terraced, timbered hillside behind the campground to the west; a similar hillside is on the east wall of the valley; Teanaway Ridge rises to the west and the Wenatchee Mountains are to the north.

ATTRACTIONS: Stream fishing; foot trails; 4-wheel drive trails in the vicinity; popular winter sports area (nordic skiing and snowmobiling).

NOTES: Some sites are close enough to the highway for traffic noise to be a minor concern, but a stand of trees between the sites and the highway muffles most of the sound. This is probably the only campground along this section of U.S. 97 which might be available for winter use.

Beautiful lake & hook up campground,

LAKE EASTON
State Park

LOCATION: West-central Washington west of Ellensburg.

ACCESS: From Interstate 90 exit 70 (15 miles west of Cle Elum, 18 miles east of Snoqualmie Pass), follow the frontage road on the south side of the Interstate easterly 0.5 mile to the park entrance.

FACILITIES: 147 sites in two sections; the primary area consists of 102 standard sites 0.1 mile south of the park entrance (directly ahead and to the left); campsites here are mostly good-sized, reasonably well separated, with straight-in parking pads; water at several faucets; recently constructed central restroom with showers; the second section contains 45 level full-hookup units 1 mile west of the entrance; about half of the hookup units are pull-throughs, the balance are straight-ins; central restroom with showers; fireplaces; presto logs are usually for sale, or b-y-o; holding tank disposal station at the park entrance; resident ranger-manager; nearest reliable source of adequate supplies is in Cle Elum.

SEASON & FEES: $6.00 for a standard site, $8.50 for a full-hookup site, $2.00 for an extra vehicle; April to October; 10 day limit.

NATURAL FEATURES: Located on the densely forested north shore of Lake Easton; the primary camping area is situated on a flat at the east end of the lake; the hookup units are located on a hilltop at the west end of the lake; tall timbered mountains are visible in most directions.

ATTRACTIONS: Fishing; boating; swimming; hiking trails; playground in the day use area; cross-country skiing (although the campground is closed in winter).

NOTES: This campground is certainly handy for Interstate travelers. However, we should note that I-90 is only a hundred yards or so from the hookup area.

River is very milky & muddy,

THE DALLES
Mt. Baker-Snoqualmie National Forest

LOCATION: Southwest Washington north of Mount Rainier National Park.

ACCESS: From Washington State Highway 410 just south of milepost 50 (8 miles north of the Mount Rainier National Park boundary, 23 miles southeast of Enumclaw), turn west into the campground.

FACILITIES: 45 level sites between the highway and the White River; sites are medium to large, with average to good separation; parking pads are oiled gravel, and most are level straight-ins; some pads are roomy enough for medium-sized rv's; there are some very good tent-pitching spots, especially in the more open sites; fireplaces; some firewood is available for gathering in the vicinity, but b-y-o to be sure; water at several faucets; vault facilities; oiled gravel driveways; adequate supplies and services are available in Enumclaw.

SEASON & FEES: $6.00 for a site, $3.00 for an extra vehicle; May to September; 14 day limit; operated by a concessionaire.

NATURAL FEATURES: Located in the Cascade Mountain Range where Minnehaha Creek flows into the White River; most sites are surrounded by towering cedars and hanging moss, but a few are in a relatively open forest setting; Mount Rainier National Park is located 8 miles south; Norse Peak Wilderness Area lies just to the east.

ATTRACTIONS: Fishing in the White River; a self-guiding nature trail leads to an old cedar tree over 9 feet in diameter; Sunrise Visitor Center is located nearby in Mount Rainier National Park.

NOTES: There are some terrific campsites here along this mountain crisp river. The drive along Highway 410 through this forested country reveals a number of first-rate views of perpetually snow-clad Mount Rainier.

Silver Creek is pretty. It runs through the campground. Driveway not level.

Washington 69

SILVER SPRINGS
Mt. Baker-Snoqualmie National Forest

LOCATION: Southwest Washington north of Mount Rainier National Park.

ACCESS: From Washington State Highway 410 at milepost 57 (1 mile north of the Mount Rainier National Park boundary, 30 miles southeast of Enumclaw), turn west into the campground.

FACILITIES: 56 sites; units are fairly well separated and medium to large in size; parking pads are level, gravel, straight-ins or pull-throughs long enough for medium-sized rv's; many excellent tent spots; fireplaces; firewood is sometimes for sale, or b-y-o; water at several faucets; vault facilities; paved driveway; camper supplies in Greenwater, 10 miles north; adequate supplies and services are available in Enumclaw.

SEASON & FEES: $6.00 for a site, $3.00 for an extra vehicle; May to September; 14 day limit; operated by a concessionaire.

NATURAL FEATURES: Located in the Cascade Mountain Range on a forested flat along Silver Creek, where it flows into the White River; a few sites are close to the highway but the tall, thick trees and fairly heavy underbrush provide a good sound barrier; some sites are right on the riverbank; Mount Rainier National Park is 1 mile south; Norse Peak Wilderness Area is to the east.

ATTRACTIONS: Fishing; hiking; foot trails lead off toward Mount Rainier and Norse Peak Widerness; nearby Crystal Mountain winter sports area; Sunrise Visitor Center nearby in Mount Rainier National Park.

NOTES: Silver Springs is the closest campground to this corner of Mount Rainier National Park. The serene setting, along the east bank of glacier-fed White River, is a super spot for a campground--especially since it's within 2 hours' drive of the Seattle metropolitan area.

Pretty campground but slightly hilly. Most sites are very uneven.

WHITE RIVER
Mount Rainier National Park

LOCATION: Southwest Washington in eastern Mount Rainier National Park.

ACCESS: From Washington State Highway 410 (Mather Memorial Parkway) at a point 4 miles north of Cayuse Pass and 37 miles southeast of Enumclaw, turn west onto a paved park road toward Sunrise Point; drive 5.2 miles to a fork in the road; take the left fork (roadway here is gravel for 1.1 miles); continue another 3.7 miles to the campground.

FACILITIES: 110 sites in 4 loops; most sites are average in size, and fairly well separated; parking pads are medium-length gravel straight-ins or pull-alongs; *most* some pads will require additional leveling; some excellent tent-pitching opportunities; fireplaces; b-y-o firewood; water at several faucets; restrooms; paved driveways; camper supplies are available at Sunrise Point.

SEASON & FEES: $5.00; July to September; 14 day limit.

NATURAL FEATURES: Located on a forested slope along the White River which flows down from the heights of Mount Rainier; moderately dense vegetation consists of conifers, bushes and ferns over a somewhat rocky forest floor; nearby Sunrise Point offers a magnificent view of Mount Rainier.

ATTRACTIONS: Amphitheater for ranger-naturalist campfire programs on summer weekends; trailhead for Glacier Basin located at the west end of the campground; Sunrise Point Visitor Center located several miles north.

NOTES: Mount Rainier National Park offers visitors a chance to commune with nature at its best. Subalpine meadows bloom with myriads of flowers near the edge of acres of tenacious glaciers. White River Campground is at one of the closest drive-in points to the great extinct volcano which the Indians called "Tahoma".

SUNSHINE POINT
Mount Rainier National Park

LOCATION: Southwest Washington in the southwest quadrant of Mount Rainier National Park.

ACCESS: From Washington State Highway 706 (Paradise Road) at a point 0.2 mile east of the Nisqually Entrance Station and 6 miles west of Longmire, turn south into the campground.

FACILITIES: 18 level sites on the riverbank; sites are small to medium with minimal separation; parking pads are level, gravel straight-ins; some pads would accomodate medium to large rv's; several large, level tent-pitching spots; fireplaces; b-y-o firewood is recommended; water at faucets; vault facilities; paved driveways; minimal supplies in Longmire, adequate supplies and services are available in Ashford, 7 miles west.

SEASON & FEES: $4.00; open all year with limited facilities in winter; 14 day limit.

NATURAL FEATURES: Located on a flat along the Nisqually River; campsites are either in the open right along the river, or just at the forest's edge; vegetation consists primarly of tall grass and tall conifers; Mount Rainier, visible to the north, is a glacier-clad 14,000 foot extinct volcano surrounded by lush rain forests and alpine meadows; the Nisqually, parented by the glaciers of Rainier, flows west past Sunshine Point on its way to Puget Sound.

ATTRACTIONS: Fishing and hiking; park roads from this point lead up the west side of Mount Rainier toward Klapatche Ridge, and also eastward toward Paradise and Sunrise Points; visitor center and museum in Longmire.

NOTES: Sunshine Point is distinctively different from the other densely forested campgrounds in Mount Rainier National Park; its climatic conditions allow for year-round camping, whereas most other camping areas are snowed-in for much of the winter.

LONGMIRE
Mount Rainier National Park

LOCATION: Southwest Washington in the southwest quadrant of Mount Rainier National Park.

ACCESS: From Washington State Highway 706 (Paradise Road) at a point 6.3 miles east of the Nisqually Entrance Station and 2.3 miles west of the intersection of Paradise Road and Cougar Rock Access Road, turn south (at the Longmire Ranger Station) onto the campground access road; drive 0.5 mile on a gently winding paved road, across a one-lane bridge, to the campground.

FACILITIES: 56 sites; sites are typically average in size and separation; parking pads are level, gravel, straight-ins; camping is limited to non-trailer vehicles; terrain is rocky so tent-pitching may require some extra preparation; fireplaces; b-y-o firewood (wood-gathering is prohibited); water at faucets; vault facilities; paved driveways; minimal supplies and services are available in Longmire.

SEASON & FEES: $5.00; *overflow camping--open only when Cougar Rock Campground is full*; 14 day limit.

NATURAL FEATURES: Located in the Cascade Mountain Range along the Nisqually River; the forest here is more open than at Cougar Rock, 3 miles east; vegetation consists of tall conifers, hanging moss and ferns; terrific view of Mount Rainier from the access road.

ATTRACTIONS: Fishing; hiker information available at Longmire; self-guiding "Trail of the Shadows"; ranger-naturalist walks are scheduled regularly during the season; Longmire Museum is open daily.

NOTES: The Longmire Campground area boasts some beautiful scenery, and is also rich in historical significance. Because the campground is open only portions of the year, it's advisable to inquire about site availability before making plans.

COUGAR ROCK
Mount Rainier National Park

LOCATION: Southwest Washington in the southwest quadrant of Mount Rainier National Park.

ACCESS: From Washington State Highway 706 (Paradise Road) at a point 2.3 miles northeast of Longmire, turn west into the campground.

FACILITIES: 200 sites in 6 loops; sites are mostly level and average-sized; forest vegetation and gently rolling hills provide separation for most sites; parking pads are gravel; most pads are average-sized straight-ins, although a few are longer pull-throughs for large rv's; some units may need additional leveling; excellent tent-pitching opportunities; fireplaces; b-y-o firewood; water at faucets; restrooms; holding tank disposal station; paved driveways; minimal supplies and services in Longmire.

SEASON & FEES: $5.00 for a site, $2.00 for an extra vehicle; June to October; 14 day limit.

NATURAL FEATURES: Located in the Cascade Mountains on the south slope of Mount Rainier; Paradise River flows into the Nisqually River at Cougar Rock; vegetation in the campground is predominantly tall trees covered with hanging moss, plus a considerable quantity of ferns and underbrush.

ATTRACTIONS: Fishing; picnicking; Wonderland Hiking Trail; Carter Falls; amphitheater for campfire programs; ranger-directed naturalist programs for children on summer weekends; Paradise Visitor Center and Viewpoint located a few miles east; Longmire also has a visitor center and museum.

NOTES: This campground is located in a rain forest-like atmosphere created by the moist maritime air flowing upward across the west slopes of Mount Rainier. The national park's attractions provide visitors with quite a variety of activities. The drive along Paradise Road offers some truly *great* scenic views.

276

OHANAPECOSH
Mount Rainier National Park

LOCATION: Southwest Washington in the southeast corner of Mount Rainier National Park.

ACCESS: From Washington State Highway 123 at a point 1.5 miles south of the intersection of the Stevens Canyon Road with Highway 123 and 11 miles north of Packwood, turn west and proceed on a paved access road to the campground.

FACILITIES: 220 sites in several loops; campsites are generally small to average in size and close together; parking pads are gravel and some may need additional leveling; a few sites will accommodate medium-sized rv's; many excellent tent spots; fireplaces; b-y-o firewood; restrooms; water at several faucets; holding tank disposal station; paved driveways; limited supplies and services are available in Packwood.

SEASON & FEES: $5.00 for a site, $2.00 for an extra vehicle; May to October; 14 day limit.

NATURAL FEATURES: Located in a densely forested valley along the glacier-fed Ohanapecosh River; Ohanapecosh Hot Springs is accessible by foot trail 0.1 mile east; campsite settings vary considerably: some sites are heavily forested while others have only a few tall trees and no underbrush; some sites are situated on small knolls while others are on a creek's edge.

ATTRACTIONS: Ohanapecosh Visitor Center offers historical information, plus exhibits about local animal life and vegetation; campfire programs are scheduled for the amphitheater during July and August; self-guiding and naturalist walks to Silver Falls, Hot Springs, Laughing Water and Grove of the Patriarchs.

NOTES: Superscenic hikes and drives are important features of this park. Mount Rainier, at 14,410 feet, towers over the rest of the park and offers visitors spectacular views from the numerous hiking trails and highways.

LA WIS WIS
Gifford Pinchot National Forest

LOCATION: Southwest Washington south of Mount Rainier National Park.

ACCESS: From U.S. 12 at milepost 138 (7 miles east of Packwood, 1 mile west of the intersection of U.S. 12 and Washington State Highway 123), turn north onto a paved, but steep and twisty, access road; continue 0.6 mile down to the campground entrance.

FACILITIES: 101 sites in 5 loops plus 23 more in a 'Hatchery' loop; sites are average or better in size, mostly level, and fairly well separated; parking pads are paved; sites in Loop A are long enough to accomodate large rv's; fairly level, medium to large tent spots; fireplaces; some firewood is usually available for gathering in the vicinity; water at several faucets; one centrally located restroom with auxiliary vault facilities; paved driveways; limited supplies are available in Packwood.

SEASON & FEES: $5.00 for a standard site, $6.00 for a 'premium' site (along the riverbank), $8.00 for a multiple site; May to September; 14 day limit.

NATURAL FEATURES: Located in the Cascade Mountains in the narrow Ohanapecosh River Valley near the confluence of the Ohanapecosh and Cowlitz Rivers; rain forest-like vegetation predominates in this area; Mount Rainier National Park is 4 miles north.

ATTRACTIONS: Hiking and fishing; the surrounding forested region has many trails--including one for exploring an "old growth forest"; Ohanapecosh Visitor Center is nearby in Mount Rainier National Park.

NOTES: La Wis Wis is located in a lush green forest of fir, hemlock and cedar, above a soft forest floor of ferns and moss. This narrow valley between the Ohanapecosh and Cowlitz Rivers is a really lovely setting for a mountain campground.

INDIAN CREEK
Snoqualmie National Forest

LOCATION: South-central Washington between Mount Rainier National Park and Yakima.

ACCESS: From U.S. 12 at milepost 159 +.4 (9 miles east of White Pass, 26 miles west of the intersection of U.S. 12 with Washington State Highway 410 near Naches), turn south into the campground.

FACILITIES: 43 sites; campsites are medium to large with average to excellent separation; parking pads are gravel and level, some spacious enough for very large vehicles; some large, level tent spots; fireplaces or fire rings; firewood is available for gathering in the area; water at faucets throughout; vault facilities; minimal supplies at a small store on the north shore of Rimrock Lake, complete supplies and services are available in Yakima, 45 miles east.

SEASON & FEES: $6.00; end of May to mid-September; 14 day limit.

NATURAL FEATURES: Located on a large, timbered flat at the west end of Rimrock Lake--a beautiful mountain lake formed by a dam across the Tieton River about 5 miles east; high timbered ridges encircle the lake; some sites offer views of the lake through the trees; sites are separated by lofty conifers and a little underbrush.

ATTRACTIONS: Swimming; boating; fishing; public boat launch located at the east end of the lake; White Pass Recreation Area is 8 miles west; Mount Rainier National Park is 30 miles west.

NOTES: All the sites in this campground are level and nicely sheltered. The lake is accessible from the campground area, but lake views are limited because of the vegetation. The level of the lake varies considerably from one season to another. Indian Creek is one of the nicest campgrounds along this route. The campground is managed by Wenatchee National Forest.

HAUSE CREEK
Wenatchee National Forest

LOCATION: South-central Washington between Mount Rainier National Park and Yakima.

ACCESS: From U.S. 12 at milepost 169 (16.5 miles west of the intersection of U.S. 12 with Washington State Highway 410 near Naches, 18 miles east of White Pass), turn south into the campground.

FACILITIES: 41 sites in 3 loops; site size is average or better with fairly good separation; parking pads are gravel, small to medium straight-ins; terrain is fairly level but a few pads may require additional leveling; most sites have good tent spots; fireplaces; firewood is available for gathering in the area; water at several faucets; centrally located restroom, supplemented by vault facilities; minimal supplies and gas at a small store 4 miles east; complete supplies and services are available in Yakima, 33 miles east.

SEASON & FEES: $5.00; end of May to mid-November; 14 day limit.

NATURAL FEATURES: Located in the Tieton River Valley on the east slope of the Cascades; 2 loops are situated along the river and a third loop is on a forested bluff slightly above it (and closer to the highway); tall timber surrounds some sites, other sites are on a fairly open riverbank, still others are along a brushy creekbed.

ATTRACTIONS: Fishing in the river; foot trails and 4-wheel drive trails lead up into the surrounding densely forested mountains; a superscenic drive leads along Highway 12 and up through White Pass.

NOTES: Though some of the sites are rather near the highway, there are also a good number of dandy sites right along a very inviting river. The Tieton River flows swiftly by, at this point, and on toward the east.

WILLOWS
Wenatchee National Forest

LOCATION: South-central Washington between Mount Rainier National Park and Yakima.

ACCESS: From U.S. 12 at milepost 170 +.3 (15 miles west of the intersection of U.S. 12 with Washington State Highway 410 near Naches, 20 miles east of White Pass), turn south into the campground.

FACILITIES: 16 sites; sites are fairly level, average-sized, with satisfactory to very good separation; parking pads are gravel, mostly small to medium straight-ins; most tent spots are level and medium-sized; fireplaces; some firewood is available for gathering in the area; water at a single hand pump; simple vault facilities; gravel driveways; limited supplies and gas at a small store 3 miles east; complete supplies and services are available in Yakima, 33 miles east.

SEASON & FEES: $4.00; end of May to mid-September; 14 day limit.

NATURAL FEATURES: Located on the east slope of the Cascade Range where a small creek flows into the Tieton River in this steep-walled Tieton River Canyon; sites are situated on 2 levels: a number of sites are right along the riverbank, others are positioned a few feet above, on a small rise; predominant vegetation is tall conifers, hardwoods, and some brush in the creekbed.

ATTRACTIONS: Fishing in the river; foot trails and 4-wheel drive roads lead from near here up into the surrounding mountains; the drive along Highway 12 and up through White Pass offers some of the best scenery in this part of the state.

NOTES: Though some of the sites are within 100 yards of the highway, there are other sites located farther from the road right along the swift Tieton River. A caution sign is posted indicating that the stream level is subject to sudden fluctuations.

WINDY POINT
Wenatchee National Forest

LOCATION: South-central Washington between Mount Rainier National Park and Yakima.

ACCESS: From U.S. 12 at milepost 177 +.5 (8 miles west of the intersection of U.S. 12 with Washington State Highway 410 near Naches, 27 miles east of White Pass), turn south into the campground.

FACILITIES: 12 level sites; sites are average-sized with fairly good separation; parking pads are gravel straight-ins, many long enough to accomodate large rv's; medium-sized tent spots; fireplaces; some firewood is available for gathering in the area; water at a single hand pump; vault facilities; adequate supplies in Naches, 12 miles east; complete supplies and services are available in Yakima, 25 miles east.

SEASON & FEES: $4.00; April to November; 14 day limit.

NATURAL FEATURES: Located on the east slope of the Cascade Range along the north bank of the Teiton River; sheer canyon walls rise sharply across the river to the south, and rocky bluffs are an important part of the scenic landscape to the north; some sites are very open, and others are well-sheltered; vegetation in the camping area consists of tall conifers and hardwoods bordering an open meadow.

ATTRACTIONS: Stream fishing; nearby mountain trails for hikers and 4-wheel-drive vehicles; the Oak Creek Game Range, located 6 miles east, is available for recreational activities and wildlife observation.

NOTES: A reasonable distance separates the highway and these campsites, a number of which are situated right along the river. Most sites offer an alluring view, northward, of fluted canyon walls. A low rail fence along the northern edge of the camping area adds a congenial touch.

YAKIMA SPORTSMAN
State Park

LOCATION: South-central Washington east of Yakima.

ACCESS: From Interstate-82 Exit 34 (3 miles southeast of Yakima), drive east on a frontage road for 0.8 mile; turn north (left) onto Keyes Road; continue for 1 mile to the park entrance; turn west (left) into the park; the campground is toward the south end of the park.

FACILITIES: 60 level sites, including 36 with full hookups; sites are average-sized and have minimal to average separation; parking pads are paved or gravel, straight-ins or pull-throughs, some are spacious enough for very large vehicles; large, level areas for tent-pitching; fireplaces; b-y-o firewood; water at several faucets; centrally located restroom with showers; holding tank disposal station; resident caretaker; paved driveway; complete supplies and services are available in Yakima.

SEASON & FEES: $6.00 for a standard site, $8.50 for a full-hookup site; open all year; 10 day limit.

NATURAL FEATURES: Located along the bank of the Yakima River; some sites are among hardwood trees bordered by a small side creek, and other sites are on an open grassy flat; Yakima Ridge lies to the north and Rattlesnake Hills to the south; a couple of small ponds are within the park's borders.

ATTRACTIONS: Pond fishing is limited to children; a children's play area with a wooden treehouse borders the creek; large day use area; birdwatching (it seems there is a gaggle of geese in residence); fishing and rafting on the Yakima River.

NOTES: The campsites vary considerably in design: some are quite close together, shaded and next to a small meandering creek, other sites are widely-spaced with virtually no separation. All sites are tolerably well-removed from the highway and nearby residences.

WANAPUM
State Park

LOCATION: Central Washington between Ellensburg and Moses Lake.

ACCESS: From Interstate 90 at Exit 136 (28 miles east of Ellensburg, 42 miles west of Moses Lake), turn south onto a paved state park access road; drive 2.7 miles south (following the west shore of the Columbia River); turn east (left) into the park and continue 0.3 mile (paved) to the campground.

FACILITIES: 50 level sites, all with full hookups, in 2 loops; sites are fairly large with minimal separation; parking pads are oiled gravel pull-through's, spacious enough to accomodate very large rv's; lawns provide excellent tent-pitching opportunities, (irrespective of typically strong winds in the area); fireplaces; b-y-o firewood; water at several faucets; centrally located restrooms with showers; resident ranger-manager; telephone at the entrance; oiled gravel driveways; minimal supplies in Vantage, 3 miles north; complete supplies and services are available in Ellensburg.

SEASON & FEES: $8.50; open all year; 10 day limit.

NATURAL FEATURES: Located on a breezy hilltop overlooking the Columbia River; park grounds are mown and surrounded by poplars planted as a windbreak; views of the Columbia River to the east, north and south, and of the vast, semi-arid Columbia River Basin in all directions.

ATTRACTIONS: Large boat ramp nearby; a trail leads from the campground down to a river beach; swimming; boating; fishing; Ginkgo Petrified Forest Interpretive Center and trail nearby at Vantage; a huge bridge spans the great Columbia River near Vantage.

NOTES: This is a nice park! Considering the surrounding terrain--rocky, sage-covered bluffs, hills and flatlands--the campground is a great stop for central Washington travelers.

BEACON ROCK
State Park

LOCATION: Southern Washington border along the Columbia River east of Vancouver.

ACCESS: From Washington State Highway 14 near milepost 35 (5 miles west of North Bonneville, 35 miles east of Vancouver), turn north/east and drive up a steep winding paved road, past the day use area, to the campground, 1 mile.

FACILITIES: 24 sites; units are of adequate size and are fairly well separated; most parking pads are short to medium, gravel straight-ins; some sites may require additional leveling; fireplaces; firewood is available for gathering in the vicinity; water at several faucets; restroom with showers; holding tank disposal station; paved/oiled gravel driveway; limited to adequate supplies are available in Cascade Locks, Oregon, 6 miles east.

SEASON & FEES: $6.00 for a site, $2.00 for an extra vehicle; April to October; 10 day limit.

NATURAL FEATURES: Located on a densely forested hill with lots of tall timber, moss and ferns; well-sheltered; Beacon Rock, the world's second largest monolith, sits on the north bank of the Columbia River, directly opposite the park entrance.

ATTRACTIONS: Several major hiking trails; children's playground and kitchen shelter in the day use area; Bonneville Dam Visitor Center, 4 miles east.

NOTES: This campground is snugly tucked away in sort of a "pocket" above the Columbia River. Due to the terrain and dense vegetation, you'll have to walk or drive a short distance to glimpse views of Beacon Rock and the superlative Columbia River Gorge.

The road into the campground is too winding, narrow & steep. The campsites are very small & uneven. Don't go in here again!

very steep / very uneven

285

HORSETHIEF LAKE
State Park

LOCATION: South-central Washington along the Columbia River.

ACCESS: From the intersection of Washington State Highway 14 and U.S. 197 north of The Dalles, Oregon (take exit 87 if you're traveling Interstate 84), drive east on Highway 14 for 1.6 miles; turn south onto the park access road and continue for 1 mile to the campground.

FACILITIES: 12 sites; the camping units are arranged parallel to each other in a crescent-shaped loop; sites are level, with medium-length parking pads, but are close together; good possibilities for pitching smaller tents, but probably meant more for vehicle camping; fireplaces; b-y-o firewood; water at faucets; restroom; holding tank disposal station; complete supplies and services are available in The Dalles, 6 miles.

SEASON & FEES: $6.00; April to October; 10 day limit.

NATURAL FEATURES: Located on the west shore of 90 acre Horsethief Lake, a secondary impoundment on the Columbia River created as a result of The Dalles Dam; hardwood trees and maintained lawns in the campground and adjacent day use area; high dry bluffs and monument-type rock formations, including Horsethief Butte, in the area.

ATTRACTIONS: Boat launch on Horsethief Lake and on the Columbia River; swimming in the lake; trails; Indian rock art can be seen just to the west of the entrance; visitor tours at The Dalles Dam.

NOTES: This 340-acre park is operated as a satellite area of Maryhill State Park, 21 miles west. It might provide you with a lower-cost and less-crowded alternative to the excellent campground at Maryhill.

Campsites are very close together. Not very nice. Rest of park is beautiful

MARYHILL
State Park

LOCATION: South-central Washington along the Columbia River.

ACCESS: From U.S. 97 at the north end of the Columbia River bridge (1.2 miles north of Interstate 84 exit 104 in Oregon, 0.5 mile south of the intersection of U.S. 97 and Washington State Highway 14 south of Goldendale), turn east into the state park entrance; the campground is 0.5 mile inside the park.

FACILITIES: 50 full-hookup sites in one large loop; units are medium-sized with minimal separation; all sites are level, and should accommodate large tents as well as medium to large rv's; about half of the sites have pull-though parking pads, the remainder have straight-ins; all parking pads are gravel; many sites have wooden windbreaks; fireplaces; b-y-o firewood; restrooms with showers; holding tank disposal station; paved driveways; nearest supplies (gas, groceries, cafes) are on the Oregon side of the river.

SEASON & FEES: $8.00 for a site, $2.00 for an extra vehicle; open all year; 10 day limit.

NATURAL FEATURES: Located in a grove of hardwoods on a mowed and watered grass flat on the north bank of the Columbia River; dry grass and sage surrounds the park; high fluted rock bluffs directly to the north; strong winds.

ATTRACTIONS: Maryhill Museum 3 miles west; Stonehenge replica, 2 miles east, is visible from the park; old railroad locomotive and coal tender on display; swimming beach; boat launch.

NOTES: This is a fine campground, particularly for rv campers. It's as flat as a ping-pong table and has all the necessities. One minor drawback that should be mentioned: an occasional freight train rumbles by on the tracks just north of the park boundary. *Lots of trains.*

BROOKS MEMORIAL
State Park

LOCATION: South-central Washington north of Goldendale.

ACCESS: From U.S. 97 at milepost 24 +.6 (12 miles north of Goldendale, 3 miles south of the summit of Satus Pass), turn west onto the campground access road; the campground entrance is 0.2 mile farther.

FACILITIES: 45 sites, including 23 with full hookups, in two sections; medium-length gravel parking spaces; most sites would probably require some additional leveling; small but nice semi-walk-in sites; fireplaces; firewood is available for gathering in the vicinity; water at faucets throughout the campground; restroom with showers; holding tank disposal station; kitchen shelter with barbecue grills; gravel driveways; resident ranger-manager; adequate supplies are available in Goldendale.

SEASON & FEES: $6.00 for a standard site, $8.50 for a full-hookup site, $2.00 for an extra vehicle; April to October; 10 day limit.

NATURAL FEATURES: Located at the base of a forested hillside; very tall pine and hardwoods in the campground; about half of the hookup sites are in the open, some other sites are in moderate timber; a creek runs along the south edge of the main camp area; very thick pine needle carpet; wildflowers bloom from March to July.

ATTRACTIONS: 9 miles of trails in the park; Environmental Learning Center; fishing in streams; Goldendale Obervatory State Park nearby.

NOTES: This park is oriented toward natural activities: hiking, wildlife observation, star-gazing. The latter is particularly rewarding in the high, dry atmosphere here. Goldendale Observatory offers the largest telescope in the country available for public viewing.

OSOYOOS LAKE
State Park

LOCATION: North-central Washington near the Canadian border.

ACCESS: From U.S. Highway 97 at milepost 332 +.7 (0.7 mile north of Oroville, 4 miles south of the Canadian border), turn east onto a paved access road; continue 0.1 mile to the campground.

FACILITIES: 80 level sites; units are average-sized with minimal separation; parking pads are gravel, mostly medium-sized, straight-ins; excellent tent-pitching opportunities; fireplaces; b-y-o firewood; water at several faucet-fountains; restrooms with showers; holding tank disposal station; paved driveways; adequate supplies and services are available in Oroville.

SEASON & FEES: $6.00 for a site, $3.00 for an extra vehicle; open all year; 10 day limit.

NATURAL FEATURES: Located on a grassy flat along the south shore of Osoyoos Lake in the Okanogan Valley; park lawns are watered and mown; some planted hardwoods; on the whole, most sites are very much in the open; dry hills and low mountains flank this very fertile valley.

ATTRACTIONS: Boating; fishing; concrete boat ramp and boat dock; an adjacent marsh area is home for various wildlife species; sandy swimming beach is situated near the expansive day use area.

NOTES: This park is located in the Okanogan Valley which is renowned for its mild climate, long growing season, and delicious fruits and vegetables. Osoyoos Lake boaters may be pleased to know that, at a few lakeside sites, their vessel can be moored right alongside their tent. Since the north end of this lake is in Canada, many boaters take the opportunity to motor or sail across the border.

BRIDGEPORT
State Park

LOCATION: Central Washington east of Bridgeport.

ACCESS: From Washington State Highway 17 at milepost 136 +.3 (3 miles east of Bridgeport, 30 miles south of Okanogan), turn east onto a winding paved access road; proceed 3 miles (past Chief Joseph Dam) to the campground.

FACILITIES: 28 sites; camp units are average or better in size and separation; gravel parking pads are fairly level, and typically long enough for larger rv's; some additional leveling may be required; large grassy tent spots; fireplaces; b-y-o firewood is recommended; water at several faucets; restrooms with showers; holding tank disposal station; paved driveways; adequate supplies in Bridgeport.

SEASON & FEES: $6.00 for a standard site, $2.00 for an extra vehicle; May to October; 10 day limit.

NATURAL FEATURES: Located in a sheltered hollow on a grassy hillside above the Columbia River; vegetation between sites consists of mown grass and a wide variety of shade trees (conveniently identified); huge monolithic boulders are perched on a rolling, grassy bluff above the campground.

ATTRACTIONS: Columbia River access, including boat ramp and dock; fishing; sandy swimming beach; playground on a hill overlooking the campground and river; golf course adjacent; view of Chief Joseph Dam from the access road; the dam forms Rufus Woods Lake in this section of the Columbia.

NOTES: Bridgeport State Park and its arboretum offer fertile relief from an otherwise dry Columbia River Basin. Although the river is not actually visible from most campsites, a terrific vantage point is just a short walk away. The camping and day use facilities have recently been expanded and improved.

LINCOLN ROCK
State Park

LOCATION: Central Washington north of Wenatchee.

ACCESS: From U.S. 2/Washington State Highway 151 (following the east bank of the Columbia River) at a point 8 miles north of East Wenatchee and 33 miles south of Chelan, turn west onto Rocky Reach Power Plant access road; drive west then north 0.7 mile (past the power plant entrance) to the campground.

FACILITIES: 94 sites, including many with full or partial hookups; most units are level and average-sized; very little separation between sites; long, paved parking pads; grass tent spots (but the lawns are watered regularly, so stay mobile); fireplaces; b-y-o firewood; water at numerous faucets; restrooms (H) with showers; holding tank disposal station; paved driveways; complete supplies and services are available in Wenatchee, 10 miles south.

SEASON & FEES: $6.00 for a standard site, $8.00 for a partial-hookup site, $8.50 for a full-hookup site, $2.00 for an extra vehicle; open all year, with limited facilities in winter; 10 day limit.

NATURAL FEATURES: Located along the east bank of the Columbia River just north of Rocky Reach Dam; forested peaks are visible beyond the bluffs to the west; mostly open and breezy; manicured lawn is dotted by a few small planted hardwoods; prominent Lincoln Rock is across the river.

ATTRACTIONS: Large boat ramp and docks; fishing; swimming; waterskiing; amphitheater for interpretive programs; spacious day use area with playground, ball fields, kitchen shelter and barbecue grills.

NOTES: Rounded foothills and towering Cascade Mountains can be viewed from virtually all the campsites. The camping and day use facilities have recently undergone expansion and improvement.

Beautiful park. A long way from anywhere. No TV. Roads not completely level for bicycling.

Washington 89

CROW BUTTE
State Park

LOCATION: South-central Washington along the Columbia River.

ACCESS: From Washington State Highway 14 at milepost 155 (26 miles west of the intersection of I-82 and State Highway 14, 54 miles east of the junction of U.S. 97 and Highway 14), turn north and follow the paved access road as it loops around to the east, passes under Highway 14, and continues south across a causeway to the park entrance 1 mile from the highway; continue another 1.3 miles to the campground.

FACILITIES: 50 full-hookup sites in one large loop; the parking spaces along the outer edge of the loop are average-sized pull-throughs; the inner sites have long straight-in spaces; all parking pads are paved; gravel table and tent pads (no tents on the grass); all sites are quite level; some sites have windbreaks; barbecue grills; b-y-o firewood; central restroom with showers; holding tank disposal station; paved loop driveway; resident ranger-manager; supplies are scarce along route 14: fill up with gas and groceries before venturing onto this stretch of road.

SEASON & FEES: $8.50 for a site, $2.00 for an extra vehicle; open all year, but weekends only in winter; 10 day limit in summer.

NATURAL FEATURES: Located at the base of Crow Butte, on an island in the Columbia River; manicured lawns; short hardwood trees provide some shelter/shade; barren hills and bluffs surround the campground; the area around the perimeter of the park is posted as rattlesnake territory.

ATTRACTIONS: Sand/pebble swimming beach; boat launch; fishing; shelter in the day use area.

NOTES: This is certainly an unexpected oasis in this rather desolate, semi-arid country. All sites have an excellent view of the river and surrounding terrain.

292

BONAPARTE LAKE
Okanogan National Forest

LOCATION: Northeast Washington between Republic and Tonasket.

ACCESS: From Washington State Highway 20 at milepost 282 +.2 (20 miles east of Tonasket, 20 miles west of Republic), turn north onto Forest Road 396 (paved); continue 5.9 miles, then turn west (left) into the campground.

FACILITIES: 24 sites in 2 loops; sites are fairly average in size with sufficient separation; level parking pads are gravel, short to medium, pull-throughs or straight-ins; good tent spots; fireplaces; some firewood is available for gathering in the vicinity; centrally located faucets; one central restroom with auxilary vaults (H); waste water receptacles for gray water; driveway is semi-paved; limited supplies are available in Republic and Tonasket.

SEASON & FEES: $5.00 for a single unit, $8.00 for a double unit, and $12.00 for a triple unit; May to October; 14 day limit.

NATURAL FEATURES: Located on the forested south shore of Bonaparte Lake; tall conifers tower over the campsites, with only a little underbrush and second growth to separate the sites; the lake is bordered by steep-sided, rocky, timbered ridges.

ATTRACTIONS: Boating; gravel boat ramp; fishing; foot trail from the west end of the campground; day use area along the shore; many of the sites have views of Bonaparte Lake through the trees.

NOTES: This is a really nice campground for any part of the country, but here in typically dry eastern Washington, it is a very pleasant surprise! This picturesque lake and nicely maintained campground are just a half dozen miles from the main highway. Another nearby forest campground, Sweat Creek, is located on a forested flat east of here at milepost 293 +.5 on Highway 20. Sweat Creek has 7 sites, vault facilities and a hand pump.

CURLEW LAKE
State Park

LOCATION: Northeast Washington north of Republic.

ACCESS: From Washington State Highway 21 at milepost 144 +.3 (6 miles north of Republic, 20 miles south of the Canadian border), turn west onto a paved access road; proceed 0.7 mile, then turn right into the main campground or continue straight ahead, then left to the lakeside section.

FACILITIES: 72 sites, including 18 with full hookups, in the main area, plus 10 additional sites in the lakeside area; sites are typically large with virtually no separation; parking pads are gravel; most pads are fairly level straight-ins; many are park-and-walk sites; tent spots are located on a grass-covered, rolling hill, but may be a bit slopey; fireplaces; b-y-o firewood; water at several faucets; restrooms with showers; holding tank disposal station near the entrance; gravel driveways; resident ranger-manager; adequate supplies and services are available in Republic.

SEASON & FEES: $6.00 for a standard site, $8.50 for a full-hookup site; 3 vehicle limit; open all year; 10 day limit.

NATURAL FEATURES: Curlew Lake is located in the rolling, grassy, tree-dotted hills of northeastern Washington; the park grounds are mown and watered; some small planted hardwoods provide limited shelter/shade; a few smaller walk-in sites in the annex along the beach have larger trees.

ATTRACTIONS: Boating; fishing; paved boat ramp and dock; sand and grass swimming beach; bath house; day use area with barbecue grills and tables; winter sports area.

NOTES: This excellent facility fills early on holidays and summer weekends. Try to arrange an off-season or midweek visit. You might consider scouting both the lakeside and main camping areas, since each has its own distinctive qualities.

SHERMAN PASS
Colville National Forest

LOCATION: Northeast Washington between Republic and Kettle Falls.

ACCESS: From Washington State Highway 20 at milepost 320 +.4 (17 miles east of Republic, 25 miles west of Kettle Falls) turn north onto a narrow gravel road; after 100 yards take the left fork and continue west a few yards into the campground.

FACILITIES: 9 sites; units are small and quite close together, although some separation is provided by trees and bushes; gravel straight-in or pull-along parking pads; additional leveling may be necessary; some secluded tent areas are squeezed in among the trees; fireplaces; firewood is usually available for gathering in the area; centrally located hand pump; vault facilities; gravel driveways; adequate supplies and services are available in Republic and Kettle Falls.

SEASON & FEES: No fee; May to October.

NATURAL FEATURES: Located in the Kettle River Range just 1 mile east of Sherman Pass at 5575'; the surrounding forest is fairly dense; moderately dense stands of conifers shelter the sites themselves; a pine-needle forest floor helps keep the dust down.

ATTRACTIONS: There are sweeping vistas through the trees from some of the sites, and even better, unobstructed views from the nearby picnic area and scenic viewpoint; Kettle Crest Trailhead is located just a few hundred yards west of the campground.

NOTES: This is a neat group of campsites perched on a hilltop above timbered ridges. Though the highway is quite near many of the sites, this is a great wayside for hikers and highway travelers. Can't ask for a better facility for the price!

CANYON CREEK
Colville National Forest

LOCATION: Northeast Washington between Republic and Kettle Falls.

ACCESS: From Washington State Highway 20 at milepost 334 +.3 (9 miles west of Kettle Falls, 31 miles east of Republic), turn south, and continue 0.2 mile (paved then gravel) to the campground.

FACILITIES: 12 sites; units are medium to large with very good separation; parking pads are gravel straight-ins, medium to long enough for good-sized rv's; some nice tent sites have been cleared and leveled; fireplaces; firewood is available for gathering in the area; water at a central hand pump; vault facilities; pack-it-in/pack-it-out trash removal system; gravel driveways; adequate supplies and services are available in Kettle Falls.

SEASON & FEES: No fee; May to October; 14 day limit.

NATURAL FEATURES: Located in a fairly dense forest at the base of Bangs Mountain; built on a bit of a hill, but the sites have been quite well-leveled considering the slope; Canyon Creek is a swiftly flowing small stream within a few hundred yards of the campsites; the Columbia River (and Franklin D. Roosevelt Lake) is 6 miles east.

ATTRACTIONS: Log Flume Interpretive Trail (H), 1 mile east off Highway 20; the starting point for the Bangs Mountain self-guiding auto tour is also at the Log Flume Trailhead; reportedly excellent fishing at Trout Lake, 5 miles north on a gravel road; Coulee Dam National Recreation Area, only a few miles to the east, has boat ramps and docks, fishing and swimming.

NOTES: This is a well-planned and nicely constructed campground with plenty of elbow room. It should seldom be crowded, and is a great buy for the money!

KETTLE RIVER
Coulee Dam National Recreation Area

LOCATION: Northeast Washington northwest of Kettle Falls.

ACCESS: From U.S. Highway 395 at milepost 247 +.9 (20 miles south of the Canadian border, 10 miles northwest of Kettle Falls), turn east, cross the RR tracks and take the left fork *down* the hill; continue 0.8 mile east on a gravel access road to the campground.

FACILITIES: 12 level sites; campsites are large but have virtually no separation; parking pads are gravel, straight-ins or pull-alongs, large enough to accomodate medium-sized rv's; some large, level tent sites on a pine needle forest floor; fireplaces; firewood is scarce, so b-y-o is recommended; water at a centrally located hand pump; vault facilities; gravel driveways; adequate supplies and services are available in Kettle Falls.

SEASON & FEES: No fee; open all year, subject to weather conditions in winter; 14 day limit.

NATURAL FEATURES: Located on a short grassy bluff overlooking the Kettle River; tall, light timber with virtually no underbrush; sparse grass; the campground is skirted by meadowland; distant mountain views from most sites.

ATTRACTIONS: Fishing in the Kettle River; boating on nearby Franklin D. Roosevelt Lake; a boat dock is located here, at Kettle River, but the nearest boat ramps are at the Kettle Falls and Marcus Island recreational sites.

NOTES: This is a nice stop, especially for Highway 395 travelers who prefer a campground not quite so close to the mainstream of the recreational area's traffic. Another nearby national recreation area campground, called Haag Cove, located on FDR Lake, has similar facilities, plus a boat ramp, but it tends to be more crowded. Haag Cove is south of here, off Washington State Highway 20 near milepost 338.

EVANS
Coulee Dam National Recreation Area

LOCATION: Northeast Washington north of Kettle Falls.

ACCESS: From Washington State Highway 25, at a point 10.2 miles north of Kettle Falls and 30 miles south of the U.S./Canada border, turn west at the "Evans Campground" entrance sign; the camping area is 0.1 mile from the highway.

FACILITIES: 56 sites; campsites are level and fairly close to each other; most units have short, paved, straight-in parking pads, some have pull-throughs; many good tent spots; fireplaces; b-y-o firewood; water at faucets throughout the campground; restrooms; cold (but free) showers at the restroom at the south end of the campground; holding tank disposal station at the entrance; paved driveways; campground manager; nearest supplies (gas and groceries) nearby on Highway 25; adequate supplies are available in Kettle Falls.

SEASON & FEES: $6.00; open all year, with limited facilities and no fee, October to May; 14 day limit.

NATURAL FEATURES: Located on an open grassy/sandy flat on the east shore of Franklin D. Roosevelt Lake (a major impoundment on the Columbia River); bordered by a small meadow; sparse pine in the campground, grass and pine covered hills and high ridges throughout this area; typically quite windy.

ATTRACTIONS: Amphitheater for scheduled ranger-naturalist programs; children's play area; boat ramp with trailer parking; fishing for a wide variety of freshwater species (trolling is reportedly the most productive method); designated buoyed swimming area with swim platform, no lifeguard; nice sandy beach.

NOTES: This very attractive, albeit well-used, campground affords tremendous views of the countryside. Definitely recommended.

MARCUS ISLAND
Coulee Dam National Recreation Area

LOCATION: Northeast Washington north of Kettle Falls.

ACCESS: From the intersection of Washington State Highways 20 and 25 at the west end of Kettle Falls, travel north on highway 25 for 5.6 miles to the Marcus Island Campground turnoff (signed); turn west onto a good paved road which leads 0.5 mile to the river level, doubles back around to the east 0.5 mile, then crosses a short causeway to the campground.

FACILITIES: 20 level sites; sites are small to medium in size, with minimal to good separation; most campsites have straight-in parking, a few have pull-throughs; all pads are paved; most sites have adequate space for tents; fireplaces; b-y-o firewood is recommended; water at a single hand pump; vault facilities; paved driveways; adequate supplies are available in Kettle Falls, 6 miles.

SEASON & FEES: $4.00; open all year, subject to weather conditions, with no fee October to May; 14 day limit.

NATURAL FEATURES: Located on a small island along the east shore of 150-mile-long Franklin D. Roosevelt Lake (part of the Columbia River system); all units are near the water's edge, and a few on the tip of a point offer sweeping views of the local landscape; campground vegetation consists of medium-dense moderately tall pine, plus tall grass; high grass and timber-covered mountains parallel the river; moderately dry climate.

ATTRACTIONS: Fishing for a variety of fresh water species including walleye, trout, salmon and sturgeon; trolling is probably the most effective means of taking fish; good boat launch and dock adjacent to the campground.

NOTES: This campground has been substantially improved in recent years, although it continues to provide more rustic camping than most of the others along the river. For that reason, it tends to be less popular (and less crowded) than nearby camping areas.

KETTLE FALLS
Coulee Dam National Recreation Area

LOCATION: Northeast Washington just west of Kettle Falls.

ACCESS: From Washington State Highway 20 at the east end of the Columbia River bridge 3 miles west of Kettle Falls, turn south onto a paved two-lane road which parallels the river; follow this road 1.8 miles to the ranger station and the campground. **ALTERNATE ACCESS:** If traveling on Washington State Highway 25, from a point 0.5 mile south of the intersection of Highways 20 and 25, turn west at a sign indicating "Recreation Area 3 Miles"; follow this paved road to the campground.

FACILITIES: 76 sites in three loops; most sites are of average size and quite level; parking pads are mostly small straight-ins, some are medium pull-throughs; excellent tent-pitching opportunities; fireplaces; firewood is a bit scarce in the immediate vicinity, so b-y-o is suggested; water at faucets throughout; restrooms with camper service sinks; holding tank disposal station near the ranger station; paved driveways; adequate supplies and services are available in Kettle Falls, 5 miles.

SEASON & FEES: $6.00; open all year, with limited facilities and no fee, October to May; 14 day limit.

NATURAL FEATURES: Located on a gently rolling flat along the east shore of Franklin D. Roosevelt Lake (actually the impounded Columbia River); campground vegetation consists of moderately dense timber with little ground-level vegetation except tall grass.

ATTRACTIONS: Super-nice picnic area with playground and swimming beach 0.2 mile south of the campground; fishing; marina nearby.

NOTES: This is an agreeably pleasant, sheltered campground. It's usually quite busy on mid-summer weekends, but definitely worth considering due to its good facilities and proximity to the community of Kettle Falls.

GIFFORD
Coulee Dam National Recreation Area

LOCATION: Northeast Washington south of Kettle Falls.

ACCESS: From Washington State Highway 25 at mile-post 56 +.4 (1.5 miles south of the hamlet of Gifford, 14 miles north of the community of Hunters), turn west onto a paved access road which leads 0.1 mile down to the campground.

FACILITIES: 42 sites; sites are average-sized with nominal separation; most units are suitable for tent or vehicle camping, but may require some additional leveling; gravel parking pads; a few walk-in sites are in a little cove at the south end of the grounds; fireplaces; very little firewood is available for gathering, so b-y-o is recommended; water at faucets; restrooms; holding tank disposal station; paved driveways; campground host; very limited supplies are available in Gifford.

SEASON & FEES: $6.00; open all year, with limited facilities and no fee, October to May; 14 day limit.

NATURAL FEATURES: Located on the east shore of Franklin D. Roosevelt Lake; most spots are right on the edge of the lake and/or have a lake view; fairly well sheltered, except for the spots closest to the lake shore; has a very "open" atmosphere; campground vegetation consists of medium height pine and tall grass with a thick carpet of pine needles; usually quite windy; lots of little coves and sandy beaches nearby.

ATTRACTIONS: Boat ramp; several floating docks; rock jetty; fishing for more than 30 species, including walleye (the number one game fish in the lake), rainbow trout, perch and kokanee.

NOTES: Camping here provides you with excellent views north and south along the lake. The walk-in sites are a couple of the nicest you'll find in this part of the state.

HUNTERS
Coulee Dam National Recreation Area

LOCATION: Northeast Washington south of Kettle Falls.

ACCESS: From Washington State Highway 25 at milepost 42 +.3 in the small community of Hunters (37 miles south of Kettle Falls, 42 miles north of Davenport), turn west at the "Hunters Campground" sign onto a paved access road; proceed 0.8 mile to the campground.

FACILITIES: 52 sites; sites are medium to large, with minimal separation; sites have been well leveled; some double-occupancy units; mostly pull-through gravel parking pads; adequate space for large tents; several walk-in sites on the beach; fireplaces; very little firewood is available for gathering, so b-y-o is recommended; water at central faucets; restrooms with naturally cool and refreshing showers; holding tank disposal station; paved driveways; ranger on duty during the summer; limited supplies in Hunters.

SEASON & FEES: $6.00; open all year, with limited facilities and no fee, October to May; 14 day limit.

NATURAL FEATURES: Located on the east shore of Franklin D. Roosevelt Lake, (part of the Columbia River system); moderately forested, with little undergrowth, within the campground; sandy beach; interesting, heavily eroded bluffs opposite the campground on the west shore of the lake; better-protected from the elements than other camping areas near here.

ATTRACTIONS: Boat ramp; floating docks; rock jetty; fishing; swimming; picnic area with barbecue grills; children's playground; Hunters community fair held annually in late August.

NOTES: This is terrific country around here! In summer, its colors are rich green and gold and blue and brown. All sites have some sort of a lake view, and many are on or near the lake shore. The walk-in sites, in particular, have a super view.

FORT SPOKANE
Coulee Dam National Recreation Area

LOCATION: Northeast Washington north of Davenport.

ACCESS: From Washington State Highway 25 at milepost 23 +.1 (23 miles north of Davenport, 19 miles south of Hunters), turn east into the campground.

FACILITIES: 62 level sites in several large loops; virtually all spots are quite spacious, with minimal separation; paved pull-through parking pads; most sites are equally well suited for tent or vehicle camping; quite a few double-occupancy units; fireplaces; b-y-o firewood; water at faucets throughout; restrooms; holding tank disposal station just inside the entrance; paved driveways; limited supplies in Hunters; adequate supplies and services are available in Davenport.

SEASON & FEES: $6.00; open all year, with limited facilities and no fee, October to May; 14 day limit.

NATURAL FEATURES: Located at the confluence of the Columbia and Spokane Rivers, (the Spokane River is within easy walking distance of the campground); light to moderately dense very tall pine in the campground; ground cover consists of some shrubbery, but mostly pine needles and grass.

ATTRACTIONS: Visitor center and ranger station 0.2 mile south of the campground; self guiding tours around the well-maintained remnants of Fort Spokane; amphitheater on the bank of the Spokane River at the north side of the campground for planned ranger-naturalist programs; fishing; boat launch.

NOTES: Fort Spokane is a very popular place, but is it *nice!* There's a pleasant open-air feeling here. They really did a good job on this park. It's definitely filled on holiday weekends. The drive down Highway 25 from the north passes through some of the most impressive scenery in this sparsely settled region.

SPRING CANYON
Coulee Dam National Recreation Area

LOCATION: North-central Washington east of Grand Coulee.

ACCESS: From Washington State Highway 174 at milepost 24 +.2 (3 miles east of Grand Coulee, 20 miles west of Wilbur), turn north onto a paved access road; continue 1.2 miles and turn west (left) into the campground.

FACILITIES: 78 sites, including 66 for trailers; parking spaces in the trailer area are pull-alongs in a level, paved parking lot; a few sunshades are provided for trailer spaces; tent sites have small to medium gravel parking pads and large tent spaces, which may need some additional leveling; fire rings; b-y-o firewood is suggested; water at several faucet-fountains; restrooms; holding tank disposal station; paved driveways; adequate supplies are available in Grand Coulee.

SEASON & FEES: $6.00 for a site; Memorial Day to Labor Day; 14 day limit.

NATURAL FEATURES: Located on a sage and grass slope overlooking Franklin D. Roosevelt Lake; some mown grass areas with planted hardwoods for shade; the lower loop has nice tent areas on a natural grass hillside; typically breezy.

ATTRACTIONS: Within view of Grand Coulee Dam; Bunchgrass Nature Trail; interpretive programs scheduled during the summer; children's playground; swimming beach; boat ramp and dock nearby; boating, fishing and waterskiing; visitor center at Grand Coulee Dam has auto tour information.

NOTES: Franklin D. Roosevelt Lake was created by Coulee Dam across the Columbia River. This camping area provides a great view of the lake, the dam and the surrounding countryside. All things considered, Spring Canyon is one of the nicest campgrounds in semi-arid central Washington.

304

STEAMBOAT ROCK
State Park

LOCATION: Northeast Washington south of Coulee Dam.

ACCESS: From Washington State Highway 155 at a point 8 miles south of Coulee Dam and 20 miles north of Coulee City, turn west onto a paved park access road; continue west 2 miles to the campground.

FACILITIES: 100 full-hookup sites in 2 loops, 0.5 mile apart; sites are level and of average size with very little separation; parking pads are paved and most can accomodate very large vehicles; sand or grass surface for tents; fireplaces; b-y-o firewood is recommended; restrooms with showers; paved driveways; resident manager; limited supplies from a concessionaire in the park; adequate supplies and services are available in Grand Coulee.

SEASON & FEES: $8.50 for a site (no sites are available without hookups), $2.00 for an extra vehicle; open all year, with limited facilities in winter; 10 day limit.

NATURAL FEATURES: Located near the shore of Banks Lake which was formed by Dry Falls Dam across the Columbia River; lush grass and a few small trees planted in the camping area; dry rocky bluffs flank the lake east and west; Steamboat Rock is a prominent landmark.

ATTRACTIONS: Boat launch; fishing; swimming; waterskiing; windsurfing; nature trail; biking and jogging paths; horse rentals in nearby Northup Canyon; winter sports area; Grand Coulee Dam Visitor Center located 10 miles north.

NOTES: Steamboat Rock State Park offers fine, more-developed camping facilities in a very distinctive setting. Most sites have views of a bay on Banks Lake and of the rocky bluffs which the campground and lake are nestled between.

Beautiful park & campground. Interesting rocky bluffs. Nice sandy swimming area. Level for bicycling. No TV reception.

305

SUN LAKES
State Park

LOCATION: Central Washington southwest of Coulee City.

ACCESS: From Washington State Highway 17 at a point 17 miles north of Soap Lake and 4 miles south of the intersection of U.S. 2 and Highway 17, turn east at the well-signed entrance to the park; follow a winding, paved access road 1.0 mile (past a private campground) to the public campground entrance; turn left into the campground.

FACILITIES: 100 sites, including 18 sites with full hookups; sites are level and quite close together; most parking pads are small or medium pull-alongs; large level tent spaces; fireplaces; b-y-o firewood is recommended; water at several faucets; restrooms with showers; holding tank disposal station; paved driveways; camper supplies at a small store nearby; adequate supplies and services are avalable in Coulee City, 5 miles north.

SEASON & FEES: $6.00 for a standard site, $8.50 for a full-hookup site; open all year, with limited facilities in winter; 10 day limit.

NATURAL FEATURES: Located on a small, open, grassy flat at the base of steep, rocky canyon walls deep in Grand Coulee of the Columbia River; a few shade trees along the perimeter of the camping area; Blue Lake, Park Lake, Deep Lake and other smaller lakes are nearby.

ATTRACTIONS: Boating; fishing; swimming at a protected cove on a lake across the road from the campground; golf course, boat and horse rentals nearby; playground; nature trails; Dry Falls Interpretive Center.

NOTES: The camping area is nicely situated considerably below the main highway, so traffic noise is at a minimum. This oasis offers a welcome change from central Washington's typically dry and barren landscape.

MILLPOND
Colville National Forest

LOCATION: Northeast corner of Washington northeast of Metaline Falls.

ACCESS: From Washington State Highway 31 at milepost 16 +.4 (2 miles north of Metaline Falls, 11 miles south of the Canadian border), turn east onto Sullivan Lake Road (Forest Road 9345); continue east, then south for 3.7 miles; turn southwest onto a gravel access road leading 0.2 mile down into the campground.

FACILITIES: 11 level sites; campsites are average-sized and have good separation; parking pads are medium-sized, gravel straight-ins; some large, level tent spots; fireplaces; firewood is available for gathering in the area; water at a single hand pump; vault facilities; gravel driveways; limited supplies and services are available in Metaline Falls, 5 miles west.

SEASON & FEES: $5.00; May to October; 14 day limit.

NATURAL FEATURES: Located in a heavily forested creek valley with a small pond near the west end of the campground; considerable vegetation provides excellent separation between most of the sites; tall forested peaks surround the immediate area; Sullivan Lake, a 3.5 mile long glacially-formed lake, is situated a few miles south.

ATTRACTIONS: Hand-launch boat area; nearby Sullivan Lake has a launch for larger boats; sand and grass beach; several foot trails in the area; Crawford State Park's limestone cave, located south of Metaline Falls on Highway 31, is available for tours during the summer months.

NOTES: This is a small, basic, but really neat campground, located toward the northern edge of the popular Sullivan Lake Recreation Area.

SULLIVAN LAKE
Colville National Forest

LOCATION: Northeast corner of Washington northeast of Metaline Falls.

ACCESS: From Washington State Highway 31 at milepost 16 +.4 (2 miles north of Metaline Falls, 11 miles south of the Canadian border) turn east onto Sullivan Lake Road (Forest Road 9345); continue east, then south for 4.7 miles; turn east (left) onto Forest Road 22; continue 0.4 mile and turn south (right) onto a gravel access road; continue 0.3 mile to the campground entrance.

FACILITIES: 41 sites in 2 sections; sites are fairly good-sized with reasonable separation; parking pads are level, gravel straight-ins, spacious enough for medium to large rv's; many large, level spots for tents; fireplaces; firewood is available for gathering in the area; water at several faucets; vault facilities; holding tank disposal station; gravel driveway; limited supplies and services are available in Metaline Falls.

SEASON & FEES: $6.00 for a standard site, $8.00 for a "preferred" site; May to October; 14 day limit.

NATURAL FEATURES: Located along the north shore of Sullivan Lake, a glacially formed lake, 3.5 miles long and up to 275' deep; tall cedars are the predominant vegetation; the campsites are fairly well-cleared of underbrush.

ATTRACTIONS: Boating; fishing; swimming; a grass airstrip makes "fly-in" camping possible; a foot trail leads south around the lake for 4.1 miles to Noisy Creek Campground; benches along the shore line and a Sullivan Lake Viewpoint provide lake-watching opportunities.

NOTES: The relaxed atmosphere of this campground is due in part to its distance from population concentrations. The sight of this alluring mountain lake surrounded by pristine forested hills is, in itself, worth the trip.

NOISY CREEK
Colville National Forest

LOCATION: Northeast corner of Washington northeast of Ione.

ACCESS: From Washington State Highway 31 at milepost 3 +.1 (at the south edge of the town of Ione) turn east onto Elizabeth Street (which becomes Sullivan Lake Road and Forest Road 9345); continue east and north for 8.2 miles (paved); turn east (right) and continue 0.1 mile (gravel) to a fork in the road; take the left fork; continue 0.3 mile to the campground.

FACILITIES: 22 sites in 2 tiered loops; sites are small to average in size and fairly private; parking pads are gravel and may require additional leveling; some sites are designated for tents or small vehicles; a few of the larger parking pads are somewhat further from the lakeshore; tent spots are mostly small and slopey; fireplaces; firewood is available for gathering; water at several faucets; vault facilities; narrow, one-way, gravel driveway; limited supplies and services are available in Ione.

SEASON & FEES: $6.00 for a standard site, $8.00 for a "preferred" (lakeside) site; May to October; 14 day limit.

NATURAL FEATURES: Located on the south shore of glacially formed Sullivan Lake; Noisy Creek tumbles past many of the sites on its way toward the lake; moderately dense forest has tall cedars, hardwoods, and very little underbrush; the entire area is surrounded by towering, forested peaks.

ATTRACTIONS: Fishing; swimming; beach; boat launch; a foot trail leads north around the lake for 4.1 miles to Sullivan Lake Campground.

NOTES: This campground, on the shores of a beautiful mountain lake, is quite a popular place. Edgewater Campground is a nearby alternative. It's located on the east bank of the Pend Orielle River, just 2 miles north of Ione. It has no fee, reduced services and nice sites for the price.

EDGEWATER
Colville National Forest

LOCATION: Northeast corner of Washington northeast of Ione.

ACCESS: From Washington State Highway 31 at milepost 3 +.1 (at the south edge of the community of Ione), turn east onto Elizabeth Street (which becomes Sullivan Lake Road); continue 0.5 mile east over the Pend Orielle River bridge; turn north (left) onto Forest Road 3669 (gravel) and proceed 2 miles; turn west (left) onto a gravel access road and continue 0.5 mile to the campground.

FACILITIES: 23 level sites; sites are medium to large and have good separation; parking pads are gravel/grass straight-ins, long enough for medium to large rv's; large, level tent spots; fireplaces; some firewood is available for gathering in the area; water at faucets; pack-it-in/pack-it-out trash removal system; vault facilities; rough gravel driveway; limited supplies and services are available in Ione.

SEASON & FEES: No fee, due to "reduced services"; 14 day limit.

NATURAL FEATURES: Located on the east bank of the Pend Orielle River; sites are on a flat above the river's level in a fairly dense forest; access is through private farmland; campground elevation is 2100'; the Selkirk Mountains rise to altitudes above 6000' to the east.

ATTRACTIONS: Fishing; cement boat ramp, not always accessible due to fluctuations in the river level; Box Canyon Dam spans the river just to the north.

NOTES: The campground has some pretty nice sites, and is easily accessible from a main highway and a small community. It appears this facility is only rarely used to its full potential.

LAKE GILLETTE
Colville National Forest

LOCATION: Northeast Washington east of Colville.

ACCESS: From Washington State Highway 20 at milepost 379 +.1 (25 miles east of Colville, 11 miles west of Tiger), turn east at the "Lake Thomas/Lake Gillette" sign; follow a paved road 0.5 mile; the "Beach Unit" is on the north (left) side of the access road and the main unit of the campground is 100 yards farther on the south side (note that Highway 20 follows a north-south line in this section).

FACILITIES: 30 level sites in the main campground, plus 10 in the "Beach Unit"; sites are fairly large and well spaced; level, gravel parking pads; some sites can accomodate large rv's; excellent tent spaces; most sites have fireplaces and barbecue grills; firewood is available for gathering in the vicinity; water at several faucet-fountains; restroom (H) plus auxiliary vaults; holding tank disposal station at the main campground; central kitchen shelter; paved driveways; campground host; nearest reliable source of adequate supplies is in Colville.

SEASON & FEES: $6.00 for a standard site, $7.00 for a "preferred" site, $10.00 for several multiple-family units; May to October; 14 day limit.

NATURAL FEATURES: Located on the southeast corner of Lake Gillette, but the lake itself is not visible from most of the campsites; tall thin pine, waist level grass and a thick carpet of pine needles in the campground.

ATTRACTIONS: "Springboard" and "Rufus" self guided nature trails lead off from the east end of the main camping area; sand and gravel beach; paved boat launch and floating dock; fishing.

NOTES: The main section of Lake Gillette campground is considered by many to be the best of the three camping areas in this vicinity, although it is a little busier and less private than the "Beach Unit" or nearby Lake Thomas.

LAKE THOMAS
Colville National Forest

LOCATION: Northeast Washington east of Colville.

ACCESS: From Washington State Highway 20 at milepost 379 +.1 (25 miles east of Colville, 11 miles west of Tiger), turn east at the "Lake Thomas/Lake Gillette" sign onto a paved road; drive 0.5 mile to Lake Gillette Campground, and continue east/northeast another 0.7 mile to Lake Thomas Campground (note that Highway 20 follows a north-south line in this section).

FACILITIES: 15 sites; sites are moderately close together, with low-level brush for some visual separation; small, paved parking aprons; not recommended for trailers but suitable for smaller camping vehicles; many units have large, level, framed and gravelled tent pads; several walk-in tent spots; all sites have fireplaces, some also have barbecue grills; firewood is available for gathering in the vicinity; water at faucet-fountains throughout; vault facilities; narrow, paved, one-way driveway; nearest reliable source of adequate supplies is in Colville.

SEASON & FEES: $5.00 (one vehicle per unit); May to October; 14 day limit.

NATURAL FEATURES: Located on a somewhat steep hillside amid dense, mature pine mixed with some second growth and low brush; the campground is surrounded by moderately tall, heavily-timbered mountains; Lake Thomas is the largest of several lakes in the vicinity.

ATTRACTIONS: Fishing; boating; hiking trails in the area.

NOTES: A number of campsites have good views of the lake, since the campground is located along the south shore. Lake Thomas Campground is markedly different from nearby Lake Gillette Campground (see separate description). There are a number of other small public campgrounds in this region, but Lake Gillette and Lake Thomas are the most accessible.

312

PIONEER PARK
Colville National Forest

LOCATION: Northeast Washington east of Newport.

ACCESS: From U.S. 2 at the east end of the Pend Oreille River Bridge at the Washington-Idaho border (1 mile east of Newport, Washington, 6 miles west of Priest River, Idaho), turn north onto a paved road at the "Pioneer Park Campground" sign; proceed north 2.3 miles to the campground entrance on the west side of the road.

FACILITIES: 14 sites; campsites are quite large and well separated; small to medium, paved/gravel, straight-in parking pads; the campground is a little hilly, but is still suitable for tents, or rv's with some additional leveling; fireplaces; some firewood is available for collecting nearby; water at faucet-fountains; simple vault facilities (H); paved/oiled gravel driveways; campground host; fairly complete supplies and services are available in Newport.

SEASON & FEES: $6.00 for a single vehicle, $8.50 for two vehicles; May to October; 14 day limit.

NATURAL FEATURES: Located on the moderately forested, east bank of the wide, deep Pend Oreille (pronounced Pond-O-Ray) River; this region is generally mountainous, quite densely forested and sparsely populated.

ATTRACTIONS: Trails from the campground to the river; fishing; boat launch (gravel with concrete traction strips).

NOTES: One of the appeals of Pioneer Park is its proximity to the services available in Newport. The campground appears to be in Idaho, but it is actually just inside the Washington State line, although there is no formal indication of that fact along the access road.

RIVERSIDE
State Park

LOCATION: Eastern Washington in Spokane.

ACCESS: From Interstate 90 exit 280A at the west end of Spokane, turn north onto Walnut Street, then cross the Maple Toll Bridge onto Maxwell; drive 1.4 miles north; turn west (left) onto Pettet Drive (watch for a park sign here); follow the river 2.5 miles to a fork in the road; take the left fork 2 miles farther, then turn left into the campground.

FACILITIES: 100 sites; most sites are smaller than average and fairly close together; gravel parking pads, mostly average-sized straight-ins; small to medium-sized, level tent spots; fire rings; b-y-o firewood is suggested; water at several faucet-fountains; restrooms with coin showers; community kitchen shelter; paved driveway; complete supplies and services are available in Spokane, 3 miles south.

SEASON & FEES: $6.00 for a site, $2.00 for an extra vehicle; open all year, with limited facilities in winter; 10 day limit.

NATURAL FEATURES: Located on the east bank of the Spokane River; tall conifers and very little underbrush between sites; a timbered hillside flanks the campsites to the east; a lava formation, called "Bowl and Pitcher", is located nearby in the Spokane River.

ATTRACTIONS: Interpretive center; self-guiding nature trail; trails for orv enthusiasts and equestrians; horses for rent near the park; boating and fishing in the river.

NOTES: Riverside Park is unusual because it is an urban park. If weather conditions are right, it can be very pleasant; but a breeze up from the city can sometimes bring local industries', er, fragrance, with it. Since it's so close to Spokane, the campground fills quickly, and early arrival in summer is recommended.

PALOUSE FALLS
State Park

LOCATION: Southeast Washington north of Walla Walla.

ACCESS: From Washington State Highway 261 at milepost 20 +.6 (15 miles south of Washtucna, 21 miles north of the intersection of Highway 261 with U.S. 12), turn east onto a fairly good, wide, gravel road and proceed 2.4 miles to the park entrance.

FACILITIES: 6 sites; tents may be pitched on the grass, vehicle campers can park in the main gravel parking area; fireplaces; b-y-o firewood; water at faucets and fountains; vault facilities; pack-it-in/pack-it-out system of trash removal; adjacent picnic ground has a kitchen shelter and barbecue grills; limited supplies are available at Washtucna, 15 miles north.

SEASON & FEES: $4.50 for a site, $2.00 for an extra vehicle; open all year, subject to weather conditions; 10 day limit.

NATURAL FEATURES: Located on a small mowed grass hill above the rugged Palouse River Canyon; picturesque Palouse Falls drops 190 feet into a deep pool on the opposite side of the canyon from the park; sage and range grass hills comprise most of the surrounding semi-arid terrain; shade trees in the campground and day use area.

ATTRACTIONS: Falls and canyon viewpoints.

NOTES: From here there are terrific views of Palouse Falls as well as the main part of Palouse Canyon to the south. This is a pleasant little spot which doesn't see a lot of camping activity. It's a popular place for weekend day-trippers, but access is closed to non-campers after dark. You may, however, want to consider staying at Lyons Ferry State Park, which has better facilities, 5 miles south.

LYONS FERRY
State Park

LOCATION: Southeast Washington north of Walla Walla.

ACCESS: From Washington State Highway 261 at milepost 15 +.4 (15 miles north of the intersection of Highway 261 and U.S. 12, 15 miles south of the intersection of Highways 261 and 260 near Washtucna), turn east into the state park, pass through the day use area, then turn westerly under the highway bridge into the campground.

FACILITIES: 52 sites; mostly level, straight-in, gravel parking pads, along with a number of very large pull-throughs; adequate space for large tents in most sites; fireplaces; b-y-o firewood; water at faucets throughout the campground; restroom with hot showers; holding tank disposal station near the day use area; paved roadways; resident ranger-manager; limited supplies at a marina across the river.

SEASON & FEES: $6.00 for a site, $2.00 for an extra vehicle; open all year; 10 day limit.

NATURAL FEATURES: Located on a small sage flat in a canyon at the confluence of the Palouse and Snake Rivers; high dry bluffs and buttes all around; trees marginally shade some of the sites, but the campground is basically as austere as the surrounding countryside.

ATTRACTIONS: Boating and fishing are the main attractions; there's a terrific shaded day use area in the park, with a large grass beach; bouyed designated swimming area, no lifeguard; paved boat launch with docking facilities.

NOTES: This is rugged, sparsely populated country around here, but nonetheless very interesting in its semi-desolation. The beautifully landscaped and maintained day use area and its facilities are excellent. And the park *usually* isn't very crowded.

Train woke us up in middle of night. It went by on a high trestle, very noisy.

316

CENTRAL FERRY
State Park

LOCATION: Southeast Washington northeast of Walla Walla.

ACCESS: From Washington State Highway 127 at a point 10 miles north of the intersection of Highway 127 and U.S. 12, 17 miles south of the intersection of Highway 127 and State Route 26, turn west (immediately north of the Snake River Bridge) onto a paved access road; continue west for 0.8 mile to the campground.

FACILITIES: 60 level sites, all with full hookups, in 6 loops; parking pads are paved, medium to long straight-ins, spacious enough for very large rv's; great tent areas on the lawn; fireplaces; b-y-o firewood is recommended; water at each site plus central faucets; restrooms with showers; holding tank disposal station at the entrance; minimal supplies at a small store, 3 miles south; complete supplies and services are available in Clarkston, 50 miles east.

SEASON & FEES: $8.00; open all year; 10 day limit.

NATURAL FEATURES: Located on the north shore of the Snake River, where Little Goose Dam forms 10,000-acre Lake Bryan; tall bluffs border the park on the south side; mown lawns and planted trees provide a landscaped city park-type setting; along the river to the east are a number of geologic formations.

ATTRACTIONS: Swimming; waterskiing; beachcombing and boating on Lake Bryan; hiking; birdwatching; hunting and exploring along the Snake River Canyon.

NOTES: At Central Ferry, windbreaks have been built to somewhat protect campers from the westerly winds which commonly blast through the canyon. The park is an oasis on the southeastern Washington plains. The nice sandy beach and boat moorage facilities are a bonus.

HOOD
Corps of Engineers Park

LOCATION: Southeast Washington south of Pasco.

ACCESS: From Washington State Highway 124 at a point 0.2 mile east of the intersection of Highway 124 and U.S. 12/395 (3 miles south of Pasco, 18 miles north of the Oregon border), turn north into the park; continue 0.3 mile on a paved access road to the campground.

FACILITIES: 69 sites, all with partial hookups; sites are average to large, with minimal to average separation; parking pads are paved, medium to long, and most are fairly level; good, grassy tent spots; barbecue grills or fireplaces; b-y-o firewood; restrooms with showers; holding tank disposal station near the entrance; paved driveways; resident manager; complete supplies and services are available in the Tri-Cities area (Richland-Pasco-Kennewick).

SEASON & FEES: $8.50; April to October; 14 day limit.

NATURAL FEATURES: Located just east of McNary Dam which spans the Snake River before its confluence with the Columbia River; the camping area is mostly open, on a low, grassy hill dotted with a few planted trees; sites overlook Wallula Lake (formed by McNary Dam) and the dry bluffs across the lake.

ATTRACTIONS: Foot trails; playground in the camping area; an adjacent day use area, on a level sheltered riverbank, has picnic shelters, barbecue grills, playground, boat ramp and swimming beach; interpretive center at nearby Sacajawea State Park; Juniper Dunes Wilderness Area is located 10 miles north off Highway 395.

NOTES: Hood Park offers an amiable camping facility very close to the Tri-Cities urban area. The vegetation in this camping area is more mature than in Charbonneau Park, another Corps of Engineers facility east of here. It provides Hood Park with a somewhat more sheltered environment.

CHARBONNEAU
Corps of Engineers Park

LOCATION: Southeast Washington east of Pasco.

ACCESS: From Washington State Highway 124 at milepost 8 +.5 (10 miles west of Pasco, 38 miles east of Waitsburg), turn north onto Sun Harbor Drive; drive 1.7 miles north to the park entrance; take the right fork 0.5 mile to the camping area.

FACILITIES: 54 sites, all with electricity; 18 sites have full hookups; parking pads are fairly level, paved, some are long enough for large rv's; grassy tent areas, many on a slight slope; fireplaces; b-y-o firewood; gravel table pads; water at several hydrants; restrooms with showers; holding tank disposal station near the entrance; paved driveways; limited supplies at a nearby marina, complete supplies and services are available in the Tri-Cities area (Richland-Pasco-Kennewick).

SEASON & FEES: $8.50 for a partial-hookup site; $9.50 for a full-hookup site; open all year, with limited facilities November to March; 14 day limit.

NATURAL FEATURES: Located just east of Ice Harbor Dam which forms Sacajawea Lake on the Snake River; campsites are all on a hilltop overlooking the Snake River and a natural jetty which protrudes into the river; a few trees have been planted on a manicured lawn, but the camping area is still quite exposed to sun and wind; most sites have views of the lake and bluffs on the opposite shore.

ATTRACTIONS: Boating; fishing; swimming; large day use area, adjacent, with tall hardwoods and picnic shelters; playground; Ice Harbor Dam Visitor Center is located 2 miles west.

NOTES: This recently constructed campground, situated on a breezy hill overlooking the Snake River, offers vast views of the countryside in all directions.

FISHHOOK
Corps of Engineers Park

LOCATION: Southeast Washington east of Pasco.

ACCESS: From Washington State Highway 124 at milepost 16 (18 miles east of Pasco, 30 miles west of Waitsburg), turn north onto Page Road; drive 4.5 miles on a paved road (past the park entrance and day use area) to the campground.

FACILITIES: 76 sites in one long loop on a hillside; parking pads are paved and well leveled, considering the terrain; pads are generally medium-sized, but some are large enough for very large rv's; 8 pads are pull-throughs, others are straight-ins; barbecue grills and/or fireplaces at each site; b-y-o firewood; water at centrally located faucets; restrooms with showers; holding tank disposal station near the entrance; paved driveways; complete supplies and services are available in the Tri-Cities area (Richland-Pasco-Kennewick).

SEASON & FEES: $7.00; April to September; 14 day limit.

NATURAL FEATURES: Located on a grassy hillside on the shore of Sacajawea Lake above Ice Harbor Dam which spans the Snake River; park lawns are watered and mown, and dotted with large hardwoods and conifers; rolling sage-covered hillsides surround the park; dry bluffs border the river.

ATTRACTIONS: Boating; fishing; swimming; large day use area with beach, picnic facilities and children's playground; hiking in adjacent wildlife habitat.

NOTES: A railroad line runs along the west edge of the park so be prepared for possible periodic disturbances. Ice Harbor Dam and subsequent irrigation projects have created a welcome sanctuary here at Fishhook Park. The grassy hillsides, manicured lawns, boat launch and swimming beach stand in distinct contrast to the surrounding sage-and-orchard covered slopes.

FORT WALLA WALLA
Walla Walla City Park

LOCATION: South central Washington in the city of Walla Walla.

ACCESS: From Washington State Highway 125 at the southwest corner of Walla Walla (on the west side of the highway opposite the fairgrounds and the Plaza Shopping Center), turn west onto Dalles-Military Road (also called just "Military Road"); continue west/southwest 0.8 mile to the park. (You can't miss it--a pair of large cannons flank the entrance!)

FACILITIES: Approximately 30 level sites, some with partial hookups; sites are generally medium-sized with very little separation; parking pads are level and most are spacious enough to accomodate larger vehicles; lots of large, grassy tent-pitching spots; fire rings; b-y-o firewood; water at faucets in several locations; restrooms with showers; holding tank disposal station; gravel driveways; soft drink, ice machines and public telephone at the office; complete supplies and services are available in Walla Walla.

SEASON & FEES: $6.50 for a standard site, $8.00 for a partial-hookup site; more than 4 people per site, 50 cents each; 7 day limit.

NATURAL FEATURES: Located on watered and mown grass lawns ringed by tall hardwoods; a little creek separates the campground and a day use area; rv sites have considerably less shelter/shade than tent units.

ATTRACTIONS: Old Fort Walla Walla Museum, just to the north of the campground, can be reached via a foot bridge across the creek; county fair held in late August.

NOTES: This is a nicely landscaped and maintained park, somewhat superior to many other municipal campgrounds. Its proximity to all the services of Walla Walla may be considered an advantage by many campers.

LEWIS AND CLARK TRAIL
State Park

LOCATION: Southeast Washington north of Walla Walla.

ACCESS: From U.S. 12 at a point 5.2 miles west of Dayton and 4.4 miles east of Waitsburg, turn north into the campground entrance (on the opposite side of the highway from the day use area).

FACILITIES: 34 sites; some units are very spacious, most are small to medium sized; most sites are also well spaced and very private; group camp on the east side of the grounds; most sites are level, with medium-length dirt parking pads; fireplaces; small quantities of firewood are available for gathering nearby, b-y-o is suggested; water at faucets and fountains throughout the campground; restroom with showers; holding tank disposal station near the entrance; paved roadways; resident ranger-manager; limited supplies and services are available in Dayton and Waitsburg.

SEASON & FEES: $6.00 for a site, $2.00 for an extra vehicle; open all year, with limited facilities October to April; 10 day limit.

NATURAL FEATURES: Located on 37 heavily wooded acres on the south bank of the Touchet River, surrounded by rolling farmland and dry bunchgrass prairie; many sites are tucked into their own little alcoves of cottonwoods, ponderosa pines and lots of underbrush.

ATTRACTIONS: Self-guiding three-quarter mile nature trail with the theme "Food, Fuel and Medicine", plus other hiking trails; amphitheater for summer campfire programs; nice day use area with ball field and kitchen shelters.

NOTES: This park was named for the Lewis and Clark Expedition which travelled through this valley in May of 1806. The setting for this facility is really a surprise, considering the comparatively barren hillsides of the surrounding terrain. The dense vegetation here may remind you of parks much closer to the coast.

CHIEF TIMOTHY
State Park

LOCATION: Southeast corner of Washington west of Clarkston.

ACCESS: From U.S. 12 at milepost 425 +.9 (8 miles west of Clarkston, 21 miles east of Pomeroy), turn north, proceed across the causeway onto an island on which the park is located. (If you're coming from the east, be watchful--the highway signs are a bit confusing.)

FACILITIES: 66 sites, including 33 with full hookups; sites are average-sized with minimal separation; most pads are level, paved pull-throughs; excellent grassy tent sites; fireplaces; firewood is usually for sale, or b-y-o; water at faucets and fountains; restrooms with showers; paved driveways; concessionaire (food, drinks, camping supplies) with limited hours during the summer; complete supplies and services are available in the Lewiston-Clarkston area.

SEASON & FEES: $6.00 for a standard site, $8.50 for a full-hookup site, $2.00 for an extra vehicle; open all year, with limited facilities October to April; 10 day limit.

NATURAL FEATURES: Located on what once was a barren island in the Snake River; planted pine and hardwoods; watered and mowed lawns; considering the local terrain, there is a surprising amount of shelter/shade here, although the hookup units have less than the other camp spots; in summer, the park stands in rich green contrast to the rocky, barren Snake River Canyon.

ATTRACTIONS: Alpowai Interpretive Center with limited afternoon hours; really nice children's play area; pebble and sand swimming beach; paved boat ramp; several docks are located on the edge of the campground, so you can tie-up to within arm's length of your campsite.

NOTES: The campground stretches for nearly a half mile along the south shore of the island. All sites have quite a spectacular view. Wow, what an oasis!

FIELDS SPRING
State Park

LOCATION: Southeast corner of Washington south of Clarkston.

ACCESS: From Washington State Highway 129 at milepost 14 (26 miles south of Clarkston, 56 miles north of Enterprise, Oregon), turn east onto the paved park access road, and continue 0.6 mile to the campground.

FACILITIES: 20 sites; sites are average-sized with minimal separation; parking pads are fairly level, gravel, mostly straight-ins, with several long pull-throughs; probably a little more suitable for vehicle camping than for tents; fireplaces; some firewood is available for gathering near the park; water at faucets; restrooms with showers; holding tank disposal station; paved driveways; limited supplies in Anatone, 3.5 miles north; complete supplies and services are available in the Lewiston-Clarkston area, 26 miles north.

SEASON & FEES: $6.00 for a site, $2.00 for an extra vehicle; open all year, with limited facilities October to April; 10 day limit.

NATURAL FEATURES: Located on a lightly timbered hillside; about one-half of the camp spots are somewhat sheltered/shaded, the remainder are in the open; moderately to heavily forested low mountains and ridges in the surrounding area; more precipitation here than elsewhere in the vicinity; elevation 3900'; 0.5 mile south of Rattlesnake Summit.

ATTRACTIONS: Self-guiding nature trail; small children's play set and enclosed shelter in the day use area.

NOTES: This is a case where it's not so much the campground but the setting that's the primary attraction. There is a breathtaking (quite literally) steep, winding, 10 mile drive through a deep canyon on State Highway 129 just south of the park. If you approach from that direction, allow plenty of time for the trip.

RESERVATION PROCEDURES

Campsite reservations may be made at a number of state park campgrounds in this region. Availability, time requirements, and fees vary considerably from state to state and park to park. As a rule, reservations are obtained by mail at least several weeks in advance. For specific details, we suggest you contact the individual park you're considering.

For general information about reservations, these offices should be helpful:

Idaho
Idaho Department of Parks and Recreation
Boise, Idaho 83720
(208) 334-2154

Oregon
Oregon State Parks Campsite Information Center
(503) 238-7488 (March to Labor Day)

Oregon State Parks and Recreation Division
Salem, Oregon 97310
(503) 378-6305

Washington
Washington State Parks Campsite Information
1-800-562-0990 (from within Washington State only, summer only)

Washington State Parks and Recreation Commission
Olympia, Washington 98504
(206) 753-5755

INDEX

IDAHO

A FEW TECHNICAL DETAILS

In their most elementary forms, outdoor recreation in general, and camping in particular, require very little in the way of highly specialized or sophisticated equipment. A stout knife, some matches and a sleeping bag will get you started on the way to a lifetime of experiences.

To bring you this series, however, took the utilization of some of the most refined equipment and methods that are available to the small publisher today.

To preserve timeliness and accuracy, fully 99 percent of the information presented was gathered *first hand* in a relatively few short months prior to publication, using modern miracles of the mind like data-recording cameras, microcassette recorders, and battery-powered computers.

Design and production were completed virtually entirely in-house.

Copy was written using IBM AT, AT&T 6300, Tandy 100 and Zenith Z-181 computers.

Preliminary cover design was accomplished using computer graphics techniques.

Page composition/typesetting was performed using custom-developed software, with output through Hewlett-Packard LaserJet and LaserJet Plus printers.

Printing was done by Publisher's Press, Salt Lake City, UT.

The information, therefore, has been gathered, stored and presented using five distinct media: holographic, audio-magnetic, visual, digital-magnetic, and print.

Discovery Publishing maintains the world's largest, most complete data base dedicated to the public campgrounds of western North America.

NOTES

332

ORDER FORM

To: *Double Eagle Guides*
Discovery Publishing
P.O. Box 50545
Billings, MT 59105-0545

Please send the following volumes of <u>The Double Eagle Guide to Western Public Campgrounds</u> series:

<u>Quantity</u>

___Volume I *** Pacific Northwest *** Idaho/Oregon/Washington

___Volume II *** Rocky Mountains *** Colorado/Montana/Wyoming

___Volume III *** Far West *** California/Nevada

___Volume IV *** Southwest *** Arizona/New Mexico/Utah

___Total number of volumes

Price: $8.95 per volume, check, money order, or MC/VISA.

Please add $1.25 for shipping of the first volume. Additional volumes (mix or match) sent for $0.50 additional per volume.

Prices and shipping charges are valid for all 50 United States.

_____ Total Amount Enclosed or Authorized

<u>SHIP TO:</u>

Name _____

Address _____

City _____ State _____ Zip _____

MC/VISA # _____ Expires _____

Signature _____

<u>SATISFACTION GUARANTEED</u>

Prices are valid through December 31, 1988, or as supplies last.
Thanks very much for your order!

ORDER FORM

To: *Double Eagle Guides*
        Discovery Publishing
        P.O. Box 50545
        Billings, MT 59105-0545

Please send the following volumes of <u>The Double Eagle Guide to</u>
<u>Western Public Campgrounds</u> series:

<u>Quantity</u>

___Volume I *** Pacific Northwest *** Idaho/Oregon/Washington

___Volume II *** Rocky Mountains *** Colorado/Montana/Wyoming

___Volume III *** Far West *** California/Nevada

___Volume IV *** Southwest *** Arizona/New Mexico/Utah

___Total number of volumes

    Price: $8.95 per volume, check, money order, or MC/VISA.

    Please add $1.25 for shipping of the first volume. Additional
volumes (mix or match) sent for $0.50 additional per volume.

    Prices and shipping charges are valid for all 50 United States.

_____ Total Amount Enclosed or Authorized

<u>SHIP TO:</u>

Name_____

Address_____

City_____ State_____ Zip_____

MC/VISA # _____ Expires_____

Signature_____

<u>SATISFACTION GUARANTEED</u>

Prices are valid through December 31, 1988, or as supplies last.
Thanks very much for your order!